1

The Philosophy of
the Social Sciences

Also by Alan Ryan
JOHN STUART MILL

ALAN RYAN

THE PHILOSOPHY
OF THE
SOCIAL SCIENCES

PANTHEON BOOKS
A Division of Random House, New York

301.01
R95p
82808
apr. 1973

Contents

Preface

Philosophers and social scientists familiar with the periodical literature will have no difficulty in identifying my larger intellectual debts. Here I should like to record the assistance of friends, colleagues and pupils; Quentin Skinner, Geoffrey Hawthorn and Michael Freeman have read and commented on drafts of what follows; to Roy Enfield and Alasdair MacIntyre I owe innumerable stimulating discussions of the problems of sociological theory; Katie Furness-Lane kindly assessed the typescript for pedagogic efficacy; and finally, but for the students of the Department of Government at the University of Essex during 1968/69 it is doubtful that I should have written the book at all.

November 1969

1 The Questions that Philosophers Ask

This first chapter answers a couple of questions, raises a good many more, and indicates how we shall set about answering those questions which are only raised at this point. The first question to which an answer will be provided is that of what *kind* of problems philosophers try to solve, and thus what kind of questions are asked by those philosophers who are interested in the natural and the social sciences. The other question is that of why almost all philosophers of the social sciences — and I among them — draw so heavily on distinctions first made and employed by natural scientists and philosophers of natural science. It ought perhaps to be said at once that defending this borrowing of philosophical achievements does not for a moment mean that a good social scientist, let us say a sociologist or an anthropologist, needs to first become a good physicist or biologist; except in the trivial sense that no doubt we could all profit from having as much information as possible, this is not remotely true. I do not even want to suggest the much more plausible thesis that to be a good social scientist one must be a good philosopher of science. All that is going to be argued is that we must bear in mind the standards of explanation and understanding which we apply in the natural sciences if we are to arrive at a balanced assessment of the successes and difficulties of the social sciences. This is a case which I think history and logic alike offer very good grounds for accepting.

First, then, what kind of questions do philosophers ask, what sort of problems do philosophers characteristically raise? Paradoxically, but importantly, this is itself a question that has agitated philosophers since antiquity, and one which has not received a totally conclusive answer. The importance of this fact is that anyone who sees why this has been the case must very largely understand what a philosophical problem is; and the paradox is that this is quite compatible

1

with it being very difficult to *say* exactly what it is. Philosophy is a self-conscious discipline in a way that does not characterise any other academic discipline, a feature of doing philosophy which both accounts for the hold it exercises on many people as well as for the frustration which it is liable to induce in both its practitioners and spectators. Only rarely do sociologists or historians say such things as — 'there is no such subject as sociology' or 'history is illusory'; and when they do say such things it is clearly recognised that these utterances are not part of their work as professional historians or sociologists but are the fruits of their reflections, in other words, philosophical comments. Philosophers, on the other hand, have quite frequently said that there was no such subject as philosophy, even though it was obvious enough that this assertion was itself a philosophical proposition. (1) It seems, therefore, that one of the things which we are trying to explain is how we draw a boundary between what sociologists and historians say professionally as sociologists and historians and what they and others might say about their subjects as philosophers — whether amateur or professional does not much matter.

In the last paragraph we took it for granted that the denial that there is such a subject as history or the denial that there is such a subject as sociology would not count as the sort of thing about which historians and sociologists are professionally expert; since most people would agree that these were philosophically motivated denials, the next obvious step is to see on what there is agreement. Consider the question: 'Is there really such a subject as sociology?' What is it about this question that makes us say it is a philosophical question? What, if anything, is odd or peculiar about such questions, leading us to say that they are not questions within the discipline, but about it? One way of answering this is to suppose that we tried to make these questions problems within sociology, history or some other social science; what kind of response can the sociologist as a sociologist give us? There are, of course, sociological surveys of the careers of sociologists; they tell us what kind of people become sociologists, what training they receive, what their professional attitudes are, what their political allegiances tend to be, what success they have in obtaining academic advance-

2

ment. Again, there are histories of historical writing, inquiries into the state of the discipline in antiquity, in the middle ages, or the nineteenth century; there are biographies of famous historians, from Herodotus and Thucydides through to Ranke, Michelet and Toynbee. Now such accounts will certainly tell us such things as the origins of the profession of historian, they will tell us that there have for many years been library catalogues, university departments, professional organisations, all of them acknowledging the existence of a subject called 'history', or a subject called 'sociology' — or whatever subject it may be. We can, in short, learn about the past and present existence of groups of people who called themselves by various titles, and we can learn about the kinds of activity which they declared themselves to be performing. But this somehow fails to meet the case, as we can see if we consider the analogous example of inquiring whether people who claim to speak with the dead actually are practising a science: 'Is there', we might ask, 'such a thing as necromancy?' Sociologically, we can certainly try to classify and describe the kind of people who become mediums, their educational background, their social and professional lives; historically, we can discover how prevalent the practice of necromancy was in, say, seventeenth-century England, or how popular consulting mediums was in ancient Egypt; anthropologically, we can discover the social standing and political power of such people as shamans in societies very different from our own, we can analyse the kind of social function that such practices serve in different societies, and whether the belief in communicating with spirits is functionally equivalent to Christian beliefs about the Eucharist; even economists might be interested in the extent to which an underdeveloped country's poverty could be explained in terms of the diversion of funds into the unproductive hands of witch-doctors. But, logically and philosophically, this proves nothing at all about the cognitive status of the belief in the possibility of communication with the dead. We can certainly agree that there have been 'mediums' in all sorts of societies and at all periods of history, and yet deny that what they have been doing is communicating with the dead; similarly, we can agree that there are people called 'social scientists' and still deny that what they practise is science, or

3

deny that the science they practise is the science of society.

For, of course, what we have here are not questions *in* the sciences with which we are concerned, but questions *about* these sciences; our questions are not *first-order* or factual questions, but rather *second-order* or conceptual questions instead. (2) A summary answer, therefore, to the question of what kind of questions do philosophers ask, is that they ask second-order questions, that the problems they raise are conceptual difficulties; and hence the answer to the question of why our suggested sociological, historical and anthropological answers were misplaced is that these were factual or first-order answers to what were essentially conceptual, second-order problems. Our next task is to make sense of this summary answer by further exploring the distinction between factual and conceptual problems. The first thing to notice is that factual questions are by no means a homogeneous class. In terms of the distinction we have just drawn, it is a factual question whereabouts the Houses of Parliament are located, but it is also a factual question what the function of parliament is within the British political process, even though this second question bears a great weight of theoretical implication that the first question does not. Again, it is a factual matter how many people there are in a given family, and it is equally a factual matter whether particularistic norms are more readily transmitted in extended families than in the nuclear family. Here, too, the second question can only be answered in the light of a good many assumptions about the scientific adequacy of a sociological theory, many of which may on inspection turn out to be wrong, or in some cases nonsensical. In a non-social science context, it is a factual question how many pieces of meat there are on a plate, and equally a factual question how enzymes act in such a way as to convert those pieces of meat into utilisable protein. But behind this second question there is a formidable body of physical and chemical theory, without which the question simply would not make sense; and this is not true of the first question. For some purposes, the distinction between more and less theoretically orientated questions is important; but here, where our main interest lies in the wider distinction, it is not. So long as the theory in the context of which our questions are framed is a

4

valid theory, then all the above questions are equally factual questions. They are such, because in all these cases the answers to our questions depend on going out and looking at the data, on counting or measuring and testing; and no answer which cannot be defended in terms of the results of such processes is any good. In other words, the answers purport to be accurate reports of what the facts are like, and must be defensible in terms of the known methods for getting at the facts. But, of course, what makes second-order questions *philosophical* is that they cannot be decided by appeal to the known methods of obtaining the facts. For when we ask whether the social sciences are really sciences, what we are worried about is not the facts, but how we are to characterise the facts, what we are to say about them, what we are to see in them. It is for this reason that such questions are termed conceptual questions, for they require from us an account of the proper thing to say and think about the facts, or, in an older jargon, an account of how we should conceive of them.

One immediate response to this analysis may well be to decide that 'it's all just a matter or words'; 'history' is simply the word which we attach to whatever it is that is produced by historians, and 'historians' are simply those people who call themselves such. Equally, if there are people who wish to call themselves 'social scientists', then 'social science' just is the proper label to attach to whatever it is that they do. And, it might be argued, this is so because definitions are only conventions, and apply only because of agreement that they should apply. Surely, nothing much can hang on the mere word; so long as we remember which word we have agreed to apply to what activity, there is no reason to worry. On this account, second-order questions become a curious kind of factual question, for what is involved seems to be getting accurate reports on what verbal agreements exist, and perhaps seeing that consistency is maintained from one occasion to the next, so that we avoid calling economics a science on Monday and refusing to so call it on Thursday. Thus, philosophy would be concerned to elaborate analytic or tautological propositions, to produce statements about the identity of meaning which obtained between various expressions. The facts of linguistic usage would determine whether

5

these relationships had been accurately described or not, and where there was no stable usage to determine the issue, philosophy could legislate a usage on which everyone could agree, by laying down a stipulative definition, to the effect that such a term bore such a meaning. This seems to have been the view of A. J. Ayer at the time when he wrote 'Language, Truth and Logic', itself a book which aimed to distinguish as clearly as possible between what was to be admitted to the respectable label of 'science' and what was to be thrown out as nonsense. (3)

There are attractions in such a view, and situations where it would seem to apply. It is, for example, sometimes the case that a good deal of trouble arises from mistranslation, and that getting clear what a word means will cure this. The German word *Wissenschaft* is particularly liable to mislead English students; it is commonly translated 'science', but in German bears a much less restricted meaning than the term 'science' bears in modern English, since any body of organised knowledge is properly to be called *Wissenschaft*. Thus, when Max Weber along with a number of other German historians and sociologists in the late nineteenth century argued that our knowledge of social life was different in some crucial ways from the knowledge obtained through the natural sciences, they still talked of our knowledge of social life as *Sozialwissenschaft* and were plainly not contradicting themselves in so doing. Thus, any student of sociology who concluded that German theorists had been unanimous in claiming a 'scientific' status for sociology would be put right by this rather elementary observation about linguistic usage. But this — the tidying-up of translation — is hardly the recognised task of philosophy. And plainly there is no reason to suppose it should be. For the philosophical interest in words, in why we say what we do, is not an interest in 'mere' words. For when philosophers study what we say, and inquire into why we say it, they focus their attention on the *criteria* in virtue of which we apply the words we do, the rules in terms of which expressions are correctly or incorrectly used, and particularly they attend to the reasons which these criteria embody, reasons why we should draw one distinction rather than another, why we should characterise things in one way and not some different

6

way. (4) Of course, there are occasions when we need to invent a new word to cover a situation which we wish to describe conveniently; an example would be Durkheim's adapting the word *anomie* to cover a cluster of symptoms of social disorder, about which he was concerned to propose various explanatory hypotheses. Under these circumstances, it would be absurd to complain that he had called the symptoms by the wrong word, for, of course, the word meant no more and no less than those symptoms to which he had attached it. Even here, however, it is worth noticing that the *point* of introducing a new expression is perfectly explicable; it is no mere exercise of verbal legislation. It was because he believed himself to have a comprehensive sociological theory, capable of explaining the phenomena of anomie, that it was worth Durkheim's while to propose the new term, and there was thus a perfectly good rationale to be given of why the word should cover those symptoms and not others. (5) So, even in rather extreme cases, it seems that we do not primarily want an account of a verbal decision or a stipulative definition; what we want to be given is an account of the reasons that justify the criteria which give a term its meaning, we want to know why it makes sense to go on using the expression, or drawing the distinctions implied by it. For, of course, the words we employ draw some distinctions sharply and blur others, throw some things into sharp relief but leave others obscured. The interest of philosophers lies in the general justifications lying behind our choosing to draw *these* distinctions, and to highlight *these* features. Thus questions about whether the social sciences are *really* sciences — which is the readiest label for the multiplicity of questions philosophers can ask about the social sciences — cannot be settled by simply deciding, or refusing, to call them sciences. For the questions are demands to have explained what makes an inquiry a scientific one, to have the differences between common sense and science elucidated, or the distinction between the insight of the sociologist and the insight of the novelist, whose explanations are not scientific, but still seem to tell us something. Thus, someone who denied that there was such a thing as the science of social life would not be denying that people had actually been *called* social scientists; his situation would be much more like that of an atheist who denied that there was such a subject as theology. The atheist could agree that there had for centuries been persons who were called theologians; but, he might go on, since there is no God, the subject is a non-starter, and these persons were misnamed, for theology is in intention the study of the nature of God, and there is no studying the nature of something which does not exist in the first place; without a subject-matter, there can be no science. When Durkheim tried to explain the phenomena of religion in terms of the affirmation of solidarity with the social organism, he implicitly accepted just this argument of the atheist's. (6) The things that were said by the adherents to a faith were not to be taken as statements about God, for there were in principle no such statements to be made; thus, they had to be interpreted in some other way, Durkheim's proposed reinterpretation being that they were expressions of devotion to the social organism. The case is exactly analogous with the proposition that there is no such thing as social science; it might, for instance, be said that there are no such phenomena as social phenomena, that upon inspection, they can always be seen to be something else, as e.g. psychological or biological phenomena. A case of this strength was not made explicitly, but it was implicit in the methodological assumptions of nineteenth-century utilitarian writers, and it has been read into the views of contemporary theorists who adopt 'individualist' approaches. The view that there was no such subject as economics, because there were no such phenomena as economic phenomena, was certainly defended by Auguste Comte, who admitted to classical economics nothing more than a preliminary role in preparing the way for the new science whose name of *sociology* he had himself invented. (7) Such a view resembled that of historians of science who see myths about creation or planetary movements, or whatever it might be, as a first step towards science; these are not literally true, but they conceal what might become the truths of science. Thus, as we can see, a person who denies that the social sciences are 'really' sciences may agree that there is some other description of what 'social scientists' do that will accurately characterise their activities; in explaining why the label of science will not properly apply, he may also explain what better label will. Of course, it is not only doubts about

8

the existence or the proper description of the subject-matter which are at issue; more common is the argument that the standards for explanatory rigour that characterise physics or chemistry simply do not fit the understanding of social life, and in principle cannot. Since our notion of what makes for the scientific status of a subject is heavily dependent on these standards, it seems that our criteria of scientificity rule out the social sciences from science. In fact, a great deal of what follows in this book is devoted to following out the implications of this argument — for it is a much less simple argument than it looks at first sight. It will, I think, become clear rather rapidly that the process of elaborating our criteria of scientificity is not a simple matter of reading off the standards from the actual practice of scientists and philosophers — an undertaking which the total absence of unanimity among scientists who are asked to describe their own work rules out at once. It involves indeed a good deal of independent judgement as to the importance of one or other feature of scientific explanation, and a certain degree of willingness to place one's intellectual bets. The reason for this is both obvious and encouraging rather than alarming; our notions of what is in principle possible are to some extent determined by what progress we think the sciences, both natural and social, will make; only if we thought that there were no major revelations to come would we be justified in demanding a conclusive account of the nature of scientific inquiry, and anyone who does offer a conclusive account risks being outrun by events.

It might seem that in describing philosophy as a second-order inquiry, we have made it out to be a parasite on other more real or more respectable subjects, and have thus denied it a life of its own. But this would be a misleading conclusion; the relationship is one of symbiosis — philosophy and other disciplines draw mutual profit from each other's existence. As we shall see in the next chapter, philosophy has elaborated a set of distinctions and elucidated various argumentative techniques, together with the technical vocabulary required for such a task, and in this philosophy resembles any other substantive discipline. These distinctions, techniques and vocabulary are not arbitrary exercises of the intellect, either, for they were evolved in the knowledge that distinctions not made in everyday speech had to be made if we were to make sense of the achievements of science, or even of common sense. (8) From the viewpoint of the sciences, both natural and social, the most useful innovations have been within the field of 'applied logic', where recent sophistication allows us to talk much more accurately than before about the difference between interpreted and uninterpreted calculi — say, between pure geometry and its applications in economics — about the differences between a model of a situation and the theory of that situation, and so on. Even so basic a distinction as that between theorems which are tautologies within a system and empirical generalisations which make claims about the world requires a concern for conceptual orderliness that is not part of our everyday concerns. The drawing of such distinctions, and the inquiry into their rationale seems to be unequivocally a conceptual task, i.e. a philosophical one, and it seems to be a task requiring as much attention and carefulness over details as does any other discipline.

But many people need less convincing that philosophers can and do draw careful, non-everyday, technically described distinctions than that this exercise is a *useful* one. There are people, scientists among them, who think philosophical questioning is positively dangerous, in that it distracts us from following the tried practices of the intellectual, or moral and political community to which we belong. The most striking statement of this view was Burke's argument in 'Reflections on the French Revolution' that individual reason was at best a limited tool, and that individuals could only achieve happy and morally acceptable lives by following the implicit wisdom enshrined in the existing practices of their society; in effect, the argument asserts that like the boy on the bicycle we get along quite well, so long as we don't stop to think what we are doing. (9) Plainly, this argument looks even more plausible applied to the scientists' rules and procedures than it does applied to the moral rules and procedures of eighteenth-century English society. For the scientists' practices of measurement, calculation, observation and experiment look much less questionable than do many of our social and political institutions; and certainly the kind of qualms we may feel about the man who never raises a

10

question about his moral and political beliefs do not seem to apply to the physicist or the economist as such. *Qua* scientists, if not *qua* husbands, fathers, colleagues or friends, their interests lie in the solution of a range of first-order, clearly defined factual problems; why then should we demand of them that they become (not, in all probability, very good) philosophers?

Luckily, this question answers itself. It is a commonplace that so long as the currently accepted procedures yield results which those who use them hope that they will yield, it is very unlikely that the urge to inquire into their logical and epistemological foundations will be very widespread. (10) The community of scientists, like any other community, has limited resources and limited energy; it will not waste effort, nor money, on supporting those who do not work on the currently accepted problems in the currently acceptable way. When there is crisis, that is when the currently accepted techniques yield results which seem not just unsatisfactory, but unsatisfactory in principle, then these techniques are bound to be questioned, in no matter how muddled a way. There is no reason to commit ourselves to the view that philosophy only flourishes in times of crisis, tempting though such a view is. What we can certainly say is that when there is a crisis of scientific confidence, the line between science and its philosophy becomes much harder to delineate exactly. The job that is done by successful theoretical innovation at critical moments has often been said to be that of *conceptual revision* rather than anything which we could plausibly describe as the discovery of new facts. New theories — at any rate the more sweeping ones, such as Copernicus's helio-centric account of astronomy — do not simply let us solve old problems; they set up new standards for explanation, and change our whole idea of what it is that we are trying to explain. In short, successful theoretical innovation is often less like the first-order task of factual inquiry than it is like the second-order task of revising or reinterpreting our understanding of what it is that is involved in factual inquiry; in much the manner of revolutions in the political sphere, our standards of legitimacy are apt to change with the incumbents of positions of power. Thus, the short answer to demands to have the usefulness of philosophy explained is

11

that scientists themselves acknowledge its utility by engaging in philosophical scrutiny of their own practices once they are beset by doubts of a particularly striking sort. (11)

Hence, on the score of usefulness, we are not committed to the view that it will necessarily make a physicist a better physicist to divert his attention to the philosophy of science; but, equally, we should not be surprised that over issues such as the principle of indeterminacy, scientists themselves have argued about the logical status of what they were saying as much as over the experimental evidence. As to the implications of all this for the social sciences, we certainly cannot assume that these are in the same condition as the better understood parts of physical science where an unselfconscious reliance on existing theories and techniques is obviously in order. We must, therefore, face the question of whether the social sciences are especially problematical, whether they raise particularly numerous philosophical issues, whether inherently, or only for reasons of historical development.

It seems to me to be impossible to doubt that the social sciences in general, and *a fortiori* particular social sciences such as sociology, political science or economics, are more conceptually puzzling than are the natural sciences. Of course, it is possible that the conceptual puzzlement is only a sign of confusion on the part of the inquirer; but even then we should want to know why the social sciences induced a confusion which the natural sciences did not. No one suggests that physics and chemistry are in principle an intellectually disreputable kind of undertaking; but intelligent men have argued that the application to the study of society of the methods and the conceptual categories of the natural sciences, the employment of their ideas of causation, measurement and the like, is impossible or misguided; or else they have argued that the information thus realised is not the information which we really want; or again they have argued that the theories and explanations so generated systematically fail to represent social and political reality. Moreover, it is a matter of common complaint that the tactics employed to put the social sciences on a par with the natural sciences have not been very successful. The establishment of research institutes, the sponsoring of work by government agencies,

12

the employment of advanced computational aids, all the tactics in brief which have worked in improving our ability to launch rockets, to transplant organs and to advance our industrial technology in startling ways, seem much less effective here. Some part of the answer to such doubts does consist in showing the genuine successes of the social sciences, and some part consists in showing how the kind of success envisaged is in principle misguided; even so, there seems to persist a sort of puzzlement shared by many social scientists.

But if the doubts about the scientific status of the social sciences are widespread, the same cannot be said of any single answer to these doubts. And in many ways, the rest of this book could be said to be an attempt to supply such an answer, or, more modestly, some of the items which would have to feature in any answer to the question whether the social sciences really *are* sciences. As a preliminary only, I want to open up in a very fragmentary way three stances on this question which it is worth bearing in mind throughout what follows. The first is what is usually called the classical empiricist view. It is the position that there is no difference *in principle* between the study of social phenomena and the study of any other natural phenomena. Adherents of this view assert the unity of methodology throughout the natural sciences, and firmly place the social sciences among the natural sciences. In recent years, the philosophers associated with the 'Encyclopedia of Unified Science' were the most persistent metaphysicians of the movement, but its essential tenets were formulated as long ago as 1843 in J. S. Mill's 'System of Logic'. For Mill, any phenomena displaying regular patterns of behaviour were a fit subject for science, and all natural phenomena were presumed to display such regularities, human behaviour among them. (12) There could not be two sorts of phenomena, one natural and one non-natural; all must eventually be amenable to causal explanation, inductively established. Such a view is perhaps as near as any to the reigning orthodoxy among social scientists today. When David Easton presented political scientists with his 'A Framework for Political Analysis', (13) his explicit purpose was to bring political science into the fold of the natural sciences. What, then, accounts for what Mill and Easton

13

would agree to be the backward condition of the social sciences — for it must be remembered that what they offer us is a programme of scientific advance, predicated upon the deficiencies of the social sciences? Why is it so hard to predict the outbreak of a revolution, when we have been able to predict eclipses for centuries; why is it impossible to find an agreed causal explanation for the outbreak of the Peloponnesian War or the French Revolution, let alone advance a general theory of the causes of war or of governmental stability and instability? According to the classical empiricist view, and to those social scientists who share their assumptions with the traditional empiricists, the difficulties lie in the immense complexity of the situations studied by social scientists, and in the moral and practical impossibilities facing someone who wants to set up a tidy experimental situation. The phenomena are numerous, very difficult to quantify, and thus offering enormous obstacles to anyone who tries to assess the relative weights of various causal influences, save under limited and artificially simple situations. The attractions of voting studies are obvious in the light of such considerations as the above, for they, and studies like them, minimise these difficulties. The social scientist who argues in this way can point to the difficulties of the natural sciences, adducing such examples as the so-called Three Body Problem, to which Newtonian mechanics can in principle offer no solution. Again, the relative lack of success in social science predictions can largely be attributed to the fact that social phenomena rarely recur in exactly the same form, which is in itself a very important disanalogy with the natural sciences, like astronomy, which have produced strikingly successful predictions. Some social phenomena do display the requisite regularity, and where they do, as in the rise and fall of prices, we have the powerful explanatory theories of economics to account for them. Again, where we can engage in experimentation, much of our confidence in the results stems from the fact that we can isolate some aspects of the situation as relevant and dismiss others as causally irrelevant. The DNA molecule cannot plausibly be called 'simple', but at any rate the biochemist does not have to wonder whether the nature of DNA has changed between two experiments. But if we were to poll seventy voters to ask their political views, and

14

repeat the poll two years later, it would be in order to find out how they had changed; if, for example, the first poll had been in a non-election year and the second in an election year, we should be startled to discover that there had *not* been a drastic change or two. This example also illustrates how it is that our theoretical ignorance makes inquiry difficult; the ability to eliminate some factors as irrelevant indicates that we already have some theories which explain which causal agencies are at work; in the voting survey field, we certainly know that the imminence of an election makes a good deal of difference, but this is scarcely sophisticated enough to warrant the title of theoretical knowledge, and the number of generalisations we possess about exactly *how* the nearness of an election influences opinions is still small. Of course, we have a vast store of commonsense causal knowledge already at our fingertips – if we even begin by asking voters what they like and dislike about the policies of the candidates on offer, we are already taking for granted a good deal about the causal processes of opinion formation. But this store of common sense can be no more than the foundations of scientific inquiry, a starting point for research, and not the conclusion of it.

If we put all these considerations together, the position of the social sciences, and the way forward can be simply characterised. We must describe the facts more minutely, experiment where experiment is possible, quantify what is quantifiable, take advantage of statistical techniques and the speed in using them made possible by computers. We need, also, to put forward appropriate theoretical frameworks, lest we become swamped by a mass of undifferentiated information. (14) But if we do all this, there is no reason why the social sciences should lag behind the rest of the natural sciences. This does not mean that we shall create the fanciful world of Hobbes's 'Leviathan', where social science would be a sub-department of physics. What it does mean is that the methodological problems faced by social scientists are no more nor less insoluble than those faced by the physical scientist, that the epistemological assumptions of the social scientist need be no different, that the logic of his explanations must be the same.

One opposed position denies practically all these beliefs.

15

Its keynote is that the phenomena of human behaviour differ essentially from those of inert matter in that they have a dimension of 'meaningfulness' which the latter do not. (15) The phenomena into which the physical sciences inquire are essentially meaningless, in that the order they display is only a causal regularity; insofar as they can be said to have significance, it is only a borrowed significance which *our* theories lend them. It is human beings who endow natural phenomena with what meaning they have, for natural phenomena do not endow their own actions with meaning, as do human beings. In this way, the phenomena studied by the natural sciences are different in kind, not merely in degree of complexity, from those which the social sciences seek to understand. And, on these premises, the belief that human activity in social matters can be understood in the same terms as are employed in the natural sciences is an unwarranted extrapolation from the history of science. It may be true that primitive science assumed that stones 'sought' the earth, or that the planets meant to follow their heavenly paths, so that dropping this kind of anthropomorphism was an essential step to scientific progress; but it would be quite foolish to attempt to push this process towards the goal of taking 'anthropomorphism' out of our understanding of human affairs. If the so-called anthropomorphic categories did *not* apply to human behaviour, from whence could we have originally derived them, when we *mis*applied them to trees, stars and stones? If it was an error to adopt anthropomorphism once, would it not be equally an error to overcompensate by falling for the equal and opposite mistake at this point? (16)

If this criticism is cogent, it follows that the categories in terms of which we are to analyse and explain social and political life must involve concepts of purpose and intention, concepts which are those in whose terms the agents themselves understand their own behaviour. We are not simply interested in such regularities as social life happens to display, but in the significance which the agents themselves attach to the actions which go to create these regularities. Hence causation plays a secondary role, if any, and the depth of understanding which we aim at goes beyond anything possible in those sciences where causal regularities are the

16

only object of inquiry. This creates some problems quite unlike those of the natural scientist. It is clear upon reflection that the account which the agent gives of the intentions and goals implied by his behaviour is not the only account which it is possible to give; and there are some awkward questions to be asked about the relationship of two different accounts, say the agent's and the social scientist's. Now whatever the problem here, it is quite disanalogous to any natural science problem, for there there can be no question at all of the situation meaning something to the falling stone, the buzzing molecules and the rest, let alone of the situation meaning something different to the phenomena and to the investigator. We shall later explore some of these themes in detail, when looking at Professor Winch's 'The Idea of a Social Science'; but to illustrate the genuineness of the opposition I am presenting here, it suffices to mention now that a good deal of that book engages in a running argument with Mill.

A final point of introduction to this second position is in order. It is important to see that to distinguish sharply between the phenomena of nature and the phenomena of human activity leaves social science as much an empirical and factual inquiry as ever; we do not have to appeal to some mysterious and non-empirical faculty of 'intuition' in order to find out what a situation means to an agent. The meaning of the situation to the agent in question is a matter about which it is perfectly possible to be right or wrong, and testably so. Take the often discussed example of the various meanings which writing one's name on a piece of paper can bear. (17) A man may be writing a cheque, signing a death certificate, showing a child how to write, and so on almost indefinitely; nonetheless, one such description is the *correct* description of what he is doing, and thus the others are not; and as anywhere else, it is the facts of the case, properly interpreted, which force us to conclude which is the correct account. The social element in such situations rests on the fact that what an individual can intelligibly intend to do depends on the kinds of rules which go to make up his society; it is these social rules which provide the skeleton of meanings within which the individual can frame intentions, decide on his goals and the like. There is thus a rather closer

17

relationship between philosophy and social science than my initial distinction between first- and second-order inquiries seemed to allow, for social science on this account must be concerned to *interpret* social life, to allow us to see how it would be to live in a social world arranged in certain kinds of significant patterns, and what we should lose in their absence. This, of course, is very much to explore the empirical consequences of conceptual situations, and thus allies philosophical and sociological theory very closely. The goal of empirical work is now seen less as the establishment of regularities than as the extablishment of what rules of significant action we should have to follow to be members of some particular society or subsection of society.

The final stance on these issues does not involve coming down on one side or other in the preceding confrontation; what it tries to illuminate is the sociological roots of the philosophical debate. And it certainly raises some difficulties of principle in integrating social and natural science. The argument starts from the premise that the theories of both the social and the natural sciences are the products of particular societies, and the assumption that there is in principle some kind of sociological and historical explanation which will tell us why certain ways of viewing the world have predominated at one time, and others at another. Professor Kuhn's work on 'paradigm shifts' has aroused a great deal of interest in the sudden and often startling changes which take place in science, not just in some small theory, but in the whole scientific community's ideas about what it is to satisfactorily explain anything at all. (18) He strongly implies that the explanation for these shifts must lie in something other than the facts as such, since these can be so variously conceived. Now the natural sciences are not concerned with the sociology of knowledge in this sense, and are thus entitled to press on unselfconsciously; but the social sciences are concerned with such matters as the sociology of knowledge, and are thus involved in studying themselves in a way which is not true of the natural sciences. Moreover, the indeterminacy that hangs about social science as the product of social life is worsened by the converse consideration that social life is in part the product of social theory. For in a way that is not generally true in the natural sciences, the social description of social reality can be self-validating. If people come to believe, for whatever reason, that they are acting from a given motive, there is a sense in which they are bound to be right, and thus a perfectly good sense in which a description of their actions in such terms is quite correct. Examples can readily be found in the pages of nineteenth-century novels about social conditions, many of which — like Disraeli's 'Sybil' — feature a hard-hearted factory owner whose life is planned by himself around the assumptions of economic rationality made by classical economics. (19) Thus he acts for reasons made acceptable to him by an economic theory; the theory is made acceptable, because people's behaviour actually does conform to it; and this means that because a man believes the account of economic motivation given by Ricardo and Adam Smith to be correct it becomes correct. In everyday life, we recognise this state of affairs on all those numerous occasions when we reassure friends by telling them that if they *think* they are happy, then they will *be* happy. More importantly, it is this point which underlies most discussions of the concept of ideology, especially in its classical formulation by Marx. Lichtheim's 'Marxism' lucidly explains Marx's analysis of the relationship between 'bourgeois society' and the economic theory of the English classical economists. (20) The theory represented the processes of production and exchange as phenomena of nature, ruled by mechanical, impersonal forces; and this theory was self-validating in the sense that uncontrolled capitalism, which was allowed simply to 'happen', did indeed display all the appearances of a mechanical, impersonal, uncontrollable natural phenomenon. And for Marx, bourgeois society was defined by this blend of belief and event, of illusion and reality.

At worst, such an argument might lead us to total scepticism, and the view that truth was a matter of majority vote; at best, it certainly seems to make the line between belief and knowledge, idea and reality, rather indistinct. An air of rampant indeterminism thus seems to hang over social theory, and the obstacles to its becoming social science seem not merely hard to remove, but impossible even to come to grips with. But, it could be objected, the same thing is true of some areas of science, without rendering the whole concept

19

of science illusory. In subatomic physics there are areas of indeterminacy where the observation of the scientist interferes with the effects which he is studying; and it could equally be said that there are various kinds of self-validation possible in the realm of inert matter; if you were to stand by a loose snow slope and predict an avalanche in a very loud voice, you might very well turn out to be right. If the social origins and effects of social theory are to be a genuine source of worry, we shall have to explain in what way the problems of indeterminism and self-validation in the social sciences are of a different logical type — as they seem at first glance to be — from those current in the natural sciences.

Finally, then, I must explain the strategy of the arguments which occupy the remainder of this book, and in so doing explain why I begin by talking in perfectly general terms about the logical requirements of any scientific explanation, whether of social or any other phenomena. Whenever we raise doubts about the adequacy-in-principle of some explanation or description, we necessarily raise them with some kind of implicit standard in mind. Often enough our doubts are phrased in a way which indicates this — we say that some proffered explanation is not the 'real' explanation, as if to indicate that there is some paradigm against which to compare it, some envisaged explanation which would be the 'real' one. (21) This again is characteristic of much everyday speech; if we tell a friend that he has not got a 'real' hangover, we are appealing to a standard, a paradigm of what would constitute an unequivocal, Grade A hangover. Equally, if the social sciences are said not to be *real* sciences, there is implied an appeal to a standard or paradigm of what *real* sciences are like; and the point of beginning by elucidating the standards of explanation implied in the natural sciences is that it is they which provide the paradigm of real science. This is not the same thing as claiming that they *have* to, nor that they have always done so. As to the first point, it will become clear in due course that there is nothing intellectually disreputable about the view that our ordinary explanations of human behaviour are extremely successful, and would not at all be improved by being remodelled in the image of mechanics. And as to the second point, there have always been people who have thought science an impoverished

20

activity compared with theology or metaphysics. What is true, however, is that the most plausible way to understand such recurrent questions as 'is sociology really a science?' is as demands that we should show how the explanations offered by sociologists compare in key respects with those offered by natural scientists. From the way the question defies attempts to answer it, we must assume that there is no simple way of showing what the key respects are, nor how the comparison goes; nonetheless, the only possible way to start is by elucidating the explanatory paradigms of science to see what emulation would in principle require. In effect, this task occupies our next three chapters, and amounts to making clear what is claimed by the first position we described — the view that logically and methodologically all the sciences are on the same level. A review of the difficulties involved in this claim then leads naturally to an assessment of the claim that these difficulties are insuperable because that view is logically misguided in the first place.

The other major reason for beginning first with the logic of the natural sciences is that much of the best work in philosophy has been inspired by problems in this field. The distinctions with which we are going to have to work were elaborated in this area, and many of the problems for which they were designed have analogies in the social sciences. An example will carry more weight than mere assertion, so let us look ahead to one of the issues discussed below — in Chapter 8 — namely, whether it is possible to reduce sociological phenomena and the theory of sociological phenomena to phenomena of individual psychology and the theory of such phenomena. The doctrine known as 'methodological individualism' asserts that this reduction is possible, the doctrine known as 'sociological holism' maintains that it is not. The vigour of the debate has not much diminished since the nineteenth century, as a glance at Professor Homans's recent critique of the work of Talcott Parsons proves. (22) This is not the place to discuss this debate; but the point of mentioning it is that comparable arguments about e.g. the 'reduction' of chemical phenomena to physical phenomena, or of biological phenomena to chemical and physical phenomena have long occupied scientists and philosophers of science. In the process, it has become clear that the notion of 'reduction' in this context contains all kinds of ambiguity, such that we can only begin to clarify the debate by clarifying a number of issues about the ways in which the laws and theories of one natural science can be said to be related to those of another. But happily for the philosopher interested in the social sciences, much of this work has already been done for us, and we can climb on the backs of other men in order to see further than they. It would, of course, be a hopelessly conservative case to argue that every distinction we need has already been drawn for us, and I do not suppose anyone believes that. Yet it would be an equally egregious mistake to start by thinking that none of the intelligence lavished on such topics has paid any dividends; it is certainly true that we may need to radically rethink the application of distinctions drawn in one area and taken over into another. But here as everywhere else, a wise radical takes care to inherit what he can.

NOTES

1. L. Wittgenstein, 'Tractatus Logico-Philosophicus' (Routledge) prop. 6:54.

2. E. R. Emmet, 'Learning to Philosophize' (Longmans, 1964) ch. 3.

3. A. J. Ayer, 'Language, Truth and Logic' (Gollancz, 1936) ch. ii, esp. p. 59; see reservations in 2nd ed. (Gollancz, 1946) pp. 5-16.

4. S. Cavell, 'The Availability of the Later Philosophy of Wittgenstein', 'Phil. Rev.' (1962).

5. E. Durkheim, 'Suicide' (Routledge, 1952) pp. 241-76.

6. E. Durkheim, 'The Elementary Forms of the Religious Life' (Allen & Unwin, 1969) pp. 418-24.

7. J. S. Mill to A. Comte, 'Collected Works' (Routledge, 1963) xiii 626.

8. E. Nagel, 'The Structure of Science' (Routledge, 1961) pp. 1-10.

9. Edmund Burke, 'Reflections on the Revolution in France' (Doubleday, New York, 1961) pp. 100-1.

10. T. S, Kuhn, 'The Structure of Scientific Revolutions' (Chicago University Press, 1962) pp. 44-7.

11. Ibid., pp. 84-9.

12. J. S. Mill, 'A System of Logic' (Longmans) bk vi, ch.ii.

13. D. Easton, 'A Framework for Political Analysis' (Prentice-Hall, 1965).

14. D. Easton, 'The Political System' (Knopf, New York, 1953) pp. 66-78.

15. P. G. Winch, 'The Idea of a Social Science' (Routledge, 1958) passim (see below, chs 6 and 7).

16. F. A. von Hayek, 'Scientism and the Study of Society', 'Economica' (1942) 270 ff.

17. R. S. Peters, 'The Concept of Motivation', 2nd ed. (Routledge, 1960) pp. 12-14.

18. Kuhn, 'Structure of Scientific Revolutions', pp. 84-5.

19. Benjamin Disraeli, 'Sybil' (Oxford University Press) p. 69.

20. G. Lichtheim, 'Marxism' (Routledge, 1961) pt 4.

21. J. L. Austin, 'Sense and Sensibilia' (Oxford University Press, 1962) pp. 62-77.

22. G. C. Homans, 'Bringing Men Back In', 'Amer. Soc. Rev.' (1964) pp. 808-18.

2 Some Basic Tools of Philosophy

In the last chapter it was claimed that philosophy is a second-order inquiry, devoted to clarifying and subjecting to rational analysis the procedures involved, and the results achieved, in our first-order, factual investigations. It was said at that point how much of recent – and indeed less recent – philosophy has been concerned with the elucidation of the natural sciences. In this chapter, we shall be looking at the technical vocabulary – and more importantly the distinctions which this vocabulary is used to make – which has been created in order to make the tasks of the philosopher of science simpler to describe and more capable of satisfactory fulfilment. This technical vocabulary is essentially employed in the logical appraisal of argument and reasoning; it is a second-order vocabulary in that we use it to talk *about* arguments and chains of reasoning, rather than in the framing of the arguments in the first place. (1) The place of such a vocabulary in the philosophy of science is that the sciences, in offering us explanations, necessarily offer us arguments, chains of reasoning designed to show why one state of affairs should occur rather than some other. It is, of course, true that this could be said of explanation in our everyday affairs as well, that *all* explanation involves us in arguing for the acceptability of one set of expectations about the world rather than some other set; just as the sciences sharpen and refine our everyday, commonsense explanations, so the philosophy of science scrutinises more sharply the logical merits and shortcomings of the arguments offered by science. Such a concern for the logical requirements which must be met by satisfactory arguments is by no means the only concern of the philosophy of science, as much of the sequel to this chapter will show; and no one can become even a moderately sophisticated student of the social sciences if he does no more than learn the few distinctions spelled out here;

nonetheless, such a concern, and an understanding of the techniques it involves, is an essential first step.

Let us begin with an example as simple as it is implausible. Suppose someone makes a prediction about the results of a forthcoming election, say to the effect that: 'All the voters in Oldhaven East Ward will vote Labour'; suppose again that he is challenged to produce grounds for this prediction, i.e. to produce some sort of explanation of the predicted event, and says that all the voters of Oldhaven East Ward are members of the manual working class, and that all members of the manual working class vote Labour. If this is spelled out, what has been offered is a simple deductive argument, an elementary syllogism. A textbook of logic would set it out thus: All members of the manual working class vote Labour (the logical form of which is All As have property B), All voters in Oldhaven East Ward are members of the manual working class (the logical form of which is All Cs have property A), so All voters in Oldhaven East Ward vote Labour (the logical form of which is All Cs have property B). From two premisses a conclusion is deductively drawn. Now two things are at once obvious about this example: the first is that it is quite untrue to life inasmuch as no political sociologist would hope to produce such conclusively universal laws about the voting patterns of social classes; the second is that such an objection is essentially *factual*, not *logical*, which is to say that what is being challenged is the truth of the premisses and not the validity of the argument. It is clear that so far as the logic of the argument goes, what we have here is a syllogism of such obvious validity that no one would raise doubts about it. (2) All of which shows up the first, and in some ways the most important point which we have to make in this chapter: whatever the argument or explanation with which we are presented, there are always two different kinds of question which we can sensibly ask about it; the first concerns the logical structure of the argument, and relates to its internal validity, the second concerns the factual truth of either or both the premisses and conclusion, and relates to its external relationship with the facts. It is important not simply to remember that there are these two kinds of question, but also to see that they are independent questions – no amount of logical sophistication can make up for a mistake about the facts, and no amount of factual investigation can patch up logical incoherence. No great effort is needed to keep such a distinction in mind, for it is well enough marked in everyday speech. Quite frequently, we accept a statement, not as true, but 'for the sake of argument', indicating that what we are going to ask is what, as a matter of logic, *follows* from the statement; and just as often, we are willing to accept that one proposition does follow from another, before going on to point out that it is, nonetheless, false, so that its premiss must also be false. *If* all of the manual working class voted Labour, there would be a permanent Labour government, we might say; but there is not a permanent Labour government, as a matter of fact, and among other things this means that it cannot be the case that all the manual working class votes Labour. The more formalised logical distinctions drawn by philosophy are rooted in common sense in just the same way as the explanations of the scientist begin in the explanations of everyday life. (3)

The original, implausible example above can be employed again to illustrate the importance of the distinction between matters of logical validity and matters of factual truth. We know that in the real world both our premisses are certainly false; in no constituency are the voters so socially homogeneous as our example maintains, and in no country does a working class vote with monolithic solidarity. This might tempt us to rewrite our argument in the following way: Some members of the manual working class vote Labour (Some A are B), Some of the voters in Oldhaven East Ward are members of the manual working class (Some C are A), so Some of the voters in Oldhaven East Ward vote Labour (Some C are B). However, any inclination to believe that an argument whose premisses and conclusion are all of them so much more plausible than before must for that reason be an improved argument would be quite mistaken. It may very well be the case that all the statements in the argument are true; nonetheless, the argument is now not a valid argument at all, since the conclusion, whether true or not, just does not follow from the premisses. The difference between this argument and its predecessor can be visually illustrated by the device of a Venn Diagram, familiar from any textbook in

26

logic. (4) It can be seen at once that the Venn Diagram corresponding to the first argument yields a decisive result, while that corresponding to the second argument does not. The central idea to grasp here is that this weakness is a matter of *logic*, and not a deficiency of factual investigation. It is, of course, true that premisses such as these would not tend to mislead a psephologist into drawing invalid conclusions; rather, he would set out to discover whether it was possible to discover what separated the Labour and non-Labour manual working class, (5) and how likely it was that the voters of Oldhaven East Ward would behave like voters throughout the country; then, and only then, might he be in a position to produce a *valid* argument — though certainly, alas, too long and complex to use here — which had as its conclusion the prediction that some of the voters of Oldhaven East Ward would vote Labour. But this does not weaken the distinction between matters of fact and matters of logic, for what the psephologist's going out and inquiring into the facts shows is precisely that he needs new data in order to be able to replace the logically inadequate premisses of the invalid argument with new premisses from which the desired conclusion can be validly inferred.

This can be understood more clearly in the light of a closely related distinction stemming from our original distinction between matters of fact and matters of logic. This is the familiar dichotomy between synthetic statements and analytic statements. (6) It ought to be said at once that this is a distinction over which much philosophical argument has raged, and one whose implications have been rather fiercely contested by philosophers of different persuasions. (7) The reason for the controversies is that in the day to day practice both of everyday life and scientific investigation, it is often hard to draw the line between analytic and synthetic statements; many of the statements made in the natural sciences — including the social sciences among them — do not show their logical status so clearly in their linguistic form that we can readily assign them to one or other category. And thus, once again, we have to conclude how many more skills the philosopher needs than the ability to pose simple either-or questions. But such reflections do nothing to hide the obvious truth that for much of the time there is no great difficulty in drawing such a distinction, and that in this book we shall run no risks if we take its usefulness for granted. The connection between this distinction and the first is marked by the common equation of statements which are both analytic and true with 'truths of logic' and statements which are both synthetic and true with 'factual truths' — conversely, of course, there is a class of logical falsehoods and a class of factual falsehoods. The basis of the distinction is this: to see whether an analytic statement is true or false we need look no further than the statement itself, to the meaning of the words which make it up, but if we are to see whether a synthetic statement is true or false, we must, once we know what it says about the world, look to the world beyond the statement and draw upon evidence about the facts of that world. (8) Another way of putting this same point is to say that the truth or falsity of an analytic statement is *internal* to that statement, whereas the truth or falsity of a synthetic statement is *external* to that statement, in that it rests on the correspondence of the statement to an outside world. The most hackneyed of examples serves perfectly well to illustrate the point. The statement that: 'All bachelors are unmarried' is not in principle one whose truth a sociologist could intelligibly set out to investigate. Anyone who supposed that it would be a worthwhile activity to go and discover how many of the local bachelors were unmarried would simply indicate that he had not understood what the word 'bachelor' meant in the first place. Imagine him drawing up a list of the local bachelors: the criteria for checking on whether the names on our list are the right names are simply the criteria for checking whether they are the names of unmarried men. In other words, one of the criteria of being a bachelor is being unmarried, so that any list of bachelors is by definition a list of the unmarried, and any list that is not a list of unmarried men is by definition not a list of bachelors at all. But such statements about bachelors as: 'Many more 35-year-old Irishmen are still bachelors than are 35-year-old Greeks' are certainly the kind of statement which not merely might interest a sociologist, but whose truth is very unlikely to be more than guessed at without some kind of empirical, sociological investigation.

The importance of this distinction becomes evident on

considering how often in sociology or political science it is left unclear whether a statement is to be understood as a definitional truth, i.e. as an analytic statement, or as an empirical statement to which evidence is relevant, i.e. as a synthetic statement. This is particularly true in those areas where what we are interested in has social and political consequences of a controversial kind. One instance in recent controversy was the insistence by one critic of the Wolfenden Committee's recommendation that homosexuality should be regarded as a private matter and 'none of the law's business' (9) that *all* moral matters were the law's business; the reasoning offered by Lord Devlin was that a society was coextensive with the agreement of its members on moral issues, and hence that moral dissent was bound to tend to destroy the society, to be a kind of treason. (10) But this argument rested on a fatal ambiguity: was the statement that society is coextensive with its morality to be seen as an empirical truth, to the effect that societies suffered calamities such as civil war, economic collapse and the like whenever people ceased to agree over sexual ethics? The obvious falsity of such a view made this hardly likely. Or was it to be taken as a matter of definition, that Lord Devlin thought we ought not to call a society *one* society unless it was permeated by a single morality? Such a view cannot be factually refuted, of course; but it is such an idiosyncratic definition of society that we can hardly imagine anyone making much use of it. The answer seems to be that Lord Devlin was making the not uncommon error of patching up gaps in the facts by trying to enlist the support of definitional truths — but as we have seen, this is quite self-defeating, since to put it crudely only factual evidence can do factual evidence's job. (11) Another example from recent debates concerns the ascription of the title of 'democracy' to a country's political life. In the modern context, where it is a term of praise, the title of democracy is obviously a coveted label, because to call a country's politics democratic involves, up to a point, praising that country's politics. But it is no use *defining* democracy in terms of the politics of any particular country, for then we can no longer praise that country for being democratic — we cannot praise a society for qualities which belong to it by definition, rather than by political contrivance. Yet, when

Professor Dahl wrote his 'Preface to Democratic Theory', he displayed exactly the same doubts as Devlin, for he asked of an account of democracy that it should both set up standards for democratic performance *and* explain the qualities which belonged to the politics of the United States and countries resembling her. These demands, however, will not run in harness; the demand that we set up standards by which to assess a country's approximation to democratic government necessarily require that it is a factual matter whether any country we happen to name conforms to such standards. Thus, 'the United States is a democracy' would amount to a synthetic statement announcing the end of an inquiry, our factual results; but if the question is not this, but one of analysing the democratic politics of other countries in terms of how closely they approach the politics of the United States, then 'the United States is a democracy' is the beginning of our inquiry, and is an analytic statement which says what definition of democracy we propose to work with. In the elaborate writings of political scientists the point is often difficult to see; but once again it is recognised in ordinary speech. The statement that: 'John is tall' may wear either a synthetic or an analytic guise in different contexts: thus, if we are grading children for tallness, and we want a standard against which to grade them, we may take John as a yardstick and say: 'John is tall', so that we are for the moment defining tallness by reference to John — and now, of course we cannot subsequently claim to *discover* that John is tall by reference to that standard. But we may also have some independent standard, culled perhaps from the average height of New England ten-year-olds, and it is then a simple matter of fact whether John is or is not tall. What makes it difficult to avoid error here is that the same verbal formula may at one point be employed to announce a definition and at some other point to announce a factual discovery, without there being any confusion; but, of course, error results if it is not made clear *which* job the formula is supposed to be doing. Dahl, for example, makes it impossible for any political scientist to *discover* that the United States is a democracy, as soon as he has defined democracy by reference to American politics; but, of course, it is open to anyone else to employ a very different definition, and thus to discover that American

30

politics either are or are not democratic. A secondary consideration here is that once Dahl has defined democracy by reference to American politics, it is no longer a matter for congratulation that the United States is a democracy — for such congratulation would only amount to congratulating the United States for being like the United States. (12) A glance at the literature of political science, especially in such areas as the debate over the 'oligarchical' tendencies of political parties, shows that many political scientists have become very aware of the dangers of passing off definitions as facts, analytic truths as synthetic truths.

Of all the social sciences, the area where the danger was first recognised and most accurately guarded against was economics. The great use of mathematical and geometrical arguments in economics speedily made its students aware of the differences between seeing that something followed from the definitions and assumptions made for the sake of a theory and finding that something was true in the real world. Political experience also tended to enforce the same lesson, for the nineteenth-century radicals who made themselves very unpopular by supporting policies stemming from an attachment to classical economic theory soon saw that the world in which they were forced to live their political lives showed little sign of conforming to their picture of the perfect market. This among other things made them realise the difference between *defining* rational buyers and sellers in terms of 'economic man' and *discovering* that the English were economic men (which they never were and never became). It soon became a commonplace of their thinking that the results of pure economic theory were analytic truths, the logical consequences of the definitions and assumptions of economic theory; but before they could be used as synthetic statements about markets, prices, buyers and sellers in the real world, there had to be a process of discovering in what ways the real world could and could not conform to the assumptions of the theory; and such a process was usually thought of as generalising from experience, rather than trying to deduce something from assumptions. (13)

Now, one of the ways in which this distinction between analytic and synthetic statements relates to our earlier discussion of the difference between the factual and logical

31

elements in argument is that any valid deductive argument can be rewritten, not as an argument with a number of premisses and a conclusion, but as one long conditional statement; thus our example runs: 'If all members of the manual working class vote Labour, and all the voters in Oldhaven East Ward are members of the manual working class, then all the voters in Oldhaven East Ward will vote Labour'. And such a statement is analytically true, since it is a matter of logic that the conclusion does indeed follow. One important feature of this statement which may have been noticed is that its truth in no way depends on the truth of the constituent clauses — just as the validity of the argument in no way depended on the constituent statements being true. The point of insisting on this is that one important aspect of science is its concern with testing explanations under experimental conditions, and one of the foundations of testing, as the next chapter will explain in detail, is the fact that in a deductive argument it is perfectly possible to infer from false premisses to a true conclusion, and yet to employ a valid argument. It might, for instance, have turned out to be true that all the voters in Oldhaven East Ward voted Labour, even though both of the premisses from which we inferred it were false. That we can produce false premisses which logically entail conclusions that are true is no surprise: the entire history of science is littered with false hypotheses which nevertheless served as perfectly good premisses. Let us look, first at an old logic-book example, and then at one drawn from some rather famous sociological studies. The syllogism: All cats bark, Some dogs are cats, So some dogs bark is a valid syllogism; the simplest way of seeing this is to refer it to a Venn Diagram. (14) Yet, of course, we have here deduced a true conclusion from two premisses of a rather striking kind of falsity. The famous sociological example concerns the explanation of the low rate of promotion among Negro soldiers in the U.S. Army during the Second World War. It was thought by many people that the explanation must lie in the Negro soldier being in general a less ambitious man than his white counterpart; and this in effect means that they subscribed to the argument: All soldiers whose level of ambition is below that of the average white soldier will have a less good chance of promotion than

32

he, All Negroes have a lower level of ambition than the average white soldier, So all Negroes have a less good chance of promotion than does the average white soldier. The conclusion was true, but the second premiss, though it had been believed for many years by the plain man and the sociologist alike, turned out to be quite false. Indeed, its falsity, shown in 'The American Soldier' (15), has a notable place in history, for Professor Lazarsfeld used it to illustrate how sociology might show up as false 'what we all know already'. The validity of the argument was no evidence that its premisses were true. (16)

The explanation of this state of affairs lies in the notion of *consistency*, for the validity of an argument is a matter of consistency, not one of truth. The importance of consistency is obvious even in the most mundane matters; we all too often have seen that what someone says cannot be right, not because we know that some particular portion of it is false, but because we see that the person has contradicted himself, that some of what he has said is inconsistent with the rest. Thus, if part of what he says is true, the rest must be false, and vice versa; and thus it cannot be the case that what he has said is all right taken as a whole. It is at this point crucial to emphasise that what we perceive when we see someone contradicting himself is not that some part of what he says is false, but rather that not everything he says can be true, taken together; it is not a matter of how the parts of what he says relate to the world, but how they relate to each other. And the point about inconsistency is that it makes speech self-defeating: a man who claims first that Britain is bankrupt and then that Britain is not, fails in the end to claim anything, much as a man who offered one a watch and then took it away again would fail to give one anything at all. Saying and denying the same thing is the linguistic equivalent of handing the watch over and immediately taking it back. With this in mind, we can now see how it is that a syllogism's validity does not depend on questions about the truth or falsity of the individual statements involved in it, but on questions of how these statements hang together — or fail to. Thus the rule for a valid syllogism is that: the contradictory of the conclusion is contradictory of the premisses taken together. Whatever is inconsistent with the conclusion is

33

inconsistent with the premises; and what this means is that the conclusion asserted is the only one which is consistent with the truth of the premisses, so that it is logically improper to accept the premisses and deny the conclusion. That the arguments cited above which had strikingly false premisses still satisfy this requirement is easily enough verified: the point is not that we must accept the premisses, for we do not; it is that *if* we accept the premisses, then we cannot without inconsistency deny the conclusion. This, again, explains why it is that the analytic statements which correspond to valid arguments are conditional or hypothetical statements; what we learn from such statements is what we *would* be committed to, *if* we are committed to the premisses of the argument. A moment's thought shows how vital this requirement is, in the pursuit of truth. In any elaborate chain of explanation, we may at length come to a conclusion which we know to be false; if the explanation is cast into the form of a valid deductive argument, we know that we cannot both accept the premisses of the explanation and still deny the conclusion; so if we do wish to deny the conclusion, we know that we cannot accept all the premisses of the explanation. *If* we accept the premisses, then we must accept the conclusion; so, if we wish *not* to accept the conclusion, we must deny one or more of the premisses. We saw earlier how this might apply: a man who believed that the working class always displayed political solidarity in voting would, given such other premisses as the preponderance of the working class in Britain and the existence of universal suffrage, have to believe that there was a Labour government permanently in power. But this conclusion is false; and therefore some one of his premisses is false: if we have got the facts about the size of the working class population right, and are right about the existence of universal suffrage, it follows that he must abandon his belief in the solidarity of the working-class vote. But it is vital to note that we cannot apply this kind of argument unless we have an argument whose logical structure is that of a valid deductive argument; it is only within formally valid arguments that such tight relationships of consistency and inconsistency hold good. To the extent that there is ambiguity in the meaning of the terms involved, or looseness in the logical relationships

34

between them, to that extent we shall not know where to look for the errors we have made.

One final point worth making about the distinction between logical and factual matters is its relation to the distinction between *formal* and *material* considerations. A common expression that is often employed when talking about validity is to say that validity is a formal matter, a question of the logical form of the argument, and not of the material truth of its constituents. What this means, most crucially, is that the subject-matter of an argument has no bearing upon the validity of the argument: an argument which is of a valid logical form will be valid whether its subject-matter is drawn from cookery, sociology or classical thermodynamics; and conversely, of course, its subject-matter will not save it if it is invalid. The notation of logicians is built around this fact; the formal qualities of our argument about the voters of Oldhaven East Ward are brought out when this argument is cast into the notation of the so-called predicate calculus: (x) $(Ax \rightarrow Bx)$, (x) $(Cx \rightarrow Ax)$ so (x) $(Cx \rightarrow Bx)$. The point of such notations is obvious enough; they symbolise the relationships on which logical appraisal rests, without encumbering the page with sentences drawn from some particular subject-matter, and it is for that reason that such formulae as (x) $(Ax \rightarrow Bx)$ are as unlike sentences in the English language as are mathematical formulae like $x^2 = 2y^2 + 4y + 4$. And this has an important consequence for science; the fact that a valid form of argument retains its validity in no matter what subject area amounts to saying in the language of the logician that a given formal calculus (of which mathematics and geometry provide examples) is susceptible of an indefinite number of material interpretations. The most obvious example of this is the use of the natural numbers to count a great variety of different objects, for we employ the formal calculus which is the series of natural numbers in order to count such diverse things as people, ideas, money, animals and so on indefinitely. (17) Provided that the objects we are dealing with are stable and recountable, we can apply to them the procedures of addition and subtraction, without having to think on each occasion whether the rules of arithmetic are still valid. The example of the natural numbers may seem trivial; that it is not will be seen by anyone who reflects on the fact that students who might regard the example as trivial nonetheless find it hard to see how it is that the more complex mathematics of statistics applies to the materials of sociology or political science. But the one application is neither more nor less logically problematical than the other, however much more alarming are the problems of computation involved. A further important aspect of this matter is that it shows how one branch of science is able to borrow from another branch which has some kind of well-developed theory of a formalised kind already established. A simple example again is the borrowing of the astronomical theory of solar orbits, and the mathematics associated with that theory, in initially constructing an account of the structure of the atom. In the social sciences, there is a well-known example of such borrowing in the use of the statistical theory of the spread of epidemics from its original home in medicine to analyse the spread of such things as rumours and technical innovations. (18) The so to speak logical core of epidemiology is thus the logical core of what we might nickname 'rumour-ology'; and obviously it makes sense for any subject to try to model itself on the arguments of some other subject-matter where this can yield results. None of this, naturally, implies that an easy way to become a good scientist or a good social scientist is to develop an eye for logic and an inclination to borrow from other scientists; but it does show one of the benefits to be expected from the insistence that argumentative rigour and strictness of definition are requirements in anything that has pretensions to the name of science.

Up to this point we have concentrated entirely on problems connected with the use of deductive arguments, arguments where the implications of premisses are explored. But now we ought to turn to a different aspect of the matter, what is broadly termed the problem of inductive arguments, those which seek not to draw out the logical implications of premisses already accepted, but which seek to establish those premisses from the evidence of the facts. Many of the premisses of arguments with which we have been concerned have been universal statements of the form: All As are B, or (x) $(Ax \rightarrow Bx)$. Now we are not always interested in what follows from such statements, we are equally concerned to know why they are thought to be true. When we use such statements to explain some state of affairs in which we are interested we imply that they are true; and the question thus arises of what are adequate reasons for thinking them to be true, or what is the nature of the relationship between such statements and the particular facts or evidence from which they have been inferred. Anyone who knows the first thing about the history of philosophy will know that this question can be the first step in the direction of embroiling ourselves in the 'problem of induction'; but here we shall skirt that battlefield. The only point about it which I wish to make is that the bitter opposition in the works of recent writers on whether there is any such thing as 'inductive inference' is misleading, because it hides a very real agreement on the main differences between deductive argument and what is often called 'the logic of confirmation'. Thus Professor Popper, who has for years championed the view that there is no such thing as inductive inference, still admits that there are 'degrees of confirmation' — or as he would *not* say, degrees of inductive support; though he characterises the process of argument in all sciences as the process of 'conjecture and refutation', guessing a hypothesis and deducing testable, refutable consequences, he nevertheless agrees that a hypothesis that comes through certain kinds of testing unscathed becomes well-confirmed. (19) And this is tantamount to saying that it has been inductively established with a high degree of success. Conversely, when Mill in the nineteenth century argued that induction was the only form of 'real' inference which we employ, he nevertheless distinguished quite clearly between the support inductively offered by evidence and the entailments established by a deductive argument. (20)

The crucial point on which agreement is general is over the difference between deductive validity and inductive support. Validity is universally held to be an all-or-nothing matter, whereas inductive support is a matter of degree. In a deductive argument it either is the case that the premises logically entail the conclusion, and hence that the argument is valid, or else that they do not, and hence that it is invalid. There is no room here for a half-way house, no possibility of an argument being 'fairly valid' or 'almost valid' or 'slightly valid': if we have doubts about whether an argument is valid, perhaps because we are not clear how some of the terms involved are to be defined, we cannot settle for some kind of compromise between accepting and rejecting the argument any more than we can in the case of a mathematical proof. But in the case of inductive arguments, this is precisely what we can and often do do. Inductive evidence for a generalisation can be better or worse evidence, fairly good or pretty bad, overwhelming and conclusive or weak and inconclusive. We do here talk of degrees of support, and of some evidence being a good deal better than other evidence. And where it is characteristic of deductive arguments that all valid arguments are as valid as each other — as they necessarily must be, when there are no degrees of validity — it is the case with inductive arguments that we may well say that of two good arguments one is still rather better than the other. Indeed, a moment's thought about the role of the jury in legal battles shows just how true this is: provided that the prosecution and defence both have good lawyers, what the jury will hear is two very convincing stories backed up by a good deal of inductive evidence to show that each is true and its competitor false; the job of the jury is to decide between two good inductive stories, and assess one of them as the true one. Now, it may be said in objection here that the example weakens the force of our remarks about induction, for it is surely the task of a jury to be *quite certain* that the decision it gives is the right one, and that if inductive support is always a matter of degree, then a jury can never be *quite* certain. But this is seriously misleading as an objection, if it is thought to mean that juries can never in principle come to the right decision. For the sense in which evidential support is a matter of degree is that it can never in principle amount to such a backing as would *entail* the conclusion to which we come — and the history of the 'problem of induction' is the history of philosophers trying to evade this conclusion; but this only means that it is logically possible that the statements of evidence be true and the conclusion drawn from them be false, i.e. that there is no contradiction between asserting the evidence and denying the conclusion. But this is infinitely far from showing that on all occasions there is anything amounting to a practical possibility that the evidence is true and the conclusion false; for in good conditions, we may produce such good evidence for the truth of a conclusion that its falsity would involve us in rewriting practically everything we have ever known about the world; and while it is not logically impossible that we shall have to do this, no one could long persist in regarding it as a practical possibility. What we require for our jury is evidence that is causally conclusive, that it should be such that the falsity of the conclusions to which the jury comes *on the evidence* — for it is of course practically possible that the jury may not have heard all the evidence there is, or that the evidence may have been misleading — would necessitate the revision of our best-known causal laws. A juror who declared himself unconvinced simply because it was not inconsistent to assert the evidence but deny the conclusion advanced would be a remarkably poor advertisement for philosophy; but one who was able to point out that some of the evidence was internally incoherent or false, or who could adduce a more plausible story which would equally well account for all the reliable evidence, would be a triumph for whatever form of training he had received. (21)

The point can readily be illustrated from the social sciences. The Tikopia, a tribe of Pacific islanders studied by Raymond Firth, (22) had various rules about the allocation of rights to grow food on particular pieces of land, and these rules often involved the placing of taboos on pieces of land which it was desired not to have cultivated. If we were already in possession of generalisations about the way in which the Tikopia observed conventions of this kind, we could employ the generalisation to explain in a deductive manner the behaviour of particular Tikopia. Thus we might argue: No Tikopia grows crops on land declared *tapu*; that land was declared *tapu*; Mori is a Tikopia; so Mori will not grow crops on that land. This is a straightforward deductive argument in which the conclusion is validly derived from the premisses. But suppose we were not aware of the initial generalisation, and only knew about the behaviour of Mori: Mori is a Tikopia; that land is declared *tapu*, and Mori will not grow crops on it; so No Tikopia grows crops on land declared *tapu*. Plainly, this is not a valid argument, and no one would try to pass it off as such. Is it anything else? The only proper answer to this must be that we cannot tell until we know a lot more about the evidence: it may be that Mori is a very typical islander, and that if he tells us that he will not grow crops on land that is *tapu*, then we shall get the same story from all other Tikopia; in that case he is, though the argument as it stands produces no grounds for saying so, rather good evidence about the social behaviour of the Tikopia. But if it emerged that Mori was an excessively superstitious character, who went round in fear and trembling of old magical formulae that everyone else took with a grain of salt, then his example would be little use to us in arriving at generalisations about the Tikopia. How good the evidence was would thus depend upon all sorts of background considerations — and it is typical of inductive arguments that they do usually leave us anxious to have some more evidence, and that they suggest further inquiries to us. Sometimes we can set mathematical probabilities to the likelihood that the case we have got is a mere freak; often we cannot, and assign only a subjective probability to our appraisal of its usefulness. (23)

To conclude this chapter, let us pull together the various points we have made by reconstructing the way in which we might in one small area argue inductively to a generalisation which we can then employ as the premiss for deductive arguments. By choosing an instance which, with a certain amount of stretching, can be cast into a graphical form, we can illustrate how it may be useful to borrow from one subject in aid of another, and also how this process may well have its limitations; and all of this will enable us to draw the general moral about the progress of science through concern both for the internal logical links in its explanations and for the factual accuracy of its reports on the world. The example I take is a much modified argument from Professor Lipset's 'Political Man'; (24) before the crudeness of my argument calls out indignant protests on his behalf, let me explain his case. Lipset discovered a correlation between economic development and the establishment of liberal democracy which strongly suggested the two are causally linked via the diminishing extremism and intensity of political opinions in developed economies. Professor Lipset's conception of development includes various important considerations other

40

than people's incomes, but for the sake of illustration I propose to barbarise the whole argument – now that I have exempted Professor Lipset from any share in this barbarism – by simply taking a relationship between rising income per capita and declining political intensity. Suppose we found a great many cases where a man's opinions had moderated a good deal as his income rose; we might use this as inductive evidence – better or worse according to its reliability, quantity, diversity of origin and so on – for the generalisation that: 'Whenever income rises, the intensity of political opinions falls.' No sociologist who has heard of the 'revolution of rising expectations' could contemplate such a generalisation without a shudder, but no matter. Armed with our generalisation, we can produce such explanations as the following: Jones has a much larger income now than in 1966; whenever a man's income rises, his political opinions become less intense; so Jones's political opinions will be less intense now than they were in 1966. In offering such a simple law, by the way, we are not merely doing an injustice to Professor Lipset for the sake of exposition; we are also doing something which is perfectly legitimate in all scientific inquiry, namely stating a law in a more abstract and comprehensive way than is strictly licensed by the facts. But, of course, the converse of this process is that when we explain particular cases by way of our law, we do so with 'due allowances' made for the particular circumstances of that case. Jones's opinions, then, are likely to be predicted to have become less intense *ceteris paribus* – other things being equal. But this modification is a commonplace of the practice of any scientist, no matter what the subject-matter involved. More interesting is the next stage of our imaginative enterprise. A natural inclination would be to ask whether there was any precise mathematical relationship between the rate at which income rose and the rate at which intensity declined. So we should then be faced with the task of inventing scales along which to measure the intensity of opinion – a problem to which social scientists have devoted a lot of attention for exactly the kind of reason I am suggesting. Suppose we do this, and discover a very simple relationship, namely that on our scale of intensity, a man's opinions become twice as intense when his income halves, and conversely. We can now illustrate this relationship graphically. And this raises some interesting issues. For when we consider the graph we draw, it has a variety of possible meanings for us. As an arrangement of lines, some curved, some straight, it has no more than a passing aesthetic interest; as a graphical representation of various geometrical truths, it is an economical way of representing a large number of them simultaneously; and, we recall, they are formal truths, analytic statements. But if we were to show the graph to an economist, he would at once see it as a piece of applied geometry, for it is the way in which any introductory textbook represents the demand curve for a good with unitary elasticity of demand. (25) In this sense there is an empirical relationship asserted, when this demand curve is said to characterise some good in the real world, for such a claim can only be assessed by seeing how demand for that good actually does vary with its price. And here we have arrived at the case where the formal calculus, that is the geometry of such a curve, is equally available to both the economist and the political scientist. Its formal properties can be materially interpreted for the relationship between price and quantity or for the relationship between income and intensity. But we can also see what sort of limits are set to this process of discovering formal similarities between different subject-matters. We mentioned the problem of devising a scale for measuring attitudes as more intense and less intense: the literature on such problems indicates clearly enough that our troubles are often conceptual ones, in that we do not know quite how to describe what we want to measure, nor what the relationship is between the indicators which we employ, and the psychological states of which they are indicators. The economist has an easier time by comparison, for when he measures price and quantity he does no more than the shopkeeper and the housewife do. But even pushing such troubles aside, we soon come to worse ones: when the economist employs the graph we have described he can use one of its interesting geometrical features, the fact that all rectangles bounded by the two axes and perpendicular lines from those axes to a point on the curve have the same area; for him, this can be empirically interpreted as the proposition that the income of a firm facing such a demand curve for its good is constant;

42

price times quantity yields income, and for such a demand curve price times quantity is a constant. But here the political scientist must stop: not for him the possibility of multiplying income by intensity, for such a move would result in the sheerest nonsense. And since it would result in nonsense, there is here a conceptual barrier to further modelling of political science on economics. The kind of thing we measure in economics makes the further exploration both intelligible and useful; but this is simply to show how the concepts of economics are not those of politics. (26)

The way in which all this ties in with the distinctions we have taken pains to establish is this. The several sciences — natural sciences and social sciences alike — aim to strengthen the connections between what we know of the world and our rational expectations of how the world will continue to behave. The aim is thus to link more and more exactly our experiences and what we can infer from these experiences. In so doing, we employ various kinds of logical calculus, of which mathematics, geometry and formal logic are the archetypes. In giving empirical interpretation to such calculi, we try to tie our experiences together with the tightest links we can; and it is for this reason that both scientists and philosophers have so much admired the sciences in which axiomatisation and the employment of mathematics reached their highest pitch. (27) The 'fit' between our calculi and the real world is an empirically discovered, inductively proved matter; the 'fit' between the various parts of our calculi is a deductively proved, logically imposed matter. Thus our elementary distinctions lead us quickly to see that the line of advance in any theoretical science must proceed on two fronts, one being that of improving the tightness of the internal connections of the theories of the science, the other being that of improving the accuracy with which the theory fits the world it purports to explain. It is not surprising that our distinctions have led us in this direction, for it is precisely this truth about science which they were elaborated in order to describe. But the time has now come to spell out in some detail the view of scientific explanation which this account has presupposed.

NOTES

1. P. F. Strawson, 'Introduction to Logical Theory', 2nd ed. (Methuen, 1964) ch. 1.

2. L. S. Stebbing, 'A Modern Introduction to Logic' (Methuen, 1930) ch. 6.

3. Strawson, 'Logical Theory', pp. 78-93.

4. P. Suppes, 'Introduction to Logic' (Van Nostrand, 1957) pp. 195-201.

5. E.g. J. H. Goldthorpe et al., 'The Affluent Worker' (Cambridge University Press, 1968) vol. ii.

6. Strawson, 'Logical Theory', pp. 230-1.

7. W. V. O. Quine, 'From a Logical Point of View' (Harvard University Press, 1953) pp. 20-37.

8. Ayer, 'Language', pp. 78-9.

9. Wolfenden Committee Report, Cmd 247, para. 61.

10 P. Devlin, 'The Enforcement of Morals' (Oxford University Press, 1968) pp. 9-15.

11. H. L. A. Hart, 'Immorality and Treason', 'Listener' (1959) 162.

12. R. A. Dahl, 'A Preface to Democratic Theory' (Chicago University Press, 1956) pp. 63 ff.

13. Mill, 'Logic', bk vi, ch. viii.

14. Suppes, 'Introduction to Logic', pp. 195-201.

15. S. Stouffer et al., 'The American Soldier' (Princeton University Press, 1949).

16. P. F. Lazarsfeld: 'The American Soldier: An Expository Review', 'Public Opinion Quarterly', xiii (1949).

17. G. Frege, 'The Foundations of Arithmetic' 2nd ed. (Blackwell, Oxford, 1956) ch. ii.

18. J. A. Coleman, 'Introduction to Mathematical Sociology' (Free Press, Chicago, 1964) pp. 41-6.

19. K. R. Popper, 'Conjectures and Refutations' (Harper Torchbooks, 1968) pp. 35-59.

20. Mill, 'Logic', bk ii, ch. iii, sec. 4.

21. Strawson, 'Logical Theory', pp. 248-63.

22. R. Firth, 'We, the Tikopia' (Allen and Unwin, 1936).

23. J. O. Urmson, 'Two Senses of Probable', 'Analysis' (1947) 9-16.

24. S. M. Lipset, 'Political Man' (Heinemann, 1963) pp. 61 ff.

25. P. Samuelson, 'Economics', 7th ed. (McGraw-Hill, 1967) p. 376.

26. D. Stokes, 'Spatial Models of Party Competition', 'Amer. Pol. Sci. Rev.' 47 (1963) 368-377.

27. As in Nagel's preoccupation with mechanics, 'Structure of Science', chs 7 ff.

3 The Deductive Conception of Explanation

Although, as anyone who peruses the literature will see, there is no single, universally accepted account of the logic of scientific explanation, there is an order visible amid the competing accounts. There is one account which enjoys a position of near-orthodoxy, although it has to fight for this position under a sniping fire from more or less critical alternatives. Both as an object of attack and defence, and both as an object of interest to scientists and to philosophers, the so-called 'hypothetico-deductive' theory of explanation dominates the field. (1) Its name summarises its main contentions, and the main objects of our scrutiny in this chapter, namely that explanations require the adducing of general laws, with the status of empirical hypotheses about the natural order, from which, in conjunction with statements of initial conditions, we can deductively infer statements about empirical consequences. The elements of this account have a long history; but since the early nineteenth century it has enjoyed almost canonical status, defended by such men as Laplace, Whewell and Mill at that time, and by such writers as Popper, Hempel and Nagel today. The goals of this chapter are therefore twofold. In the first place, we must try to understand the point of insisting on the deductive nature of explanation, and try to follow the consequences of this insistence; then we must consider the view which is almost invariably a concomitant of this insistance, that the mode in which scientific inquiry proceeds is by the testing and attempted falsification of empirical hypotheses. Finally, we have to raise some of the doubts which have been brought out by critics of this account. In the process, I hope to put forward some not wholly orthodox suggestions about our interest in causal sequences in science, not so much to show that the hypothetico-deductive account is in a simple sense wrong, as to show how it misplaces what I

46

take to be our interest in explanation. There is one cat which should be let out of the bag at once; it is a cat of negative characteristics, for it is my eventual view that the social sciences do not differ appreciably from the natural sciences in the applicability to them of this picture of explanation. That is, I do not propose to argue that the hypothetico-deductive picture of explanation does apply to the natural sciences and does not apply to the social sciences; for it is my view that its merits and demerits are visible more or less evenly across the scientific spectrum; accordingly, in what follows, there is no very careful attempt to employ illustrations drawn from one area of the sciences rather than any other.

It is obvious that the analysis of explanation is a central concern of the philosophy of science, since we only embark on scientific inquiry in order to be able to explain the world more satisfactorily than we can by unaided common sense. This holds good whether the events which we explain are economic, political or chemical; no matter what the kind of phenomena in which we are interested, what we want is to explain how they turn out the way they are rather than in some utterly different way. The question thus arises at once, what is a good explanation? Now, one word of warning is here in order; a great deal of the recent literature on explanation (2) has dwelt with great enthusiasm on the fact that explanations are always given *in a context*, so that we very often offer some piece of information as *the* explanation of some phenomenon not so much because we think that in itself this piece of information is strikingly important, but because we think that in the context of what the inquirer can be expected to know, this information is the information which he is lacking. What is assumed is that since an explanation is sought because of our ignorance, then whatever it is that fills in the gap in our knowledge is an explanation; plainly this has its uses as an argument to show that, in this sense, almost any information can be *the* explanation, just as any piece of a jigsaw puzzle can be *the* piece, depending on what has been completed already. But this emphasis on the state of mind of the inquirer has one great defect as a general account of explanation, in that it confuses the psychological question of what will satisfy the inquirer with the logical and conceptual question of what constitutes an adequate explanation of the event in question. It is an obvious, if lamentable fact about human beings that as a matter of fact they have often been satisfied by all sorts of half-truths, untruths and various kinds of nonsense; what gratifies the curiosity of mankind, and what provides a logically acceptable explanation remain two different inquiries. Nonetheless, we can best approach the analysis of the logic of explanation by way of considering what it is that we are after when we demand the explanation of some particular event which we find puzzling. And as a general rule, what we look for is that information which, when appropriately put together, yields us an argument to the effect that the event in question was what we should rationally expect. Suppose, to take a distressing possibility, that you have bought a new car, and one morning notice that there is a large dent in the back of it; thus you want to know how this dent got there, or what caused it, i.e. you want to have its presence explained. It may be that inquiries reveal that a friend had borrowed the car, and had backed it violently into a lamppost while he had it. At this point you will conclude that you have the explanation; you can assemble the conditions — the friend backing up quickly, the presence of an obstacle — and from these it is possible to infer the result, the presence of a dent in the rear of the car. What this amounts to is producing an argument whose premisses concern the causal antecedents, and whose conclusion states the present sad results. (3)

To this the obvious objection is not that this is not an explanation of the dent in the car, for it is clear that it is a perfectly adequate explanation so far as it goes, but rather that it does not seem to square very well with all the talk about deduction. We ask why the car is in a sorry state, and we are told two facts, that a friend borrowed it, and that he backed it into a lamppost. If the event of the car's being dented is to be our conclusion (C), and the antecedent events are our premisses A and B, what we have here is not a deductive argument, but a sequence — event A, the car is borrowed; event B, it is backed into a lamppost; so event C, it has a dent in it. A sequence A, B, so C scarcely looks like, and indeed is not, a valid deductive argument. What any 'deductivist' would argue, of course, is that in a case such as

48

this we all tend to take the general law which governs the explanation for granted, but that once this is made explicit (as it always can in principle be) we have a valid deductive argument. (4) The singular statement 'John's backing the car into the lamppost caused the dent in the car' rests on a causal law of a general kind, which states the effects of impacts from hard objects on softer ones. The generalisation that hard objects will damage softer ones on impact is so un-challenged that we simply do not bother to state it where it can be left understood − which is simply to make again our previous point that in giving an explanation we try to tell people the things they do not know already, and not those that they do know. That the generalisation, whether stated or not, is logically necessary to the explanation can be seen quite readily. If lampposts were not made of hard substances such as concrete or cast iron, but of some yielding substance such as a soft plastic, then we could not cite the collision between the car and the post as the causal explanation, since it would no longer be covered by the backing of the general-isation which makes it relevant. When we explain an event causally by pointing to its causal antecedents, to what Popper terms the 'initial conditions' (5) of the event, this only makes sense because we appeal implicitly to a general law which states that these causal antecedents are sufficient to bring about this event. Thus a fully spelled out explanation takes the form of adducing a general law or laws, some set of initial conditions, and deducing from these the statement describing the event to be explained. The logical relationship is thus Laws $(L_1 \ldots L_n)$, Conditions $(C_1 \ldots C_n)$, so Event(s) $(E_1 \ldots E_n)$; and as in any valid deductive argument the *explanans* must entail the *explanandum*. For example, an economist who set out to explain the devaluation of the pound which was forced on the British government in 1931 might explain it in terms of the Bank of England having pursued the policy of 'borrowing short to lend long' in the months preceding. The event to be explained − the event which we term the *explanandum* − is thus the devaluation, and its causal antecedents the Bank's actions in borrowing money on a short-run basis in order to finance long-term lending on its own part; the background generalisations are rather numerous, but they will include laws about the

49

behaviour of speculators in selling a currency which they believe to be overvalued, and laws about the way in which frightened holders of sterling will sell their holdings if they believe that there will be a run on the Bank, and laws again about the way in which under a gold standard speculation can only be defeated by ample monetary reserves in gold or in currencies readily exchanged for gold. Anyone who knows a certain amount of economics will see at once what the point was of adducing the Bank's policy of borrowing short and lending long as a cause of the devaluation; he is in the position of the layman to whom the antecedents of the dent in his car give a wholly satisfactory explanation. But anyone who knows no economics will have to have the *point* of the cited antecedents explained, and this will essentially involve producing the generalisations about economic behaviour which make them relevant − and this may be a long job. (6)

Now, it is possible that a sceptic is unconvinced by this, and does not think too well of the insistence that generalisations must really be involved, even when they are not appealed to. He may go on to say that it is likely not so much that we would bring in more and more generalisations to explain our economics to the layman, but that we would bring in more and more intervening variables, that we should elaborate our story about the antecedents. Now, I do think that there is something in this objection, if it is understood as a complaint that the emphasis on generalisations is often excessive; nevertheless, this is only a complaint about the balance of emphasis in the usual account of scientific explanation, and not an objection to its logic. For the need for backing generalisations is readily explained in a very convincing way. Suppose that we want to have an event explained; one thing that is surely at the back of our minds demanding an explanation is that we want to know how it is that *this* event occurred, rather than one of the other events which we should *a priori* have thought possible. We ask why the pound was devalued, or why a street corner gang should choose to measure its members' prestige by their bowling scores, why the average output of the bank wiring room remains constant in spite of everything the company does to increase it; (7) and always we want to know why *that* outcome − why not the maintenance of the existing parity, why

50

not the measuring of prestige by simple physical strength, why not an increase in output when the company raises piece rates? In short, when we want an explanation in causal terms, what we want is to be shown how no other event was causally possible, how the event(s) in question *had* to be the way they were, given the conditions we can cite and the laws which we know to hold. This aspect of causal explanation has created endless disputes about the kind of 'necessity' involved in causation; fortunately, we can ignore them at this point, and simply note that the necessity we are interested in is causal necessity, and that it involves only the belief that when we cite causes we show why things had to turn out one way rather than another.

The relevance of deduction to this requirement is simple enough. If we can cite a valid generalisation of the form 'All A are B', what we are doing is ruling out any chance of finding a singular statement of the form 'This is A but not B'. (8) For example, the generalisation 'all Tikopia respect *tapu* ceremonies' amounts to the claim that we cannot find an instance of someone who is both a Tikopia and yet does not respect *tapu* ceremonies. If we recall the basic point about a deductive argument, it was that we cannot both accept the premisses and deny the conclusion; thus if one premiss is a general statement to the effect that all Tikopia respect *tapu* ceremonies, and the other is a singular statement to the effect that here is someone who is a Tikopia, we have to accept that he respects *tapu* ceremonies; if all A are B and this is an A, then it *must* be a B. If the major premiss of our argument was a causal law to the effect that any firm which increases its output in a market with unchanged demand will have to take a lower price per unit, and our initial conditions were that here was a firm which increased its output in the face of unchanged demand, then — supposing the premisses are true — the price per unit *has* to go down. If we want to explain the fall in the unit price of the good in question, then here is the explanation; on these premisses, no other outcome is possible. Let us look at this another way. Suppose we are explaining the fall in price, and adduce the fact of increased output. At this point we have a conclusion and one, singular, premiss. To make the argument stick, we need a general law to the effect that *whenever* a firm acts thus, the price will

51

fall, for without such a premiss, the conclusion does not *have* to follow; with it it does. If such a premiss is missing or incomplete or only roughly true, then to that extent we have not produced a conclusive explanation of the event; for the answer to the question whether there could not have been some other outcome must be that there could. So long as the statements which form the premisses of the argument do not entail the statement which forms its conclusion, we have not got a compelling argument, for we can without self-contradiction accept the premisses and deny the conclusion — which amounts to accepting what is offered as the explanation while denying that that is what it is.

One important consequence of this is worth recalling from the previous chapter, namely the implications for the false-hood of the premisses of the falsehood of the conclusion. Take our hypothetical firm once again. Suppose now that it raises its output in a static market and yet that its price per unit does not drop at all. We have here produced a case of the form: 'This is an A but not a B', that is, precisely the case which generalisations of the form: 'All A are B' rule out. The proposition that a firm raised its output and did not have to lower its prices is straightforwardly inconsistent with the generalisation that *all* firms raising their output in a static market have to accept a lower unit-price. If the generalisation were true, then it would *have* to be the case that the firm's unit price fell; if the firm's unit price did not fall, then one of the premisses of the explanation must be false, whether it is the generalisation that price per unit falls under such conditions, or the particular statement of initial conditions, that the firm did raise its output under those conditions. Thus we can summarise the requirements for successful explanation laid down by Professors Hempel and Oppenheim in a famous article some years ago: (9) a successful explanation has to obey three requirements. The first is the formal requirement that the statements laying down the laws and initial conditions should entail the statement laying down the conclusion; the second is the material requirement that the premisses should be true — or more cautiously that they should be well corroborated; the last is a consequence of these requirements, that the *explanans* should be empirically testable, by being open to refutation should it predict what is

52

not the case. Only under these conditions do we empirically or causally explain why an event had to happen as it did. And it is practically a defining quality of empiricist philosophy of science that it sets up these standards as the standards for true explanation.

Before concluding this account of the insistence on the deductive aspect of explanation, we should say something about the nature of the causal laws which we have cited as the backing for deductive explanations. We said earlier that explanations are implicitly general in that they appeal, even covertly, to generalisations, so that even a singular causal assertion is backed by a general law. Now we can expand on this. An everyday causal statement may look unequivocally singular: it may appear to relate singular events to singular events, as when we say 'It was George's calling him a coward that made Harry knock him down', or 'It was his mother's sending him to school without breakfast that made Bill so miserable that day'. Here we refer to single events of being insulted and being neglected in order to explain the event of the blow that knocked George down or the series of events that are Bill's being miserable. Not only are these single events, but we might even be very unwilling to generalise from them, even though we would be willing to assent to the particular explanation on that one occasion. There is, of course, a very trivial sense in which each occasion is unique; but this has a non-trivial consequence, namely that generalisations have to be concerned with *types* of event, and we may be extremely unsure that we can identify the *type* of case we are dealing with. (10) For example, if we try to generalise the proposition that it was being called a coward by George that made Harry hit him, what shall we come up with? Not, we may be certain 'Whenever anyone is called a coward by anyone else, he hits that person', for that is very plainly not true, even though it would certainly fit the logical role. It is not clear that we should be any happier with the law 'Harry hits George whenever George calls him a coward', either because it might well be the case that Harry had previously put up with the insult quite cheerfully, or because it was the first time George had insulted Harry and we had no idea what would generally happen. If, then, we are so unwilling to *produce* generalisations to back our explanations, what is

53

the force of the claim that we are committed to them? Firstly, it lies in the methodological demand that we should make our explanations as explicitly deductive as possible, since only then can we discover what it is that we are committed to — is it, for example, to no more than a limited generalisation about the behaviour of Harry and George, or is it to a wider generalisation about human aggression? Only if we couch our explanations in this deductive form can we bring out our commitments and answer such questions; but only if we answer such questions can we be truly said to give reasons for our beliefs. A second aspect of the case is that reasons are in their nature general, which amounts to saying that anyone who gives something as a reason for his belief on one occasion is committed to giving the same reason on any occasion exactly like it. This may seem a rather abstract point, but it has some concrete consequences. Once a person has committed himself to a causal explanation, he is committed to that explanation in all relevantly similar cases; thus if there is some second case which looks identical to the first, but he does not wish to explain it in the same way, then he is obliged to explain how the second case is really different from the first. To revert again to the case of the insulted Harry, we might find a second occasion on which George called Harry a coward and Harry did not hit him at all. At this point, the explanation of the first case comes into question, and if it is not to be refuted by this apparent counter-example, relevant differences between the two cases must be cited: it may be, to take one possibility, that Harry is now sober, and before he was drunk, and that he is always more prone to take offence when drunk; in this way we make our original explanation more complex, and bring out some of the qualifications which we wish to attach to any generalisation employed in such circumstances. But all this presupposes the claim we made, that explanations are implicitly general. Anyone who still had doubts about this claim could only have practical doubts — to the effect that any generalisations produced in this way will be immensely long and filled with hedges and qualifications; and thus, of course, the unwillingness to produce generalisations which I earlier suggested we might feel appears to be a practical unwillingness, and not an objection on logical principle. (11)

54

The final claim for generalisations which is usually made by philosophers of science leads us into deepish waters. This is the analysis of covering laws as contingent universal statements of regularities in the natural order. There is no logical link between the first two elements of generality in explanation and this one; yet this third claim is a more or less constant concomitant of them: almost all those who have defended an analysis of explanations along the hypothetico-deductive pattern have also offered an analysis of causal generalisations as statements of *de facto* regularities. Although this is true also of those philosophers who have discussed the social sciences I think there are some good reasons for not accepting the whole package, and indeed for taking the first two points, but not this third one. But before I turn to this part of the case, let me begin by listing those aspects of causal laws on which everyone would agree. The first aspect to be clear about is that laws are not the same as merely accidental generalisations, and hence that we have to distinguish between enumerative and 'nomothetic' generalisations. (12) The distinction here insisted on is less easy to describe than it is to illustrate; but the illustrations are simple enough. A statement to the effect that: 'All the men in this room are called Smith' or 'All the balls in this bag are black or white' is an enumerative generalisation; it has two important characteristics. The first is that it can be shown to be true by exhaustive enumeration, i.e. by listing all the men in the room and seeing that each is called Smith: 'This man and this man and ... is called Smith, and these are all the men there are in the room.' In other words, the statement amounts to a string of singular statements and the assertion that these cover the case. The second feature of such generalisations is that they will not license what are termed 'counterfactual' statements, that is hypothetical statements about what would have been the case had some non-actual possibility been realised. This amounts to saying that we cannot employ them as laws in arguments which tell us what would have happened in some other case than the present. Thus we cannot infer from 'All the men in this room are called Smith' that had Jones come into the room he also would have been called Smith; equally, we cannot infer from 'All the balls in this bag are black or white' that a red ball placed in the bag would have been black or white. This second point is of the utmost importance, because it is central to the whole idea of testing and experimentation which most people associate with scientific procedure. A generalisation from which one *can* predict in this counter-factual way is one which can – if only in principle – be tested experimentally. Thus, to employ our example of the relationship between prices and output, we can infer from the law that all firms which raise their output in a static market have to accept a lower unit price a proposition like the following: 'If we, Allied Engineering, raise our output next year, in spite of the fact that we can see no possibility of rising demand for our product, we shall have to sell at a lower unit price' – and obviously, such an inference is of the utmost use if we are to decide rationally whether to increase output or not. Because we can make such predictions, we can set out to test our generalisations: if we, Allied Engineering, are sceptical of the truth of the generalisation, we can test it by raising output regardless and seeing whether unit price does indeed fall. Thus we are both in a position to guide our conduct by generalisations accepted as true, and to test the truth of such generalisations by our conduct. In brief, the distinguishing feature of a causal generalisation is that it *will* license future and counterfactual statements – predictions and explanations – whereas a merely enumerative generalisation will not. It is, in fact, one of the central concerns of social science and natural science alike to try to *extract* causal generalisations from the data which surveys and the like yield in the form of enumerative generalisations, often of an imperfect kind. It is a frequent criticism of social scientists' work that they present us with something less than adequate explanations, that they are prone to leave us with mere enumerative generalisations, without causally analysing them. Thus the pioneering work on voting behaviour, called 'Voting' (13) was sometimes criticised because it told us e.g. only that a certain proportion of Catholics vote Democrat; the authors of 'Voting' failed to tell us *why* Catholics tended to vote Democrat rather than Republican (and even more interestingly what were the causes behind the deviation of those Catholics who voted for some other party). It was, of course, enormously important to have had the data collected

56

and sorted with such care; nonetheless, what was produced was the material out of which genuine causal statements could be produced, not those causal statements themselves.

The second major point on which all critics are agreed is the need to distinguish between causal connection and logical connection. (14) A causal statement associates a change in one property with a change in some other, logically independent property, as when we say that 'earning more money makes a man more moderate in his politics'. It is important to recall that such a statement, however well-founded on the evidence it may be, is still a contingent statement, and not a statement of logical connection. This, in effect, is to insist again that in terms of the distinctions we drew in the last chapter causal statements are synthetic truths (or falsehoods). What this amounts to is the reminder that earning more money and being politically moderate are properties that are defined independently of each other, so that logically it is possible (though, of course, our causal statement claims that factually it will not happen) that a man will be found who earns more money and becomes less moderate. We may now add to the points we made before about the distinction between synthetic and analytic statements that this line also marks the line between causal statements and definitional truths, and recall all that we said earlier about the importance of distinguishing between those statements to which evidence is relevant, and whose truth can be empirically tested, and those statements whose truth is a matter of the definition of terms. Obviously, this has implications for testing and experiment, in that a causal proposition which asserts that two logically independent properties are causally related can always in principle be put up for test by bringing about the existence of the one property and seeing whether this does indeed bring about the existence of the other. (15) Thus, suppose we are a government which fears working-class radicalism; relying on our earlier generalisation, we may launch the policy of planning for economic growth together with a measure of redistribution of income, in the hope that this will then raise the incomes of the working class and moderate their political views. I need hardly say that I do not offer this as a piece of practical advice to any government in such a situation; the point it illustrates, however, is that here the properties we are concerned with are logically distinct, and therefore it makes sense to think of trying to bring about one of them in order to produce the other. But where the properties are logically linked, there can be no question of producing one as a means towards producing the other. We cannot test the generalisation because nothing can *count* as a test; for the state of affairs which would count as producing one property would also by *definition* count as the state of affairs of producing the other — hence, of course, the notion of the counter-example, in which the antecedent does appear, but the consequent does not, simply makes no sense in these conditions. Let me illustrate this. In various areas of sociology, such things as the choices people make of education for their children or of accommodation for themselves are explained in terms of the social class of those who do the choosing. Now class is well-known to be a very dangerous concept, because so much hangs on the definition with which any given sociologist decides to work. If, for instance, we try to explain a disregard for educational advancement in terms of 'class values', but include within working-class values such things as a disregard for education, what happens is that it becomes an analytic truth that the working class care less for education — simply because being working class has been defined in terms of this very fact. Again, it is sometimes proposed to use housing rental as a test of class, so that one of the defining characteristics of the working class is that it lives in low-rental housing. (16) But at this point it becomes impossible to assert as a causal generalisation that being working class makes people live in low rental areas, for it has become a necessary truth, not a contingent one. Only where the criteria for class membership and those for housing occupancy are distinct can there be any causal statement about the relationship between them. It is not exactly a golden key to academic success to keep this distinction firmly in mind; nonetheless, it is of considerable importance. At every point it is worth asking of any sociological statement: 'Is this intended to be a causal generalisation; can we conceive of an experimental test for it?'

But though I share the general concern that the distinctions marked above should be carefully attended to, I

58

want now to suggest that we ought to reject the analysis of causal laws as statements of *de facto* regularities. There are three points worth making, at a length which does not involve our pursuing the issue for ever. The first point is to see that there is some sense in the often-heard complaint that a lot of explanations do not tell us why something happens, but only that it always does. (17) It does seem a fair complaint that to be told only 'it always happens that way' is not a very helpful explanation, and this surely is what a statement of *de facto* regularity does tell us. The familiar example of the explanation of the alternation of night and day illustrates this well enough. We have come to explain this alternation in terms of the rotation of the earth about its axis, so that any given portion of the earth is alternately in the light of the sun or in shade. To have offered the generalisation 'night always follows day, and vice versa' as an explanation of the way day and night follow each other would clearly have been no good at all. What explanations offer us — even the rather primitive, if long-lived one which saw the earth as a flat disc above and below the rim of which the sun used to pass — is plainly something other than a statement about *de facto* regularity. This brings me to the second point, which is that *de facto* regularities appear almost always as data or evidence, not as part of explanatory laws; by themselves they are of little use in explaining anything. A case in point is the discovery by two nineteenth-century statisticians of the unsuspected regularities in the crime rates in France for many years. (18) What they discovered was certainly interesting, namely that for many crimes, the rate at which they were committed was seemingly very stable over a long period and did not seem to be influenced by social and political changes of great importance. The question arises of whether the generalisations thus produced can be said to explain crime. The answer is obviously that they did not. Of course, what such generalisations could do was in the first place *suggest* causal generalisations about crime, which would explain how it came about that such stable rates were produced, and in the second place *test* existing explanations of criminal behaviour, since these would have had to show how the rates came to be the way they were or else be refuted. That is, anyone con-

59

fronted with the regularities might have guessed at some account of how criminals were motivated which would account for their apparent independence of political and social changes, perhaps he might have done as Lombroso did and tried to account for it in terms of genetic defect; (19) alternatively someone who thought that crimes of all kind were rising rapidly due to the insubordination of the poor in the early nineteenth century would have had to throw away that hypothesis as refuted by the evidence. This raises the third point, the nature of such explanatory hypotheses. The current literature on the philosophy of science neglects one aspect of explanation which appears to me to warrant more emphasis: this is the notion of *causal narratives*. (20) By a causal narrative, nothing more is meant than a story of how one event would follow another, either in terms of a familiar sequence − or an analogue to it − or at any rate in terms of a controlled process. We saw at the very beginning of the chapter that an ordinary explanation seems very often to be couched in terms of a causal history; what I now suggest is that causal statements are not statements of *de facto* regularities, but recipes for constructing causal histories. Certainly, no harm comes of calling them causal generalisations, for they are indeed general; their generality consists in the fact that they offer (at best) rules for constructing an indefinitely large number of actual and hypothetical histories. And they are certainly related to regularities in the sense that they assure us that a repeated sequence of one property or variable will be accompanied by a repeated sequence of some second property or variable. It is only an account along some such lines as this which will do justice to the traditional stumbling blocks of empiricist philosophy of science − for example, to the difficulty that a universal law about the behaviour of a body moving in a right line and unaffected by any impressed force was accepted as true, although we know that there is certainly no case of even one such body, let alone a regular stream of them. The point, once seen, is readily grasped; so let us simply re-construct one of our former examples in the light of it. Take our piece of elementary economics: it is certainly true that we can construe as a causal generalisation the statement that all firms which raise their output in a static market will have to lower their unit price. But it can hardly be a statement of *de facto* regularity simply because it is very dubious whether there has been a firm which raised its output in what it knew to be a static market — as we had occasion to notice in the last chapter, economics is characterised by a high degree of abstraction and idealisation. But what makes it a bona fide causal law is its place in the construction of causal histories along the following lines: if we come to a particular case, we can say that since we know that price is the result of the demand for the good and the supply of it, and we also know that people's desire to buy depends on the price they are asked, we can see that what will make a person buy more is a drop in the price (other things remaining unchanged); but suppose a firm produces more than it did, and everything else is unchanged, what inducement can it offer to buyers to clear this extra quantity of output? Only a drop in price. What gives the causal law its explanatory force is that it refers us to a causal history of this kind, it shows us how we fit together the chain of events with which we are confronted, and how to construct a great many alternative, hypothetical chains. The claim made here is that the explanatory value of scientific explanations depends in general on their allowing us to construct such causal histories, and that this feature is central to anything which we can call a causal inquiry. Of course, this does not imply that we shall necessarily be able to give such histories although the debate about the absence of causality from quantum physics shows clearly enough what a blow it is when we cannot; all it implies is that where we are in possession of causal laws, this is what their utility is. An added merit of this account which will only emerge in the next chapter is its suggestiveness for an adequate account of the difference which theories make to science.

Now, however, it is time to ignore deductive requirements for a while, and to turn to the 'hypothetico-' element in the hypothetico-deductive account. This in essence involves us in explaining the concept of 'falsifiability'. (21) The simplest brief statement of this is that the causal generalisations which serve as the backing for our explanations have the logical standing of empirical hypotheses, which can be conclusively falsified, though not conclusively verified, by way of their deductive implications. The logical status of laws is that of

61

hypotheses, in that we guess at, or speculate about some causal law which would provide the looked-for explanation, and then deduce from it consequences which either are or are not in accord with the facts that we either come across or contrive to produce experimentally. If we cannot deduce empirical consequences from a hypothesis, it is not an empirical hypothesis at all; thus, for instance, the hypothesis that artificial satellites are kept in motion by flights of invisible, intangible, non-corporeal angels would not be an empirical hypothesis, since there would be no way of conclusively discovering that angels were not there. On the other hand, the hypothesis that their motion was the result of air rushing from in front of them to fill the vacuum behind them and so impelling them forward is conclusively falsified once we know that there is no air at that distance from the earth. That this latter hypothesis — that bodies are kept in motion by the movement of the air about them — is falsified conclusively at least means that it was an empirical hypothesis; indeed, it was part of medieval physics. (22) The point can be equally well illustrated from political science. Much thought has been devoted to the question of how liberal democracies contrive to keep in existence a fairly peaceful and coherent system for changing leaders, policies and the like. One hypothesis posits the existence of a general will whose characteristic mode of operation is to give good and careful decisions so long as the people at large pay attention to it. But it was pointed out by such critics as Joseph Schumpeter (27) that the explanatory value of this hypothesis was very slight since the only criteria for the operation of the general will were good and careful public decisions, while the only criteria for its absence were their absence. And this made the connection between good decisions and the operation of the will an analytic not a causal matter. However, there have in this area been decisively falsified hypotheses also. For instance, political scientists frequently thought that democracies operated peacefully and effectively because their citizens were well educated, public-spirited and politically highly motivated. (24) This hypothesis gave rise to a story about the ideal voter who was ready to change allegiances when the public good required it, who balanced alternatives and so on, all in the hope of making peaceful

62

change possible. But the first effect of voting research was precisely to falsify this story. It was found that voters practically never changed their party allegiance, that most electoral change was the result of higher and lower turnout, not of decisions by voters to change sides, and, most damaging of all, that the man who did change sides – the 'floating voter' – was typically less educated, less motivated, more politically ignorant than the average of citizens. So whatever does account for the stability of democratic regimes, it cannot be that story. (25)

Why is falsifiability so important? The first reason hangs on a point we noted in the previous chapter: there is an asymmetry between the premises and conclusion of an argument, such that false premises may lead to a true conclusion, although a false conclusion necessarily means that one at least of the premises is false. As we saw in the example drawn from 'The American Soldier', the truth of the conclusion is very weak evidence for the truth of the premises. But a *false* conclusion is logically much more powerful, in that it is conclusive evidence for the falsity of one or other of the premises. And this is one of the reasons why it is important to cast explanations into a deductive form – only then are we able to see what we are committed to, and hence able to set about subjecting it to the kind of tests which will show it up as false, if it is false. The first point about falsifiability, then, is that it amounts to the requirement that our explanatory generalisations should be exposed to tests designed to falsify them if they are false. The second element rests on the fact that causal explanations are general, i.e. that they apply in principle to a variety of cases. Since a generalisation claims that *whenever* a property varies in a certain way, then some other property also varies in a specified way, the obvious way to secure that we only utter well-founded generalisations is to see what the limits of this 'whenever' are. We know, of course, that as a matter of fact many of our generalisations have fairly precise limitations: a law such as 'if you push a book off the table it will fall to the floor' holds good only during ordinary conditions – it will not be true under conditions of weightlessness, nor in an aeroplane dropping rapidly through an air pocket. But how do we know this? In two ways: firstly through the employment of theories which account both for the truth of the generalisations in those conditions where it does hold and for its failure in other circumstances, and secondly because we all recognise the importance of experimental tests. Given a generalisation, we want to see if it holds under unusual conditions, and where it does not, to account for the breakdowns. Offered a chemical formula, what is more natural than to see if it holds at very high temperatures or very low ones, very high or very low pressures? Offered a generalisation about political behaviour, what is more natural than to see whether it covers politics on the verge of civil war as well as politics after a century of domestic peace, whether it covers the politics of super-powers as well as the politics of small tribes? In all this we recognise the role alike of the generality of causal laws and the importance of trying to falsify our hypotheses about the world. And as elsewhere, the analogy between the knowledge founded on causal laws and the behaviour displayed in accordance with moral principles is instructive: if someone claims to believe in a certain principle, we are always tempted, whether kindly or in malice, to see whether they would stick by it in hard cases — for across the board the test of principles is the case in which they are least likely to succeed. And this is because there is little point in merely piling up examples where a hypothesis yields successful results — for it is still as vulnerable as ever to the falsifying result. Successful causal laws are those which apply under the most *im*probable conditions. (26)

The acceptance of this account of scientific explanation has generally involved a certain picture of scientific progress which does much to explain the hopes and doubts of social scientists. The essence of the account is that progress depends on a more or less Darwinian struggle for survival among competing hypotheses; by ensuring adequate competition, the scientist can ensure that only the fittest hypotheses survive. The great merit of scientific hypotheses is to be both comprehensive and accurate, to apply to the widest range of cases possible, and at the same time to apply with the greatest degree of precision possible. The attraction of this view for social scientists hardly needs stressing in view of the recent enthusiasm for model-building associated with writers such as Easton (27) or Gabriel Almond. (28) And the justi-

64

fication adduced by model-builders generally is precisely that they aim to produce generalisations which will give order and coherence to the lower-level, partial regularities with which we are acquainted, but with which we cannot be content. The aspiration to comprehensiveness and accuracy is entirely in harmony with the stress on the need for empirical testing of hypotheses. Comprehensive laws are those which will tell us both when our more limited laws will hold and when they will not; and accuracy is plainly central to our being able to say what will count as the refutation of a hypothesis — and thus to telling us when we must look for disturbing causes or try to find some more general law to account for the break-down of our initial story. The more exactly we can deduce results from our hypotheses, the more searching can be the competition between them — for the more readily will competing hypotheses yield incompatible predictions, such that one is bound to be wrong.

This is by no means to suggest that these are the only ingredients of progress. To take two simple points only: it is obvious that in a science of any degree of complexity, there will be enormous difficulty in deciding whether a projected experiment does genuinely constitute a test of the theory in question. There have to be innumerable supplementary hypotheses in order to operationalise any tolerably compli-cated theory, and it is unfeasible to test all these at once. Hence a great many experiments test nothing more than whether the experiment was the right kind of experiment to set up in the first place — and the history of science is littered with experiments which did not prove anything one way or the other. The other point is that it is only possible to set out to test a hypothesis when we have some means of assessing the results. Thus it was not until the invention of the Galilean telescope that it was possible to directly test the astronomical theory which claimed that Jupiter could not have any moons of its own. Nonetheless, the way in which science has been committed to the goals of comprehensiveness and accuracy is evident. The classical case where this was decisive was the replacement of the Aristotelian laws of motion by those developed by Galileo and later by Newton. Aristotle's laws of motion were founded on the assumption that bodies had a natural terminal velocity, and generalising from bodies in the near neighbourhood of the earth he put this terminal velocity pretty low. Now, Aristotle's law was very accurate within the available limits of measurement, and for the kinds of motion he was in fact able to observe. Indeed, what Aristotle produced was the law of acceleration of bodies in a viscous medium, such as air or water, and even after Galilean physics was accepted, Aristotle's laws of motion could still be inferred as special cases of those developed by Galileo. Near the earth, Galileo's laws were no more accurate than were Aristotle's when applied to the same phenomena; but where they scored was in being able, as Aristotle's were not, to account for bodies in free fall, and for bodies in celestial motion. It was evidently the case that simplicity and comprehensiveness would be served by dropping the cluttered Aristotelian apparatus at that level. (29) Now what is important about this example is how well it illustrates the major tenets of falsifiability. It was true of Aristotle's physics that it had been accepted for hundreds of years, and had thus scored a great many successes; nonetheless, what mattered was not its successes but its failure, for at the point where a competing hypothesis about motion could cover the same cases as did Aristotle's laws, and also cover those cases which were refuting counter-examples to them, the new hypothesis had to be accepted as superior. In short, it was the experimental crux that proved decisive. And in this instance, the hypothetico-deductive story about explanation is illustrated to perfection — a universal hypothesis about motion was put up in competition with another one which was known to have a variety of flaws; it was unrefuted where the other was refuted; it could account in its own terms for both the successes and the failures of the other hypothesis; hence it succeeded in the struggle for survival.

The final strand in this account which I ought to mention before coming to its weaknesses concerns the importance of the notion of falsifiability in assigning what we say about the world to various logical categories. It is evident that we do not only use the language of science in talking about the natural and the social world. Indeed, we use that language rather rarely by comparison with the talk which is poetic, religious, expressive in one way or another. The notion of falsifiability not only enables us to formulate clearly the aims

66

and the logic of scientific investigation, it also enables us to distinguish between the statements which are empirical hypotheses about the world and those which have some other conceptual status. At one point, this was claimed to mark the line between sense and nonsense, as Professor Ayer's 'Language, Truth and Logic' demonstrates. (30) But I wish to make no such claim and to give no impression that I would be sympathetic to it: it is no deficiency in a novel to be something other than a piece of social psychology, and it is no defect in an ode to the moon not to be a piece of astronomy. However, there is one kind of statement which does seem to occur in the sciences and which does not seem to be obviously testable. This is what we can call 'metaphysical' assertions, or 'transcendental' hypotheses — such as the assertion that space must be Euclidean, or that every event must have a determinate physical cause. These statements look both like and unlike scientific hypotheses in that they seem to make claims about the world, but yet not be susceptible of conclusive falsification; if we believe that all events have causes, then we shall look for causes, but if we do not find them, we shall conclude only that we have failed to find a cause, not that there is not one to be found. If we rule out the possibility of some sort of special metaphysical insight into how the world is ordered, there seem only two possible roles for such statements — they are either loosely framed empirical hypotheses which need to be made more exact and therefore testable, or else they are analytic truths, mere definitions. There is, however, one more complicated suggestion about them, which is perhaps more plausible than those alternatives. That is that they are methodological instructions, rather than statements of a simply true or false kind; that is, they are rather like pieces of advice, or remarks about the way to conduct science, and thus are not in any simple sense falsifiable, though they are certainly not definitional truths either. Like any advice, they are to be assessed as more or less fruitful or fruitless. They are, in a sense, indirectly testable, in that it will certainly be something about the empirical observation of the world which decides whether they are fruitful or not. The classical example which will illustrate this is Kant's assertion that space was necessarily Euclidean. Kant claimed that this was a

67

'synthetic *a priori*' truth — i.e. that it was not discovered by experience to be true, but that its truth was still a truth about the world, not a matter of definition. It was, however, clear by the time relativistic physics was established that this belief, though not directly refuted, made for grave difficulties when applied to the calculations involved in stellar mechanics — and so another geometry was adopted. Now, this is not a refutation, in the sense that it is very unclear how one *could* refute Kant's assertion, and also that it seems to be in principle possible (though in practice absurd) to translate the stellar mechanics of non-Euclidean space into the stellar mechanics of Euclidean space, although there are doubts about this. It thus seems most sensible to analyse the belief as a methodological claim about the geometry applicable in astronomy and physics, and a claim which we have now come to reject as fruitless. (31)

We can now turn to the third of the tasks of this chapter, that of making this rather elegant account of scientific explanation look a great deal less tidy than I have so far made it out. Many of the criticisms opened here will carry rather more weight as the argument develops in subsequent chapters, but here at any rate we can look at four different issues, the first of them the problem of probabilistic explanation in the light of the 'hypothetico-deductive' picture, the three latter all concerned with the way in which the existence of theories must modify this account. The problems posed by the existence of theories can be summarised as, first, the picture of scientific progress offered above does various kinds of violence to the actual course of scientific advance, second, that the statements occurring in theories do not seem in any clear way to be generalisations of, or from, the statements describing the events they explain, and third, that a more coherent account of the nature of theories and of explanation generally can only be given when we give due weight to the importance of causal sequences, as suggested above. These last three points will be somewhat dogmatically treated now, but ought to carry a good deal more conviction by the end of the next chapter.

The way in which probabilistic explanation forms a difficulty is this. We often use explanations which have a non-deductive character, because they rest on premisses of a

68

less than strictly universal kind. Medicine, for instance, is full of probabilistic claims: a doctor gives a patient penicillin, saying something to the effect of 'This will probably do the trick'. The question arises of what kind of backing this sort of probabilistic prediction receives; and the answer seems to be that it is a partial generalisation of the form 'Nearly everyone given penicillin for inflammation of the ear recovers quite rapidly'. This, together with the initial condition that you are given penicillin for inflammation of the ear, licenses the probable prediction that you will recover soon. The critical logical point about such an argument is that it is not deductively valid, and as we saw earlier this means that it is wholly invalid. Since we seem unlikely to cease to employ explanations of this sort in the near future, the fact that we cannot analyse it in deductive terms seems more of an objection to the model of explanation so far offered than it does to this kind of explanation. There are various possible answers to this criticism. One is to say that though we do employ such explanations in everyday life, they are essentially incomplete and unscientific. They are no more than the rough materials out of which deductive explanations will eventually be created; at the moment, doctors who have to work under harsh exigencies of time and conditions cannot unravel the successful from the unsuccessful cases of such treatment, but this does not mean that there are no universal connections to be discovered. All the word 'probably' means here is that we are not certain in advance of the event whether the patient belongs in the class of patients all of whom recover or in that class all of whom do not. The approximate law which we use is only the outward evidence of two strict laws which we have not yet discovered; and it is only our assurance that this is so which enables us to call this an explanation at all. A second answer is that in those cases where we seem unable to find a strictly universal law, we *cannot* explain single events at all, but only classes of events, the behaviour of whole populations; and it is claimed that the relationship between a probabilistic law and an inference about a class of events is strictly deductive. This does mean that we cannot form causal stories about the way in which a particular event turns out, and this is undoubtedly a blow to the determinist conception of science, but no more is lost

69

than this. The example over which most of the argument has taken place is quantum physics; but the social sciences offer equally good grounds for argument. The statistical law that 85 per cent of the working class has authoritarian attitudes towards the bringing up of children would not — on this view — explain the presence or absence of authoritarian views in any particular member of the working class, but it would enable us to predict that an indefinitely large number of working-class parents would split 85/15 along the authoritarian/non-authoritarian divide. But it is crucially still the case that this will not explain particular cases. (32)

There is a good deal of truth in both these replies; it is certainly the case that we usually believe that some more precise law underlies the visible partial regularity we discover at first; and it is undoubted that the establishing of nothing better than a probabilistic law indicates a weakness in our understanding of the causal connections involved. Nonetheless, this is a far cry either from establishing that we do not employ what is properly to be called probable explanation or from showing that we are wrong to predict particular cases with probability rather than certainty. After all, for a very great deal of the time we have to take decisions in the light of whatever evidence we can lay hands on, and a refusal to choose on the balance of probabilities rather than unavailable certainty would be simply perverse. A doctor who refused to prescribe us a pain-relieving drug simply because he had scruples along the lines suggested by the 'hypothetico-deductive' picture would be no friend to the needy. The better reply, surely, is to refer back to our concern with causal sequences, and to regard causal laws as rules for generating sequences as before: universal laws thus emerge as laws which *guarantee* our sequences, where probabilistic laws only *support* them, more or less strongly. We may or may not believe that if we were to analyse a sequence more carefully we should always uncover certifying laws, but whether we believe this or not, we should try to do justice to the fact that we do adduce less than universal generalisations in support of our expectations on single occasions. Moreover, to the objection that we cannot have causal inferences based on probabilistic laws, the answer is surely to deny that it is an all-or-nothing matter: causal laws have often enough been

70

described as telling us which lever to pull in order to bring about what event in the world; it is on this analogy surely plausible to say that we can have an idea what lever we need to pull, even if we cannot so fully describe the machinery connecting cause and effect as we should like. We cannot say what has gone wrong if the event does not occur, and this is obviously a limitation on the reliability of our inferences. Nonetheless, a partial and not wholly reliable causal law is not the same thing as no causal law at all. (33)

The introduction of theories into science adds a further dimension of complexity to the discussion. The first complication concerns the way in which theories come to life and die in the actual practice of science. The account we gave of the way in which Aristotelian physics was superseded by Galilean physics suggested a rationalist account of the process, in which two competing theories faced the facts, and one was refuted. But it has been argued by Professor Kuhn in 'The Structure of Scientific Revolutions' that this story is a 'rationalisation' of the history of science as it really happened. (34) The process as it happened was much more uneven than the account we gave before suggests it should be. Scientists hang on to theories long after they have been refuted in the sense of failing to square with large numbers of facts, and the attractions of a 'good' theory seem to depend a great deal on such extra-scientific qualities as its aesthetic qualities, its coherence with religious attitudes and the like. The process of change is indeed like that of a revolution in that the new theory does not simply explain the same old facts in a better and more accurate way, but rather that it renders the old theory totally meaningless — in much the way that a successful revolutionary regime annuls all the acts of the pre-revolutionary regime. On Kuhn's account, until an old theory is discredited, we simply cannot help seeing the world in the terms it suggests to us: once it is discredited, we no longer see how we believed in it. In other words, theories operate as world-views, or what Kuhn calls 'paradigms', which do not so much confront the facts as tell us what we should see in the facts. This view of science leaves little room for falsificationist analyses, because the facts against which we should falsify our theories have become so much less visible. There are, I think, only two comments we need make here, since I shall say something more about the impact of this argument at the very end of the book. The first is that Kuhn presents us with both a logical and a historical problem here. The logical problem is to account for the processes of the acceptance and rejection of theories in terms which do justice to Kuhn's observations, and which also do justice to the techniques and methods of experiment and observation which are usually described as enabling us to get at the facts. The historical problem is that anyone who adheres to an account like the 'hypothetico-deductive' account must find some way of explaining why the practice of scientists diverges so widely from what that account would lead us to suppose. We need, in other words, a historical explanation of the way in which their methods somehow did conform to the hypothetico-deductive account. (35) Kuhn's own story, of course, accounts quite readily for the popularity of the hypothetico-deductive account among natural scientists; for it tends to suggest that the mechanical sciences are the peak of human intelligence, and this is an agreeable consequence for most of those scientists who have written about science. The second comment worth making here is that it is worth bearing in mind that Kuhn's account would apply just as forcefully and perhaps more forcefully to the social sciences. Thus the classical economist's theory would not have appeared merely because the mercantilist's theory was 'refuted'; rather, classical economic theory would only have appeared because it served the needs or interests of various social groups, or for some other extra-scientific reason. Of course something much like this has been said before by Marxist critics of the social sciences, who thought classical economic theory was one aspect of the bourgeois ideology; but their objections seemed usually to leave the natural sciences untouched. Now we see that if the social sciences are suspect for Marxist reasons it is because they are more suspect than a natural science which is itself suspect.

The second doubt introduced by the existence of theories is that theories do not seem to be explicable as generalisations from evidence describable in everyday observational terms. Theories are notable for introducing all kinds of non-observable forces and entities as much as for anything else — as when observable diseases are said to be caused by

72

non-observable bacterial infection; and in the social sciences, they seem noted for requiring us to understand one form of behaviour in terms of some other form of behaviour, as in Professor Downs's 'An Economic Theory of Democracy', where political parties are said to 'sell' policies for votes, and to 'buy' votes with promises. (36) The relations between theories and facts cannot be simply explained; the images which dominate the literature are those of 'maps', 'models', 'analogies', 'hidden mechanisms' (37) – and none of these things looks remotely like a generalisation from the events they are explaining.

Our third point, which is one of the reasons behind this second objection, is that whether we explain their effectiveness in terms of mechanisms, maps, analogies or whatever, theories certainly seem to cater to our need to render causal sequences intelligible to us. If political parties *are* groups of people selling policies and buying votes, then we can follow the steps by which two parties in a political system with a centrist public will try to sell the same policies under different labels – in other words we can borrow what we know of how competitors behave under various market conditions in order to follow step by step the actions of politicians and voters in a democracy. The use of the analogy in such a theory is that it allows us to fill in gaps in a causal sequence; and this surely is a vital role of theory in all sciences. But to suggest this is to do two things, to cast further doubt on the adequacy of the usual account of scientific explanation and to bring us to the explicit account of the role of theories in the next chapter.

NOTES

1. C. G. Hempel and P. Oppenheim, 'Studies in the Logic of Explanation', 'Phil. of Sci.' (1948) pp. 135-79.
2. R. Brown, 'Explanation in Social Science' (Routledge, 1963) p. 41.
3. Hempel and Oppenheim, in 'Phil. of Sci.' (1948) pp. 135-6.
4. C. G. Hempel, 'The Function of General Laws in History', in H. Feigl and W. Sellars (eds), 'Readings in

Philosophical Analysis' (Mayflower, 1949) pp. 459-67.

5. K. R. Popper, 'The Poverty of Historicism', 2nd ed. (Routledge, 1960) pp. 122 ff.

6. Hempel, in 'Readings in Philosophical Analysis', pp. 466 ff.

7. G. C. Homans, 'The Human Group' (Routledge, 1951) chs vii, iii.

8. G. H. von Wright, 'The Logical Problem of Induction' (Blackwell, Oxford, 1957) pp. 10-11.

9. Hempel and Oppenheim, in 'Phil. of Sci.' (1948).

10. Ibid., p. 142.

11. W. Dray, 'Laws and Explanation in History' (Oxford University Press, 1957) pp. 31-7.

12. Nagel, 'Structure of Science', pp. 49-52.

13. B. Berelson et al., 'Voting' (Chicago University Press, 1954).

14. Nagel, 'Structure of Science', pp. 52-6.

15. Mill, 'Logic', bk iii, ch. vii, sec. 3.

16. Brown, 'Explanation in Social Science', pp. 168 f.

17. Dray, 'Laws and Explanation', p. 61.

18. L. Radzinowicz, 'Ideology and Crime' (Heinemann, 1966) pp. 29 ff.

19. Ibid., pp. 46-50.

20. Dray, 'Laws and Explanation', pp. 68-72.

21. Popper, 'Conjectures', pp. 33-41.

22. S. E. Toulmin and J. Goodfield, 'The Fabric of the Heavens' (Penguin, 1963) pp. 101-14.

23. J. Schumpeter, 'Capitalism, Socialism and Democracy' (Allen & Unwin, 1965) ch. xxi.

24. Berelson et al., 'Voting', pp. 305-13.

25. Ibid., pp. 322-3.

26. Popper, 'Conjectures', pp. 217 ff.

27. Easton, 'Political System'.

28. G. Almond and J. A. Coleman, 'The Politics of the Developing Areas' (Princeton University Press, 1960).

29. Toulmin and Goodfield, 'Fabric', chs 5 and 6.

30. Ayer, 'Language', pp. 39-45.

31. Nagel, 'Structure of Science', ch. 8.

32. M. Brodbeck, in H. Feigl and M. Scriven (eds), 'Minnesota Studies' (University of Minnesota Press, 1956 onwards) iii 248.

33. Mill, 'Logic', bk iii, ch. xxiii, sec. 2.

34. Kuhn, 'Structure of Scientific Revolutions', pp. 1-4.

35. Ibid., pp. 145-50.

36. A. Downs, 'An Economic Theory of Democracy' (Harper & Row, 1965) pt i.

37. R. Harre, 'Theories and Things' (Sheed & Ward, 1965) pp. 22 f.

4 The Role of Scientific Theories

In the three preceding chapters I have frequently said that the views I was explaining were part of a general philosophical consensus. From now on, this claim is nothing like as plausible. In the case of elucidating the nature of scientific theories there is no general consensus to be found, in spite of an enormous literature seeking to unravel the distinction between theories and such close relations as models, maps, metaphors and analogies. (1) It is, of course, true here as elsewhere that there is widespread agreement on the considerations which we have to take into account; but there is no one view about their implications which has gained overwhelming acceptance; and thus there is no one story to be told about the implications for social science. Accordingly, I shall mostly be concerned simply to explain why theories matter – whether in the natural or the social sciences – and in such a way as to be compatible with any of the more common accounts of the nature of theories. But after this point I shall move on to discussing the rival claims of 'realist' and 'operationalist' accounts of the entities talked about in theories; and I shall, finally, say something about the relationship between theories, models, 'conceptual schemes' and analogies – without, however, claiming for what I say more than a heuristic value.

The great importance of theory in a developed science is obvious. Indeed, it is easy to wish it were less obvious when confronted with the rather desperate attempts of social scientists to provide theoretical frameworks for their own discipline. The major point about theories, however, is that their explanatory power does not rest on any improvement they make to the formal or logical qualities of explanation. An easy way to see this is to consider that well-worn example, the kinetic theory of gases. (2) Suppose we were to begin by performing some experiments of the kind familiar from schoolrooms everywhere: we should discover that when gas was trapped in a balloon and the gas was heated, then the gas expanded. Given a certain amount of good fortune, we might even discover an approximation to Boyle's Law as the law which governed our experimental results. But it should be noticed that Boyle's Law is *only* an experimental law; it does offer generalisations to cover the heating and expansion of all gases, but this is only a generalisation of what is immediately observable. Thus the generalisations which link observable volume and temperature are essentially of the same logical kind as 'glass is brittle', in other words dispositional generalisations from immediate experience. Throughout the history of science, such laws have been held to be of little explanatory value, to be distinguished as 'low-level' laws or 'merely empirical' generalisations; at worst they have been misrepresented as in the famous passage of Molière where the pedant ascribes the fact that opium puts people to sleep to its possession of a 'dormitive power'. But this *is* a misrepresentation in the following sense: we may satisfy the demand for an explanation by employing a low-level generalisation of this kind, if it succeeds in eliminating other alternatives under review. Thus we may account for a broken pane of glass by adducing the fact that glass is brittle, and for an extremely lengthy prison sentence by adducing the repressiveness of military regimes. These may succeed as explanations in the sense that the first may rule out the alternative that the projectile possessed immense, though non-obvious, force, and the second may rule out the alternative that the crime for which the man was sentenced was really, though non-obviously, very heinous. In this respect, the frequent use of such low-level generalisations in explanation is plainly justified. (3) But so also is the complaint to which we paid attention in the last chapter, that such generalisations tell us what happens but now how, or that they lack explanatory 'force'. Why, if there were nothing in such complaints, would people have troubled to think up the kinetic theory of gases, or have attempted to unravel the molecular structure of crystalline substances, or have tried to analyse the motivation, information and *Weltanschauungen* of military rulers? Only by analysing what such attempts at theoretical underpinning set out to achieve can we understand what the role of theories is.

77

A low-level law, such as Boyle's Law, covers innumerable conceivable and actual cases of the expansion of gases by heating and their contraction through cooling; it is a genuine causal law, in that it yields counterfactual predictions about how gases *would* behave under various conditions. And it covers explanations of both an idle and a practical sort — it will explain that a half-inflated balloon lying on a warm radiator will swell up, and equally that it is a bad idea to try to set the pressures of car tyres when they are warm after a journey. But the law itself needs explaining, and this is achieved by way of the kinetic theory of gases. It is easy to overlook the fact that two kinds of explanation go on in this process, and that we need to pay some attention to both of them. In both cases, what we attend to is the question of why it is that heat causes an increase in pressure, and in both cases we need to employ the premiss of the kinetic theory to the effect that gases are made up of molecules in constant motion. Now, one thing that is achieved by the introduction of the theory is to show that the things that go on when a gas is heated are the same things as go on in a great many other cases — and thus to bring gases under the scope of wider generalisations than merely experimental laws. The other thing that is achieved is to produce an answer to the question of how heat comes to be changed into pressure by way of showing how heat brings about more and more violent motion on the part of the particles that compose the gas. With the aid of the usual schoolroom analogy about the impact of billiard-balls on the cushions of a billiard table, and similar kinds of imagery, we come to see the pressure changes as manifestations of an underlying activity. We now, as one might say, have a more complete picture, with the details filled in. The point which needs to be noticed is that this second aspect of explanation does not in any sense improve the formal or logical qualities of our previous explanations; so far as these go, there was no room for improvement. The explanation before could be cast into a valid deductive argument, and that is all that can be asked of any argument. If we have a well-tried empirical generalisation about the rate at which some given gas expands when heated, and we have a sample which we heat through so many degrees, we can validly deduce the amount by which it expands, and that is all there (logically) is to it. Since, on this reading, it cannot be improved as a logically valid argument, whatever improvement in its explanatory force is made by the kinetic theory of gases must be accounted for in terms other than improving the logical links between *explanans* and *explanandum*. The obvious way to do this is to revert to our claim in the last chapter that what we require from explanations is an intelligible account of causal sequences — or, if this is too strong, a coherent story about natural processes. Thus the role of theories seems to lie more in the improvement of causal narratives than in the ensuring of deductive rigour. This is not to deny the role of deductive rigour, and in particular it is not to deny that the mathematical and logical rigour introduced by many theories is of overwhelming importance; nonetheless, it is to assert that this role is contributory to the goal of coherent narrative, and not wholly independent of it. (4)

A similar analysis can be given of the example which Professor Toulmin makes so much of in his 'Philosophy of Science', the geometrical theory of optics. (5) Here again we begin with everyday observations and measurements, let us say a series of measurements linking the length of a shadow to the height of the object casting the shadow, the angle of elevation of the sun and so on. We might arrive at some perfectly good inductive generalisations about the length of shadow cast at particular times on various days, explained by the generalisation about the relationship between the angle of elevation, height and length. But it is likely we should do something more than this, and this something more launches us on the path of geometrical optics. We should probably draw a diagram to illustrate our generalisation; and we might stop short at illustration. But more than likely we should move on to theorising about what was happening in the picture, i.e. we should tell a story about the behaviour of light. We should say that light passes from its source in a beam which touches the top of the object and the edge of the shadow; and from this we might launch out to guess that these beams fan out in all directions from their source, and travel in Euclidean straight lines for an indefinite distance unless obstructed by opaque substances; and then we might start wondering about the effect of mirrors, prisms and the like. At this point we have a story about light which suggests all kinds of probable results and hence all kinds of experiments; light is described in terms of 'rays' which 'travel', and thus we are given a mechanism for the behaviour of shadows, refraction and a host of other phenomena. (6)

Once again, we can see how the existence of a theory fits in with our desire to fill in causal links. But we can go further and draw an implication which is vitally important for the social sciences. When we produce a story about how the mechanisms of the natural or the social world operate, we give a point to scientific investigation which it would not otherwise possess. A successful theory provides what Kuhn calls a 'paradigm'; (7) it provides a model of the story which we ought to be able to tell, and in this way it provides a focus for research and experiment which would otherwise be unavailable. If we had no idea of what story we ought to be able to tell about natural or social processes, we should simply have no idea (other than that vital form of everyday theory, common sense) what facts to look at, what information to seek. That this is not a process only applicable in the natural sciences can be illustrated from a somewhat surprising place, namely traditional political theory. The importance of this example lies incidentally in the fact that recent political science, and to a lesser extent sociology, has been somewhat intimidated by the apparent lack of 'paradigms' for their research. If the suggestion which I am about to make, that the 'social contract' theory of political obligation formed such a paradigm, is correct, then some part of these feelings of inferiority is unjustified. Suppose the Lockean notion of a 'social contract' were such a paradigm, what would its role and purpose have been? (8)

On Kuhn's account, the job of a paradigm is to set puzzles and also to set the standards for their solution. According to his characterisation of 'normal' science, this is a period in which there is general agreement both on the nature of the problems and on the nature of successful solutions. Thus, when we set up the kinetic theory of gases, we begin by abstracting from the total of the real qualities of molecules such things as energy losses due to friction and internal gravitational attractions between particles; we are then left later with a 'puzzle' — namely, the incorporation of these

80

complicating factors into the theory, and hence the elaboration of a more complete theory which will cover a greater variety of conditions. Political scientists such as Professor Easton accept this characterisation of how paradigms help us to proceed, and argue that this accounts for their urgency in the social and political sciences. (9) The 'facts' and low-level generalisations which a political scientist might discover are all too literally infinitely numerous, and political scientists will drown in a sea of undifferentiated data without some sort of model which will rule in relevant research and rule out the rest. Equally, the name of Talcott Parsons is associated with an attempt to provide just such categories for the collection and analysis of sociological data in the hope that thus — and only thus — will progress be made towards a social *science*. (10) Both of them, but more particularly Easton, give the impression that theories have been somewhat thin on the ground, and rate as urgent the need for paradigms of research.

But could it be claimed that the social contract fulfilled such requirements, even inadequately? The usual answer in political science would be no, on the grounds that the social contract belonged to a tradition which was concerned to produce normative theory and not explanatory theory, and hence that the social contract was part of a theory which aimed at telling us what we ought to do, rather than at a series of generalisations about how men actually behave in political and social matters. (11) Certainly these are impressive considerations; but they are not conclusive. For let us look at the other side of the coin. If society is viewed as founded on a social contract, then certain kinds of behaviour at once emerge as rational and intelligible. On a Lockean view, for example, the activities of the American colonists in fighting for independence from the British government are readily explicable as the actions of men whose contract with their rulers has been unilaterally abrogated. In the light of this abrogation, they were as free to set up a new government as if they had never owed allegiance to the Crown. And the language of many of the founders of the new American republic certainly lends colour to the supposition that this was exactly how they visualised their own conduct, as the establishment of a new social contract.

The theory certainly suggested enough puzzles to satisfy the most demanding Kuhnian; in part, such puzzles were caused by the need for internal clarification of the theory, as when it was unclear whether it was the origin of society or only political organisation that depended on the contract; again, it was not clear — though it could be made clear — whether the notion of the social contract was to be employed historically, in accounting for the historical origins of existing political societies, or whether it was to be understood structurally, as implying that there was a continuously made and implemented contract implicit in all forms of everyday social and political behaviour. The other major aspect of puzzlement centred on the relations of the theory with the outside world: was it, for example, a refutation of the theory of the social contract if men did not think that their relations with their rulers were contractual, but were laid down by divine ordinance? Was the social behaviour of savages a better guide to the essential condition of mankind — a better experimental situation — than the behaviour of the inhabitants of more developed societies? We may say that the paradigm was a poor one in that it never achieved the universal allegiance that Newton's mechanics did; or again, we may say that it was a poor paradigm in the sense that the puzzles it set up were never satisfactorily resolved in the way that analogous puzzles in geometrical optics were. Still, even a poor paradigm is admittedly a paradigm. And we can defend its performance against these strictures, at least far enough to make it not too badly the loser in the comparison. It is surely right to think that human societies are more complex kinds of system to explain than, say, the solar system — for one thing explanation has to contend with the way in which human beings come to visualise their lives, a phenomenon of self-consciousness which no natural science has to trouble itself about. Hence it is easier to forgive social paradigms their weaknesses than their counterparts in the natural sciences. And the fact that the social paradigm has to play a practical part in allowing us to see how to construct a social and political order (12), the point of remarking on the normative character of political theory — no doubt adds to the difficulties of elaborating a successful paradigm. But both as a matter of logic and a matter of history, the social

82

contract played a paradigmatic role in social thought; and to this extent we can assign to theory as much importance in the social sciences as in the natural sciences.

When it is complained that the social sciences lack theories, is there nothing in the complaint? So far I have talked of the social contract theory as if there were no question that this is what it was, and when we referred to Downs's 'An Economic Theory of Democracy' we did not scruple to regard it as a *theory* of political behaviour. (13) Is there nothing to be said in qualification? There is, though it is none too easy to say it clearly. One aspect of the worry is the apparent absence from social science of 'theoretical entities'; it will be recalled that many of the schoolroom examples of scientific theories refer to such entities as 'molecules', or to beams of light which are said to be made up of 'photons', particles of light. Without anticipating our discussion of the logical status of such entities we can say that what disturbs people is the absence of entities corresponding to these unobservable objects which are introduced into the story to account for the observable processes we wish to explain. This, unfortunately, is one of the areas in which linguistic legislation is all too easy; one might claim equally that if we all call the 'Quantity Theory of Money' the quantity *theory*, then that's just what it is, or else that calling that piece of explanation a theory merely shows that we are using the word wrongly. Happily, we can escape being embroiled in this argument by pointing out one simple truth, that the social sciences *do* employ theoretical entities. Thus, when Durkheim introduces the concept of the 'conscience collective', he insists that there really is such a thing as the 'conscience collective', that it has a factual existence and that it is causally effective. (14) Now, what is true is that such an entity is not an *atomic* entity on a par with molecules or particles of light; but then the concept of a universal gravitational field hardly refers to an atomic entity either. But here perhaps we do have a genuine difference of emphasis, if not in the sciences, at any rate in our everyday view of them. We may say, approximately, that in much of theoretical science we look for 'infilling' causal explanations, explanations which will display the micro-structure of the phenomena with which we are concerned. And this is not

83

true to anything like the same extent in the social sciences, where very often we are looking for the macro-structure of the phenomena, looking, that is, for theoretical laws which will show how the actions and aims of individual people result — in a non-arbitrary way — in changes at a societal level. (15) It is in this sense that economics is unequivocally a theoretical science. It takes an infinity of particular decisions and from them accounts for such societal phenomena as the price level, total social product and the trends in these which we refer to as inflation and deflation, booms and slumps. In Chapter 8 we shall explore some of the consequences of this inquiry, and there is no need now to anticipate that discussion. It is, however, worth pointing out how approximate is such a characterisation of the typical aims of social science. For the boundary between the social sciences and all other scientific inquiry is a mere matter of convenience and interest; such disciplines as cognitive psychology or theoretical linguistics employ an ample store of theoretical constructs in explaining how we possess a language, how we recognise objects and organise our knowledge; these concepts refer to processes not visible either to the persons performing them or to the casual observer; and that they are not concepts of *social* science is an accident of current knowledge. If the results of these disciplines prove to have important consequences for understanding how individuals behave in social situations, we shall simply call them aspects of social science, and their theories will simply be part of the theoretical equipment of social science. (16) In this way, then, the fear that there are no social science theories is seen to be confused, and a fear not to be shared.

The arguments offered above to explain why theories matter to science do not beg any of the issues between the two rival accounts of theories known respectively as 'operationalism' and 'realism'. They do however pose a problem for the deductive conception of explanation, the problem to which 'realism' and its rival offer answers. The problem is this. The point of employing a theory is to explain some observed phenomena, say the swelling of a half-inflated balloon left on a radiator, or the apparently unmotivated suicide of a young man in twentieth-century London, or the sudden anger of a worker in the face of a request from his employer. In explaining these phenomena we introduce theoretical concepts of one sort and another, as when we describe the gas in the balloon as a swarm of dancing molecules, or introduce the idea of *anomie*, the absence of intelligibly structured norms, which we claim to be the social origin of suicide, or we bring in the notion of unconscious projection to explain the worker's behaviour as an infantile rage provoked by ascribing to the owner hostility which he himself feels. Now such descriptions are usually, if not always, of a different logical type from the descriptions of the observed phenomena. Thus it could be argued that a well-formed theory of molecular excitation would enable us to strictly deduce laws about the accelerations and decelerations of particles in a gas; and it could certainly be argued that well-formed experimental laws about the relations between heat and pressure would enable us to deduce strictly accurate predictions about particular experimental cases. It is a good deal less plausible to suppose that Durkheim's notion of *anomie* or Freud's concept of the unconscious would even in principle yield us anything comparable to the elegance of particle mechanics. Nonetheless, in these cases also we have the crucial discrepancy between the story told in the theory, and the story which the bare facts will license. Pressure is not particulate motion; *anomie* is not the reason which the suicide would give for making away with himself; and unconscious projection is plainly not the same thing as conscious anger at one's boss. Thus there is a logical gap between the two kinds of story, a difference in the *kind* of events described in the two accounts. To link the story — or deductions — of one context to those of the other we have to have some kind of *transformation rules* which will empower us to say, crudely, that expanding gases are swarms of excited particles, that certain kinds of suicides are anomic individuals, that certain angry individuals are displaying the process of unconscious projection. The importance of these rules is of course that they allow us to move from the laws of the theory to the observable data. It is not just that the laws of the theory describe a wider range of phenomena than do the experimental laws they support — though it is characteristic of theories that they should aid the process of bringing more and more phenomena under fewer and fewer rules — it is that they represent the phenomena differently. Hence, there can be no simple deduction of the experimental results from the theoretical assumptions; there must be some linking statements which assert that the two kinds of phenomena are to be identified. These rules or linking statements have been given various names: Hempel, for example, calls them 'bridge statements' while Nagel cautiously describes them as statements 'associating' experimental and theoretical results. The question which dominates the discussion is naturally that of the logical status of such statements. It will be recalled that we earlier made a good deal of the distinction between analytic statements which asserted equivalences of meaning and logical relationships, and synthetic statements which made assertions about what in point of empirical fact was so. The question arises: are we to say of transformation rules that they are analytic or synthetic? What hangs on this is the following: are we to say that a statement like 'many forms of anger are caused by the unconscious projection of infantile hostility' is to be read as 'talking about anger often *means the same as* talking about unconscious projection', or are we to read it as 'someone who is angry is *as a matter of fact* likely to be going through a process of unconscious projection'? Must we, indeed, be confined to these alternatives? (17)

Before setting out to answer this question, we should see what its importance is. We saw earlier how vital was the insistence that the propositions of empirical science should be testable, that predictions should be made which can be put up against the facts with the aim of either validating or refuting the assumptions from which they are derived. Not only do the empirical sciences seek to bring the phenomena of the natural world within the compass of an explanatory hypothesis, they also seek to bring the explanatory hypothesis up against those facts about the world which will show it up as false, if false it is. It is only when this process is possible that empirical laws can be said to be *empirical* laws at all. Now, at the level of experiment and observation we have observationally defined terms both in our generalisations and our conclusions; but in the case of theoretically defined terms, we don't *ex hypothesi* believe this to be the case. The very point of referring to 'theoretical' entities is to draw the distinction between the experimentally and the

86

theoretically defined. This means that if theories are to be tested they must be so by being linked in a tightly controlled way to the laws and descriptions which apply to the observed phenomena. Only if this is unequivocally done will we know whether we have indeed got a test case on our hands or not – which is not to say the task of experimental specification is a simple one, only that it is essential. There are examples of physical theories where the process of making the links seemed in the end so impossibly difficult that the hypothesis was abandoned as in principle untestable. One such hypothesis was the existence of the luminiferous ether: by the last years of the nineteenth century it was felt that hypotheses about its nature could not be rigorously generated and brought to experimental test, and so astronomy and physics just ceased to employ the concept of the ether. (18) Many psychologists have felt the same way about the concept of the unconscious, arguing that the link between statements about what goes on in the unconscious and what goes on in observable behaviour were in principle so loosely specified and so nearly impossible to tighten up satisfactorily that the concept ought to be dismissed from science. (19) In sociology the situation has been similar in the case of several concepts – Durkheim's 'conscience collective', Marx's 'alienation', Talcott Parsons's 'pattern variables' are only some of the examples of theoretical terms whose introduction has been resisted on the grounds that they do not generate testable hypotheses with the required rigour. What all these complaints have in common is that they are predicated on the need to link theoretical and experimental generalisations in such a way that the latter will provide a check upon the former. If we insist that the statement of this link must be either analytic or synthetic but not both at once, we have the two standard accounts of the relationship between theory and fact – operationalism and realism. (20)

Theoretical realism amounts to the following claim: the entities referred to in theories are as real, and as real in the same sense, as are those referred to in experimental laws and reports on observation. When a gas is said to be made up of minute particles, this is to be construed quite literally as an empirical statement about the make-up of what we observe. Again, if the geometrical theory of optics analyses light as a stream of photons, minute particles in rectilinear motion across empty space, then that is what light is, and photons just are the objects which the theory is about. Photons and shadows are as real as each other, one sort of object being what high-level theory is about, the other being what everyday observation is about. In sociological theory, a position very much like this was argued by Durkheim, who went to great lengths in insisting on the facticity or what he called the 'thinghood' of social forces; (21) and it is argued also by Siegfried Nadel, when insisting that his conception of social structure is of empirical properties of social behaviour, not merely of a useful mental construct of the scientist. (22) And many, perhaps most physicists have been staunch defenders of the reality of such strange entities as electrons and other sub-atomic particles, holding them to be every bit as good candidates for objective status as are chairs and tables. On these terms the relationship asserted in the bridge statements is always an empirical one: it is a fact about the world that when such and such a theoretically characterised event takes place, it is observed in such and such a way. (23)

This view is subject to one obvious difficulty. We began by assuming that there is an easily drawn, commonsense distinction between experimental observable data and unobservable theoretical constructs; but if we adopt the realist position this distinction has to go. The reason is simple: if we say that the connection between experimental and theoretical terms is an empirical one, this must mean that the terms are in principle logically independent of one another, hence that we could at any rate conceive of how in principle we might investigate the behaviour of the posited theoretical phenomena without studying the particular experimental data the theory is explaining. If the statement of the link is an empirical one, we must in principle be able to conceive of its being false; and this must mean that we can imagine what it would be like to make a check on the behaviour of the theoretical entities other than through the experimental data they are invoked to explain; for if we could not conceive such a test the relationship would be an analytic one, not a synthetic one. Hence theoretical entities must in principle be observable, and the initial distinction untenable as anything more than a rough and ready kind of

88

approximation. But many scientists are more than happy to accept this conclusion; they would move on to the attack as well. The practice of science in its unreflective moments offers no sharp distinction between theoretical and observational results: a physicist will tell you he has *seen* electron tracks in a cloud chamber, though he will also tell you why there is in principle no hope of straightforwardly watching electrons. And anyone who wished to preserve a sharp line between theoretical and non-theoretical explanation must face some sharp questions about the line between observation and inference; do we *see* things when we see them on the television? (24) Is seeing through a microscope a straightforward case of seeing or not, and is there a line to be drawn between seeing through an optical microscope and seeing through an electron microscope? A scientist's willingness to say that he has seen a theoretically defined entity seems to rest not at all on any *a priori* notions about the nature of observation, but almost wholly on the reliability of the theory in question. Borrowing the point from Professor Ryle's analysis of verbs like *see, hear, feel,* (25) we can say that their primary point is to make claims about what is there rather than about the nature of the experience through which we come to know what is there. Hence in all our talk about the world we make claims about its contents, and the idea that we could even in principle talk about the observations *alone*, from which all else is inference, is mistaken. The scientist who abandoned talking about electrons in order to talk only about meters and pointers would impoverish science without getting any further towards the in principle unattainable goal of describing pure observational data. A sociologist might try to characterise what went on in a law court in terms of mouth movements, changing physical movements of bodies and so on; but this too would only succeed in rendering sociology impossible, without getting us any nearer an observation untainted by theory. Thus realism becomes the only plausible view of science's use of theory, whether the sciences be those of physical nature or the social order. One of the most eloquent defences of this view was Eddington's famous distinction between the table revealed to common sense, at which as we say we sit, from which we eat, and so on, and the real table revealed by science, which consisted of a cloud of particles swarming in an empty space. For Eddington, it was not only that realism was the order of the day, but even that philosophical doubt was more properly attached to everyday beliefs than to the results of physics. Such substance as ordinary knowledge possessed was borrowed by it from the theories of the sciences. (26)

However exaggerated Eddington's extension of the argument has become, (27) the realist position certainly does provide a straightforward answer to the question of the connections between theory and observation. It means that when we have a coherent theory we can link it empirically to lower-level, visible regularities; and hence we have three levels of argument, in the case at any rate of developed and mathematically formulated theories. At the core of the theory we have the abstract logical calculus about which none but formal questions can sensibly be put; we then have the theoretical specification of this, and finally the empirical regularities we observe and order by experimental generalis-ations. The line between these latter steps is a fluctuating one, and varies with our information and our experimental techniques. Thus e.g. we might have the set of equations which govern the reproduction rate of bacteria as a piece of straightforward mathematics; then we might first guess at the existence of bacteria multiplying in this way to account for the observable progress of an infection; but with more powerful microscopes we should actually come to observe the bacteria we have posited, and thus bring their behaviour within the scope of experimental law. (28)

This is a conclusive case. There are, however, some residual doubts, especially relevant to the social sciences, and in clearing these up, we can see what the attractions of 'operationalism' are. This will incidentally explain why operationalism has had a much greater acceptance in the social sciences than in the natural sciences. The residual doubts seem to arise in two kinds of case. The first is that of concepts which typically refer to processes rather than entities (a line which will readily be seen to be less than absolutely stable). The second is the case of 'ideal type' theories in which entities and processes alike appear which could not possibly occur in the real world, and hence of course could not be observed even in principle. The first

90

worry, that about the ontology of processes, has an interesting history, which reveals among other things that which processes most worry thinkers depends a good deal on the existing state of science. Thus the idea of gravitational attraction took a good deal of swallowing at the time of Newton; even Newton himself referred to his 'Principia' as the 'mathematical' principles of nature because he shared those doubts. (29) To qualify as the 'philosophical' or 'scientifical' principles of nature they would have had to explain away the notion of action at a distance, a notion which the contemporary mechanistic paradigm could not make any sense of. The paradigm ruled in mechanical *push* as an intelligible process, but ruled out gravitational *pull*. Of course, it appeared soon enough that familiarity bred acceptance of action at a distance, and its discrediting by the critics of scholasticism ceased to interest anyone but historians. And much the same thing was true when the notion of the electrical field was introduced into science, and again with the notion of electromagnetic wave motions. The social sciences give rise to similar doubts whenever there is proposed some kind of structural analysis of a form of social behaviour; for the temptation is always strong to say that while it is true that we can see people behaving in various ways, it makes little sense to say that we can (in any other sense than this) observe the structure of their actions. Or when kinship relations are explained on the analogy with fields in physical theory, we are tempted to say that it is much easier to see the relations than to see the field and *its* structure. Yet, of course, we realise that theories involving such concepts are essential to the sciences, and that they must therefore be reputable enough. Yet this respectability is not accountable for on realist grounds. The same thing goes for covert processes. We may want to analyse the way a child learns a language in the first few years of its life as a process whereby it constructs a grammar according to predetermined principles; that is, to adopt Chomsky's formulation, we may regard the infant as a pre-programmed device which fits the sounds it hears into patterns specified in a very abstract way by the rules of the programme. These rules are of course not ones of which the child is conscious, and they are not rules which we as adults could conceive of using consciously. And

91

we may have absolutely no idea of how the 'programme' is physically represented in the human organism; nonetheless, there is nothing outrageous in claiming on theoretical grounds that a child learning its own native language follows such rules. (30) The case of 'ideal types', however, is of more obvious relevance to the social sciences. Max Weber coined the term 'ideal type' (31) to describe the process of reasoning about a kind of 'entity' which we quite clearly know could never have existed, in order to explain the salient features of the social phenomena we are concerned with. One obvious example of an 'ideal type' — not in an area where Weber applied the notion for sociological purposes — is the rational man of economic theory whose sole object in life is to buy cheap and sell dear, whose information is both costless and complete, and so on; plainly such a man neither exists nor could in principle be observed, even though he was indispensable to classical economics in its efforts to gain understanding of actual economic phenomena. But sociology has a great stock of equally ideal examples: the attainment-oriented man is just as much an ideal type as his counterpart the ascription-oriented man; and this goes just as much for entire social and political systems as well — as Aristotle long ago pointed out in his 'Politics', when he offered his famous and long-lived classificatory schemes. But the social sciences are not unique in their employment of such a notion. The Newtonian concept of the 'point-mass' is an ideal type in just the same sense in its context as is economic man in his.

These considerations give rise to what is known as operationalism, sometimes also referred to as a 'black box' theory of theories. (32) On such a view the relationship between theories and descriptions of observational results is analytic in the following sense: the only terms which have any existential implications for what the contents of the world actually are are those referring to experimentally observable states of affairs. Theories are essentially instrumental in that they are good means for linking together statements about observations to other statements about observations. They are heuristically useful because they suggest to us new experiments which make us aware of connections between observable states of affairs that we should not otherwise have noticed. Thus the idea of 'unconscious projection' may serve

92

a useful purpose in suggesting to us how we should link the anger a man displays now to fears he had when he was a child, and it may be that this suggests to us certain therapeutic moves in that we see how to cure certain kinds of emotional distress by providing an environment in which a process rather like relearning emotional habits can take place. (33) We do not have to claim that there *really is* an unconscious mind at work; the network of successful analogy is its own justification. And correspondingly the failure to generate consistent and interesting experimental consequences is what spells death to a theory. In this sense the theory is a black box: we feed in experimental data as an input and we obtain further experimental data as output, i.e. as predictions which we can test. What it is about the box which allows it to do this we do not have to know or care; it may be that a story about the insides of the box will have fruitful implications for suggesting new inputs, but this is a bonus and not part of the logic of theories. A good box is one which transforms true statements as inputs into true predictions as outputs; it should not, in principle, disturb us if we were somehow able to break open the box and find it empty. And plainly, for anyone who holds this view, concepts such as 'economic man' or 'the spirit of capitalism' are seen as complex ways of shuffling our information and arguing about our data.

Although I do not think this is an adequate account of all theoretical concepts, it has a good deal of point over a limited range. And once again this is particularly true in those areas which have particularly interested political scientists. This is because recent political science has indeed been characterised by a great deal of analogical argument, and a great many attempts to borrow plausible models of explanation from elsewhere among the sciences. Thus, for instance, there have been attempts by such ingenious writers as Karl Deutsch in 'The Nerves of Government' to borrow the analysis of self-regulating mechanisms which have to process a great deal of information and react to it with frequent self-monitoring by way of various feedback devices. (34) Now it is quite plain that no one thinks that, say, the United States *is* a machine in any straightforward sense; and again it is plain that no one thinks that it produces an output in quite

93

the way that a motor with a governor will turn a flywheel so many times a minute, or an amplifier will feed a steady five watts into a loudspeaker. Rather, what we end up with is a lot of suggestions about the causal connections implicit in political activity, a set of ideas which tell us what lines of research might be worth exploring, a way of more systematically linking the opinions of the public and the responses of their rulers. And with such a 'theory' we are better able than before to order, classify and scrutinise our results — all of these things being part of the tasks which paradigms were said to perform.

But the defects of this analysis lead us on to the final arguments of this chapter, namely a short characterisation of some differences between models, theories, maps and analogies. The very first thing to insist on is that nothing whatever turns on the verbal usage which I adopt here and someone else might reject. What matters is not the words we use but the distinctions which they mark, and it is important that there should be agreement on which distinctions we have to mark. The deficiency of operationalism, then, is that it blurs the distinction between theories and models, between analogies which state that the phenomena behave *as if* they were the visible outcome of some underlying mechanism or quasi-mechanism, and theories which maintain that the phenomena behave as they do because they *are* the visible outcome of such and such a mechanism. (35) And this distinction holds equally good for the sociological or economic theory which asserts that the phenomena possess such and such a structure as contrasted with the merely analogical claim that they behave *as if* they did. Thus we are led to revise our acceptance of Downs's 'An Economic Theory of Democracy' as a *theory* of democracy, for it now emerges that in our present sense it is a *model*, for people are said to behave in political matters *as if* the political system were a certain kind of market. For what Professor Downs does is to model the behaviour of politicians and voters onto a form of behaviour which is more adequately theoretically explained, namely the behaviour of buyers and sellers in a market situation. And as with almost all models, one of his aims is to show how the real-world situation diverges from the results predicted in the model, for in so doing we can

94

show how politics is not quite like economics. But if Downs had been able to deduce consistently accurate predictions about the behaviour of, say, American voters and politicians from the model, we might well have come to assign it a rather different status and to have begun to believe that the model's assumptions were true of politicians and voters as we know them in political life, and thus that it was a genuine theory of democratic politics. Indeed, we can see how too sharp a distinction between model and theory would be misleading; for a model may become a theory, if it is thought to have existential import. (36) Thus we can imagine argument arising as to whether the American political system really was a sort of market, and about how we might test such an existential claim; and this would be an argument as to whether this was a genuine theory. But, of course, there are models which will plainly never approach this condition of so to speak candidacy for the status of theories. Suppose that we were to model international conflict between two super-powers in terms of a game of draughts — not a fanciful suggestion in view of the interest in game theory in conflict analysis. In such a case we should not remotely contemplate claiming to have produced a 'draughts theory of international conflict'; if we were to produce a theory at all it would be one about the structure of conflict generally, of which both draughts and international disputes might be cases.

Those who produce models do not make existential claims about the world; but those who produce theories generally do; and this is why realism is the more plausible account of the matter — scientists are not content merely to say that things happen as if a certain mechanism is at work; they claim that there is a mechanism at work, and this claim is a claim about the contents of the world. (37) We can, therefore, contemplate failing a theory because its claims about what is actually there are mistaken. In other words, we do not let an account through merely because things happen as if the account were a true account of the way things work but because we believe that it is a true account. When Copernicus claimed not to have made any revolutionary changes in cosmography merely by adopting the heliocentric picture of the solar system as a useful calculating device, he deceived almost nobody; it was clear that the point of the heliocentric

95

theory of the solar system was not merely to free calculation from the drag of Ptolemaic epicycles, but to give a rational account of how the solar system really was structured. Equally, the kinetic theory of gases has to be taken as claiming that there are swarms of particles going to make up gases if there can be any question of drawing further consequences about such matters as the internal gravitational attractions within a dense gas; the history of science is on the side of the plain meaning of the claims made in theoretical statements — when a gas is said to be composed of particles, that is what is meant. Again we see how this ties in with our previous claims for the importance of causal chains, and it explains why the imagery of 'maps' should be popular; for a map shows us the way from one place to another, the sequence of steps which will get us from the beginning to the end of a journey, and a map like a theory sets out to tell us what is actually there on the ground; like a theory it abstracts from most of the properties of the objects in the country-side, but like a theory it fails to be accurate if we arrive and find the object depicted is missing. Models and theories alike assist us to fill in causal sequences by showing how one thing follows on from another; but the weakness of models relatively to theories is precisely that they *only* have a heuristic usefulness, they do not tell us that this is the sequence which really takes place.

All of which leads to one last comment about the situation in the social sciences, more particularly in the field of political science. There has recently been something of a proliferation of 'conceptual frameworks' — of which the most noted examples have been Professor Easton's so-called systems analysis (38) and Professor Almond's modified structural-functional model (39) — offered by writers who hope to provide not theories about political behaviour, but an agreed terminology within which theories can be constructed. But this process comes a little oddly, for the following reason. If we consider any well-attested theory, one thing we can do is ask causal questions about the results to be expected if we alter some factor or other in an experimental situation; and this is a distinct question from asking what, as a matter of logic, is the relationship within an analogy or model — for as we have said, the theory claims to be about the real world in a way that the model does not. But when we are offered a 'conceptual framework' it is not clear that we can ask either of these questions, for avowedly the framework is a pre-theoretical product. Where we can ask either of the questions, it is important to be able to distinguish clearly between what we might call proto-theories, i.e. loosely formulated, but genuine, theoretical claims about causal sequences, and merely analogical formulae of one or another sort. But in most sciences, and in the social sciences until now, conceptual schemes – which is another way of saying classificatory schemes – have always arrived only in the wake of, and as aids to, genuine theoretical advance. The classificatory schemes of anatomy only developed to any use when physiological theory developed; and no one reading Aristotle, Montesquieu or Marx could possibly believe that their 'conceptual framework' would have been produced other than in the process of their producing theories of politics. There is thus a strong case for supposing that conceptual frameworks are either theories whose authors are afraid to assert them like men or else a wasted labour; a more adequately validated supply of causal generalisations would inevitably generate the vocabulary necessary to their adequate formulation; to suppose that this process of generation could simply be reversed suggests already a lack of attention to plausible causal sequences.

NOTES

1. M. Brodbeck, 'Models, Meaning and Theories', in L. Gross (ed.), 'Symposium on Sociological Theory' (Harper & Row, 1959) pp. 373-403.

2. C. G. Hempel, 'Philosophy of Natural Science' (Prentice-Hall, 1966) p. 73.

3. Brown, 'Explanation in Social Science', ch. vii.

4. Dray, 'Laws and Explanation', pp. 79-82.

5. S. E. Toulmin, 'The Philosophy of Science', rev. ed. (Hutchinson, 1967) pp. 17 ff.

6. Ibid., ch. iii.

7. Kuhn, 'Structure of Scientific Revolutions', pp. 10 ff.

8. S. S. Wolin, 'Paradigms and Political Theories', in P. King and J. Parekh (eds), 'Politics and Experience: Essays Presented to Michael Oakeshott' (Cambridge University Press, 1968) pp. 125-52.

9. Easton, 'Political System', pp. 52-63.

10. T. Parsons, 'Essays in Sociological Theory', rev. ed. (Free Press, Chicago, 1954) pp. 212-19.

11. Wolin, in 'Politics and Experience', p. 128.

12. Ibid., pp. 149-52.

13. See Ch. 3, n. 36.

14. E. Durkheim, 'Rules of Sociological Method' (Free Press, Chicago, 1950) p. 14.

15. S. F. Nadel, 'The Theory of Social Structure' (Cohen & West, 1957) ch. i.

16. N. Chomsky John Locke lectures delivered at Oxford University, June 1969.

17. Nagel, 'Structure of Science', ch. 6.

18. J. A. Coleman, 'Relativity for the Layman' (Penguin, 1959) chs 2, 3.

19. A. C. MacIntyre, 'The Unconscious' (Routledge, 1958) pp. 2-4.

20. Nagel 'Structure of Science', pp. 129-52.

21. Durkheim, 'Rules', p. 14.

22. Nadel, 'Theory of Social Structure', pp. 4-7.

23. Harre, 'Theories and Things', pp. 22-6.

24. Austin, 'Sense and Sensibilia', pp. 14-19.

25. G. Ryle, 'The Concept of Mind' (Hutchinson, n.i. 1967) pp. 222 f.

26. A. Eddington, 'The Nature of the Physical World' (Everyman ed., 1935) pp. 5-8.

27. L. S. Stebbing, 'Philosophy and the Physicists' (Methuen, 1937) pp. 47 ff.

28. Hempel, 'Philosophy of Natural Science', p. 82.

29. N. Chomsky, 'Language and Mind' (Harcourt, New York, 1968) p. 7.

30. Ibid., pp. 75-8.

31. M. Weber, 'The Methodology of the Social Sciences' (Free Press, Chicago, 1949) pp. 89 ff.

32. Hempel, 'Philosophy of Natural Science', pp. 81 f.

33. MacIntyre, 'The Unconscious', pp. 80-3.

34. K. W. Deutsch, 'The Nerves of Government' (Free Press, Chicago, 1963) ch. 5.

35. Harre, 'Theories and Things', p. 26.

36. Ibid., pp. 26-8.

37. M. Polanyi, 'Science and Reality', 'Brit. Jnl Phil. Sci.' (1967-8) pp. 177-96.

38. D. Easton, 'A Systems Analysis of Political Life' (Wiley, 1965) pp. 10-25.

39. Almond and Coleman, 'Politics of Developing Areas', pp. 9-16.

5 The Causal Explanation of Behaviour

The topics discussed in this chapter not only merit lengthy investigation — they have received it in dozens of books, philosophical and psychological journals, introductory text-books and elsewhere. Accordingly, our approach in this chapter will be determined by the overall programme of this book: what we must ask is in what sense a causal account of the actions of individuals is a necessary constituent of the social sciences. We must then go on to ask whether the establishment of the envisaged causal explanations of our actions is only a matter of factual discovery, or whether it calls into question our pre-existing ideas about human behaviour — i.e. whether it would involve a major conceptual shift and raise acute philosophical problems. I shall not raise in any detail the obvious and fascinating question of how one might anticipate the practical changes which any large-scale revision of our image of human nature would bring about. It is clear, however, that our conception of moral praise and blame, of social and political responsibility, and thus our conceptions of the reasons behind such social practices as punishment, or the maintenance of police and military forces, are all heavily dependent on our assumptions about how human actions are to be explained; radical changes in these assumptions would obviously necessitate radical changes in the most basic aspects of social organisation. This is a matter on which there has been a good deal of speculation by novelists, science-fiction writers, and off-duty scientists,(1) but there is room for doubting that even they have seen the extent of the revisions which might be forced upon us.

The account of explanation in the sciences which we have offered raises the question of how far the human sciences can model themselves on the natural sciences. So far, we have not suggested that there are any limits to this process, for our criticisms of various aspects of the 'hypothetico-deductive' account of scientific explanation have all rested on weaknesses of that account which appear no matter what field it is applied to. But now we must face the question of how the account of explanation which was developed in the last two chapters applies to the explanation of human behaviour. One school of thought holds that there can be no trouble involved in such an application. (2) Everyday life already involves an immense knowledge, unorganised though it may be, of the regularities implied in human behaviour. It is argued, and very plausibly, that no child could survive to adulthood without becoming aware of these regularities, for without such knowledge he would be unable to regulate his behaviour with regard to other people. He must have learned some approximate generalisations about the responses of people to whom one is polite and of those people to whom one is rude; he must have learned some approximate generalisations about the relationship between offers of meals and their actually appearing, and so on indefinitely. The child could only learn about these generalisations and form expectations based upon them if the behaviour of those around him actually did display regularities of a discernible and reliable kind. The point can be generalised: all social life would be quite impossible if we could not expect that people would behave in a regular manner. Governments, for instance, know that people will not generally part with their money willingly, and thus no government operates an entirely voluntary taxation scheme; indeed, the whole apparatus of taxation operated by all states rests on the generalisation that people will not of their own free will set about providing the finances required for the maintenance of the machinery of government. Equally, the assumption behind the creation of a police force is that most people who break the rules of their society will endeavour to escape the consequences of their actions; and plainly, we can repeat examples throughout every area of social life. Such generalisations may be approximate generalisations only, and subject to exceptions; but as much could be said about many of the generalisations found in the natural sciences. Does the existence of these generalisations settle the question at once; are they incontrovertible evidence that we have the raw

101

materials for a science of human behaviour?

To traditional empiricist philosophers — whether Hume in the eighteenth century, Mill in the nineteenth, or Ayer in the nineteen-thirties — the answer was plainly that it did settle the issue to produce such daily examples. There are two main planks in this assurance, the first a matter of philosophical principles about what kind of phenomena there are in nature, and how they are to be explained, the second an image of the internal logical structure of a well-developed science. The two planks are to some extent independent, although the first is often used as a support for the second. The philosophical assumptions underlying the more 'metaphysical' aspect of the argument were mentioned briefly in the first chapter. The world as understood by science is a sequence of particular events, of which the events that form human thoughts and actions are one subclass; if there are regularities in human actions and human thought, as it seems impossible to deny that there are, then these actions and thoughts must occur in the same kind of law-governed way as do all other events. The question boils down to whether human behaviour is governed by invariable laws: if it is, then human behaviour can be studied by a psychological science which is integrated in the unified science of the natural world, both human and non-human; to answer that it is not seems to contradict not merely the evidence of our daily life, but also to leave room for some slippery metaphysical attempts to show that human beings are somehow not part of the natural order they inhabit. (3) Obviously, for any empiricist thinker impressed by the physical sciences, it was unthinkable that there should be radical discontinuities between everything else in the universe and the human inhabitants of it. In this way, we come to the heart of empiricist ambitions. The programme for the causal account of behaviour has been part of a traditional drive towards the reduction of all types of explanation to physical, preferably mechanical explanation, a programme which has both excited the western mind and frightened it very thoroughly for nearly four hundred years. Contemporary psychologists who claim in all honesty to speak not as philosophers but as psychologists commit themselves to such a programme with almost as much enthusiasm as did Hobbes some three hundred years earlier. Hobbes believed as firmly

102

as one could that all behaviour, whether of animate or inanimate matter, was ultimately to be explained in terms of particulate motion: the laws governing the motions of discrete material particles were the ultimate laws of the universe, and in this sense psychology must be rooted in physiology and physiology in physics, while the social sciences, especially the technology of statecraft, must be rooted in psychology. (4) There is a plausibility about Hobbes's picture that persists in spite of its many crudenesses and logical deficiencies. Its basic tenet is that the outcome in any physical system is in principle open to prediction, because it is causally determined; physical determinism holds everywhere, for the laws governing physical matter are universal laws. Now, whatever else one wants to say about the nature of human beings, they are certainly physical objects, and thus must be subject to physical causality along with the rest of the physical world. Although no modern scientists spend their time defending such extremely general assumptions, the practice of, say, physiology since Hobbes's time would seem to show that these general views form working hypotheses about the nature of the connections to be looked for. Moreover, this programme has long recognised what cyberneticists have familiarised us with since the Second World War: human beings form organised systems, with self-regulating mechanisms that operate on apparently holistic principles to maintain integration and promote survival. This creates logical problems for anyone who wishes to generate the properties of the entire system from the mechanical principles explaining the working of the parts; nonetheless, it does not cast any doubt upon the assumption that the working of the parts *can* be mechanically explained, nor that the overall properties of the system are in some sense inferable from the operations of the parts. To say that this amounts to the claim that human beings are mere machines, as opponents of this view are inclined to do, is clearly of no avail. It is true that the claim is that the operation of the so to speak components of the human organism must be explicable on mechanical principles, or if the term 'mechanical' be too restrictive, on 'physical' principles; but this does not impose any restrictions on the kind of total system we are dealing with — a Cartesian

103

physicist would be amazed by the achievements of the electronic computer, and because of its construction certainly would not see it as in his sense governed by mechanical principles, but present-day physicists are happy to regard computers as machines. (5) Thus we must understand the programme of causal explanation envisaged here, not as claiming that men are merely machines. but rather that the principles by which we are to explain human behaviour are the same as those by which we explain complex physical phenomena. If human beings are physical objects, governed by causal laws, it seems to follow that human behaviour is straightforwardly amenable to causal explanation. Ideally, therefore, a truly adequate explanation of a human action would involve our being able to trace in detail the physiological — and in the end the physical and in this wide sense 'mechanical' — processes by which the action comes to be produced. The demonstration of these processes is obviously a matter of enormous complexity, far exceeding the difficulties of the traditional physical sciences, and it cannot be claimed that psychologists or physiologists have so far succeeded in analysing the behaviour of even relatively simple animals in these terms, let alone suggesting successful hypotheses to explain human behaviour. It can in addition be argued with some justice that so excessively simple have the experimental situations been in which the attempt has been made that much more successful experiments would still yield little knowledge of the real capacities of even the maze-trained rat. Yet a standard introductory work like Dr Broadbent's 'Behaviour' commits itself to the belief that essentially this programme is the correct one; (6) much progress has been made over the past half-century, and much more can be anticipated; and such striking work as that done on the brain by Dr Grey Walter operates within the same explanatory framework — a dominant image throughout the account is that of electric switchgear, used in starting and stopping motors, an image which was put to use in the construction of one of the most famous of laboratory pets, the Grey Walter 'tortoise', so lucidly described in 'The Living Brain'. (7) Both psychologists and physiologists recognise that much of the characteristic behaviour of complex organisms stems from principles of organisation within the organism, as

104

well as from the physical properties of the parts of the organism; there is thus a two-pronged attack to be mounted, one concentrating on the organisational principles, the other on the physical properties of the parts. But in all this, the basic assumptions remain those which were set out above, and the goal remains that of integrating the causal processes of human behaviour with the processes we discover to be operating elsewhere in nature.

The programme envisaged above raises some awkward problems about the sense in which the psychological processes of thinking, choosing, feeling and so on can be said to be 'reduced' to, or be 'the same as' physiological processes, and it is time to mention some of these. They are difficulties of a recurrent kind, wherever the topic of 'reduction' is mentioned, so a short account of them at this point will serve as introduction to our later discussions as well. The major difficulty is that the terms involved in psychological description seem not to belong to the same logical category as those involved in physiological or physical theories about psychological events. For instance, if we consider the question of temporal duration, we find that a one-one correlation between a mental event and a corresponding physiological event is highly implausible. Suppose someone says that he has been 'thinking about his family': it makes no sense to inquire of him how long he took to think about them, though it does make sense to ask how long he spent thinking about them; yet if thinking about his family *were* a physiologically determinate event, then it must make sense to ask how long it takes for such an event to occur, even if the answer is to be given in micro-seconds. Or again, take the issue of spatial location: we have in everyday speech a host of spatial metaphors about thought, as when we say that an idea is 'at the back of our mind', or that something 'slipped our mind', and some philosophers have assumed that such metaphors were pre-scientific recognitions of the physical truth about the brain. But quite aside from the scientific doubts posed by the relative lack of success of physiology in locating cognitive operations in different areas of the brain, there is the prior logical problem that spatial metaphors simply cannot be pressed. It makes no sense, for instance, to inquire whether one thought was *further* towards the back of my mind than another — except as a joking way of asking whether I was even less likely to remember it spontaneously. Again, it makes no sense to ask whether my memory of eating strawberries as a child is to the left of my memory of seeing steam engines hauling trains; yet if memories are straightforwardly to be identified with physiological events, then they must happen in a determinate place, and must therefore enter into definite spatial relations with each other, since we do of necessity locate all physical processes in a common space. (8) Another kind of logical hiatus occurs in the criteria we use for identifying, and distinguishing between, mental phenomena on one hand and physical phenomena on the other. Once made, this is an obvious point; we say of a great variety of different pieces of behaviour that they evince nostalgia — a man sighing over a photograph, reading a poem about the old days, collecting ancient theatre programmes, all these may make us say that he is feeling nostalgic. Yet it would be extremely difficult to suggest a remotely plausible physiological theory that would pick out identical physical states to correspond to what we call the same emotion. For the physiological theory would have to pick out events by their physical properties, such as spatio-temporal location, perhaps their frequency if they were understood as firings of neurons, or their wave form if they were seen as electrical outputs of some area of the brain; and these properties are quite unlike any which we say emotional states have in common. To revert again to the well-worn example mentioned in the first chapter, the man who writes his name on a piece of paper performs what is crudely to be described as the same physical movements, yet what he is doing can be variously described; the converse case is that of the man who is said to be doing the same thing, but may employ a great variety of physically distinct means for doing it, as when he hands over bank notes, signs a cheque, merely nods, or says 'O.K.' — and in each case is bankrupting himself. (9) The description of what a person does, or thinks, or feels, seems to involve quite other ways of picking out events than would any physiological or physical account of what he is up to. If this is so, then there seems to be grave difficulty in the way of anyone who proposes to 'reduce' psychological — or everyday — accounts of human behaviour to a causal account

106

of events rendered in physiological terms. A third kind of difficulty which is allied to the above is that the *way* in which we come to know about psychological events is quite different in kind from the way in which we come to know about physiological events. Suppose we did say that the real event that occurred when we thought of home was some sort of physical process in the brain; now this would suggest that the way to find out what we were thinking was to look at the state of our brains — and yet this is plainly preposterous, since we know (whenever we are conscious) what we are thinking, without there being any question of our having to go and look. There seems to be something terribly wrong with the suggestion that I am not the final authority, under normal circumstances, on what I am thinking; there seems even to be something wrong with the suggestion that in general I need to *find out* what I am thinking. Certainly, other people have to find out what I think, and vice versa; but this does not hold good for the knowledge which we have of our own thoughts and feelings.

I shall go on to say something about the inconclusive nature of such arguments; but first I want to say a few things about one proffered alternative to the causal account of human behaviour as first presented. It can be argued that the problems of physiological reduction do not matter, because there is no need to reduce psychological explanation to physiological explanation. All that matters is that we should be able to establish some basic psychological laws from which we can go on to explain human behaviour. The practice of psychologists is ambiguous enough to allow both theories of independence and interdependence to be proffered. An analogy offered by psychologists is that with our strategy if we were faced with a computing device of unknown construction, but whose inputs and outputs we could measure: it would be possible for us to try to discover what programme the computer was running, even if we had no idea at all how this programme was physically mapped inside the computer. This slightly abstract argument can be concretely imagined if one considers the difference between the homely cash register with mechanical linkages rather like those of a typewriter, and its contemporary electronic version: in one the counting is done by rotating cogs, in the other by

107

transistors and capacitors, but someone who knew nothing of the internal workings of the machines could easily enough discover that what they did was register and total the sums of money put into and taken out of the till. In like manner, we might try to discover the various 'programmes' written into human behaviour without positing any particular physiological mechanism onto which these programmes were mapped. (10) The view offered by numerous empiricists has been that psychological processes followed causal paths which were discovered independently of anything which we might come to learn about their relationship with bodily conditions. A political scientist might uncover a causal sequence in which a man who enters a polling booth is in a certain mental set — he believes certain facts about the policies of two competing political parties, he values certain outcomes above others, and he has various expectations about which outcomes will be promoted by what policies; the total mental set amounts to predisposing causal conditions, on which new perceptions will have an effect. The man now sees various names under the Democrat label, and various others under the Republican label; this perception triggers the decision to vote for one party rather than the other; and accordingly, he sets the machine and pulls the lever to register his vote. The social sciences, therefore, can rest on so to speak mental mechanics rather than physiological mechanics. Possibly the most elegant formulation of this programme was the employment of psychological premises in classical economics; but once again, the practice of the social sciences in general indicates that social scientists feel an interest in and an affinity with the work of psychologists, and thus displays the perhaps not very explicit belief that there is at any rate interdependence of the several human sciences. The case of classical economics is an 'ideal type' here, since nineteenth-century economic theorists tried explicitly to root their science in what they took to be the fundamental laws of human nature, a process described in Lord Robbins's 'The Nature and Significance of Economic Science', (11) and in the nineteenth century by Mill's essay on 'Definition and Method in Political Economy'. (12) The argument is not, of course, that economics is a branch of psychology, for the laws of economics both abstract from all

108

aspects of human action save those concerned with the gaining of reward in the conditions of the market, and also invoke numerous physical laws about the conditions under which human beings have to work for their rewards. Such 'laws' as that of diminishing marginal productivity rest not only on what we know about human motivation, but also on our knowledge of the scarcity of good land, easily mined minerals and so on; and, of course, economics studies something other than the *intended* outcomes of human behaviour − from the psychological premisses about what men intend to achieve in the market, it derives generalisations about the unintended results of their actions, for example about the catastrophic fall in prices which will be brought about if everyone attempts simultaneously to realise a profit at the height of a stock-market boom. Naturally, no one wants to bring about a fall in prices, yet this is what they as a group achieve, under the appropriate conditions. In such a way, then, economics rests on, or employs, psychological generalisations about the aims and behaviour of individuals to generate theories about entire markets or entire economies. If the status of economics is good evidence for the soundness of the underlying methodological assumptions, it seems that the classical empiricist belief in the existence and usefulness of psychological generalisations, whether or not founded in physiological knowledge, is amply validated.

This would certainly settle doubts about the viability of reductionism as a psychological programme, but it raises its own difficulties. One of these is the venerable philosophical problem of how minds and bodies can be related to each other. Clearly those writers are correct who say that psychological and physical phenomena are different in the sense that I can know that I feel fear without knowing anything about the adrenalin gland, or I can tell that you are an excitable kind of person without knowing anything about the output of your thyroid gland. But if we take this to mean that mental events are somehow not events in the ordinary physical order of things, then there is a good deal of difficulty in seeing how they can have any effect on the physical world; but they must have those effects which are required if mental events can play any role in the causal explanation of behaviour. If, for instance, my wanting a

Conservative government to come into power was not a fully fledged causal antecedent of my voting a particular ticket in local elections, then producing this want as part of an explanation would not fit the causal pattern of explanation. But if it is a causal antecedent it implies that we understand how wants bring about actions; but do we understand this? Let us look at the supposed causal chain here. Suppose we want to explain my having voted for the Conservative slate in the local election: the event of voting, we might assume, can be described as the physical occurrence of my intentionally pulling the lever that stamps my ballot in the appropriate way. Its causal antecedent is the decision which I take to pull the appropriate lever, in the knowledge that this is the appropriate means towards bringing about the goal I desire. But to this there is the old, but powerful objection that this causal connection is unintelligible: we can see that the impact of one billiard-ball upon another will push the second into motion, we can see that a lever inserted beneath a large block of stone will move it; but how can anything so immaterial as a decision bring about anything so material as the movements of the arm and hand which go to make up the action of pulling a lever? All accounts that have envisaged 'acts of will' or 'volitions' have come to grief on this point; there seems to be a categorial jump at the point where the act of mind causes the act of the body, the machinery which would get us across this gap seems to baffle the imagination. And, of course, it is one of the attractions of the reductionist programme that it seems to offer a solution to just this problem. (13)

Rather than embark on a superficial account of the ramifications of the mind-body problem, let us look at the implications of the problem for two aspects of the argument of this book. The first is that it displays the ambiguity of our notions of causation; the second is that it shows the importance of the notion of theoretical realism, and in explaining the impact on this problem of the idea of theoretical realism, we can explain also the second of the reasons why a causally construed psychology should be thought to be a necessary element in the social sciences. On the issue of causation, we can see the difficulties raised in asking whether mental events can be causes of physical events by considering what possible replies there might be. One obvious one is that which all empiricists since Hume would tend to give — and in this class I think we can include most social scientists who accept the predominant strains in the philosophy of science. For them, it is perfectly in order for there to be such a categorial gap between cause and effect, because there is no question of causal connections having to be intelligible. (14) All causes are equally inscrutably linked to their effects, for causes are never more than antecedent conditions universally linked to their consequents; wherever we can truthfully utter the generalisation: *whenever event A then event B*, we have a causal connection. There is no further causal nexus than this, and in this sense we can never see further into what the causal power of one event over another consists in; the transmission of motion from one billiard-ball to another — if we may use the well-tried example proffered by Hume — is not intelligible, it is merely familiar. It is true that we permeate the world of science with our anthropomorphic imagery of pulling levers, or pushing objects about, and thus deceive ourselves about what actually goes on; but what actually goes on is no more nor less than regular sequence. Where there is regular sequence, there there is causation. The account of explanation offered by Professor Popper in 'The Poverty of Historicism' is explicitly intended to carry over this analysis from the natural sciences into the social sciences; a causal account is an account where a deductive explanation is in place, and Popper is emphatic in defence of the view that when we explain human actions we do so in the deductive mode; it is plain therefore that his talk of 'situational logic' is talk about causal accounts of human actions. (15) When we explain Caesar's crossing the Rubicon in terms of his ambitions, we appeal to a causal generalisation linking ambition with the taking of bold and decisive action at key moments, and Caesar plainly fits into the particular conditions of being an ambitious man at a point where striking action at a key point is possible and called for. The nature of mental states is not in question, nor whether such things as 'ambition' are wholly mental or partially physical phenomena; all we want are generalisations which will act as 'covering laws' for the particular events we need to explain. If cold can cause ice to form, decisions can cause actions; in

111

both cases we have covering laws, and thus in both cases we have causation. And this holds good throughout the social sciences; we may discover from voting surveys generalisations such as 'being perceived as working class tends to make people politically authoritarian', and these are straightforward causal generalisations.

In assessing such arguments, we do not get much help from ordinary speech. We obviously do talk of causing people to do and to feel: a striking example cited by Professor MacIntyre comes from the Book of Common Prayer, where the marriage service describes the officiating priest as *causing* the couple to be joined together; (16) and certainly we ask questions such as 'what caused him to get so angry?' or 'what caused that sudden burst of kindness?' In terms of generalisations, we have already seen that there are plenty available in everyday life; and if we look at some of the other possible senses of causation, these also seem to be implicit in what we ordinarily say. MacIntyre suggests that one of the two most common senses of causation is where we want to talk about sufficient conditions for an event – that is, those conditions which are adequate to bring about an event, but which do not have to be present, i.e. are not necessary. Stabbing is a cause of death because it is a sufficient condition of death to be stabbed through the heart, but not a necessary condition, since there are many alternative things that will kill one. In sociology, it is much more plausible to hope to find sufficient conditions than conditions which are both sufficient and necessary – we may suppose that, for example, we can discover that agrarian discontent coupled with inflation at the expense of the middle classes will sometimes cause revolution, without for one moment ruling out military defeat as a cause operating on some other occasion. (17) The other most common sense of causation is where we pick out what seems to be the final necessary condition which will jointly with other conditions make up the sufficient antecedents: thus, given a man whose temper is pretty bad, but generally under control, the third drink may suffice to make him really angry. He may always be absolutely calm to outward appearing when he is sober, but drink may be the one additional necessary condition to make him become angry. Sociologists again are much concerned with necessary
112

conditions; indeed, many sociological works are much more adequate accounts of some of the necessary conditions — though very rarely of *all* the necessary conditions — than anything else. Bureaucratic efficiency may readily be discovered to necessitate intelligent and well-trained staff; but it is far from true that these will be sufficient to produce bureaucratic efficiency. In short, it is possible to find in ordinary speech innumerable uses of causal terms in describing human behaviour and in explaining it; and the sense in which these are causal expressions seems to be homogeneous with the sense in which explanatory notions in sociology or political science are causal notions. This does not, I think, show that common sense is committed to the idea that a fully fledged causal account of human behaviour is quite unshocking, as we shall see below. Still, at this point, we can say only that everyday speech seems to leave room for causally explaining human behaviour, and seems not to imply such a conception of causation as would be radically at odds with that generally described by the philosophy of science.

Nonetheless, there are still shoals ahead, created by our attachment to theoretical realism. For the puzzles involved in explaining the causal connections underlying our everyday generalisations about human behaviour stem from the attractions of a particular kind of causal connection — mechanical connection. The contemporary image of the machine is that of the electronic computing device; but even in this widened, modern sense of 'mechanical', mechanical causation causes us as many difficulties as did the narrower sense for our predecessors. The importance of theoretical realism is that it requires that theoretically validated explanations must give some account of the 'machinery' explicitly said to be operating, and thus accounting for the observed phenomena. In the previous chapters, it was argued that causal histories play a vital role in science, and that the goal of theoretical explanation is to show us what causal linkages are to be found upon analysing the phenomena with which we are dealing. This is not only achieved by explaining how a gross physical event is to be broken down into smaller events, though this is certainly the dominant interest in the traditional account: more importantly for social science, we may

113

construct a theoretical account to show how the smaller events with which we are initially acquainted form a structured system, which has properties deriving from this structuring. (18) But what does seem crucial to theoretical explanation is the ontological commitment to the existence of typical patterns of causal sequence as empirical properties of the subject-matter in question. Now, what this seems inevitably to entail in the case of psychological phenomena is that a causal account of human behaviour must seek to fill in the details of the sequences between cause and effect, i.e. to offer us an account of the mechanism through which the causal sequence operates. Thus, to take a simple example, the causal statement that being perceived as working class makes people vote Democrat can certainly be unpicked in several ways. The obvious way is the following: we might think that men vote for what they take to be their interests, hence that a man who supposes both that he belongs to the working class, and thus to the less well-off part of the community, and who also supposes that Democrat policies are in general more likely to benefit the poorer members of society than are those offered by the Republicans, has a perfectly good motive for voting Democrat; thus the details of the causal connection between class and political allegiance can be spelled out. And equally important, the psychological theory, if we can so dignify it, that asserts that human actions are governed by perceived costs and benefits comes up against evidence which may support it or weaken it. In this way we seem in the everyday explanation of behaviour to envisage a causal chain, which becomes a more satisfying explanation the more detailed we make it. But we are still left with the problem of explaining how this causal sequence, the psychological one, fits in with the other causal sequence which we presume to be at work, one more familiar to physical science. For it looks as if we can give two sequential accounts here, one which details the various psychological steps between thinking of oneself as working-class and deciding to vote Democrat, another which would explain what physiological processes occurred as these various psychological events took place. The impact of theoretical realism on this assumption is that it makes the physiological processes seem more unequivocally the *basic* processes, since

114

they fit, in a way the psychological processes do not, the picture of that well-ordered scientific corpus in which the processes analysed by physiology can be shown to depend on those analysed by chemistry, and these in turn on various physical processes. And for this reason, a good many psychologists would want to say at the very least that psychological explanations were not scientifically satisfactory until they could be backed by an account of the physiological mechanisms which showed us how the psychological processes could take place. (19)

And in essence, it is this image of the well-ordered relations between the several branches of science, committed as it is to a realistic account of theoretical explanation, that accounts for the importance of a causal account of behaviour to the social sciences. Against this the sceptic might argue that just as we have psychological generalisations unconnected with the physiological facts that may or may not underlie them, so we could have sociological or political generalisations not at all linked to generalisations about individual psychological processes. In this sense, then, individual psychology is simply irrelevant to social science, in much the way that physiology is irrelevant to psychology, physics to chemistry and so on; it is in all these cases true that we may discover that when events of one kind occur, then we can also say that events of another kind occur — when water turns to ice, molecular energy levels are dropping — but we can develop chemistry independently of physics, and sociology independently of psychology, and that is all that is at issue. But we have already seen that while there is a good deal in this sceptical approach, it is not as much as suffices to make it a knock-down argument. There are two fronts on which the sceptical case can be confuted, that of practical scientific investigation and that of theoretical coherence. As to the first, it is quite impossible to say anything both informative and adequate to all the sciences. But what is evident from the history of, say, chemistry in the nineteenth century is that its linking with atomic theory, and hence with physics, was an enormous step forward, for all sorts of theoretical advances became possible. The relationship between psychology and physiology have yielded no such striking results as yet, but it is surely true that they

115

might; and it is certainly true that it is unthinkable that psychologists would advance accounts of behaviour which demand physiological processes which were known to be impossible, or conversely that physiologists would put forward accounts of physiological processes which ruled out psychological performances known to be possible. (20) This may seem a relatively obvious restriction, but that only shows how close the interdependence is. The same thing seems obviously true for the social sciences: it is plainly no use putting forward generalisations which would demand individual behaviour which we know to be impossible, and it would be no use putting forward psychological generalisations which would yield social results we know to be impossible. As to whether psychology will suggest sociological results in the way in which advances in physics have been 'borrowed' for the benefit of chemistry, it is surely pointless to speculate in advance of the attempt — if one could predict that kind of progress, one would already have made it. On the theoretical side, the sceptical approach is plainly right, as we have previously seen, in supposing that there are at any rate puzzles about the sense in which we can 'reduce' theories about one kind of phenomena to theories about some other kind of phenomena. But the matter does not end there. For even though the kind of sequences we posit are different at different theoretical levels, we still need to render it intelligible that there should be these different levels of description and explanation of the phenomena, by showing how the processes described by one inquiry can be mapped onto the processes described by another. Thus the pressure that makes for a physiologically backed psychology operates as strongly in making for a psychologically backed sociology, economics, political science or whatever other social science it may be. Certainly, there is an independence of sorts; but equally certainly, there is a more impressive interdependence.

If this suffices to explain why the possibility of a causal account of human action seems an integral part of the claims made by a social science modelled on the more successful physical sciences, this by no means shows either that such a science will as a matter of fact prove to be readily established, nor that it will fit easily into our existing account

116

of our behaviour. Let us now see why the second of these points is so debatable. Up till now, I have taken it for granted that the kind of sequence offered by commonsense psychological explanation is a straightforward causal sequence, and that there are no important divergences between the physical sequences envisaged in, say, the kinetic theory of gases and the psychological sequences which we appeal to when explaining, say, the phenomenon of a boom or a slump. The time has come to challenge this assumption. One way of doing this is to show how a psychological explanation seems to appeal, not to causes, but to reasons for behaviour – or to put it another way, to show how the causes of human behaviour are reasons, not mechanical causes. (21) In the process, we have to illustrate some of the disanalogies between causal knowledge and the knowledge which an agent has of his reasons for what he does. One important difference between reasons and causes is that reasons can be assessed as good and bad, proper or improper, whereas a proffered cause either is or is not the cause of whatever we are explaining. Suppose we discover that a friend habitually steals small articles from a local store, and that he does this to maintain status within a group to which he belongs; we may condemn this as a bad reason for behaving in this way, or even declare the entire aim of belonging to this group mistaken while still accepting that it was the reason. But we do not and cannot say this kind of thing about causal sequences; a cause either does or does not bring about a given effect, and that is the extent of our interest in it. If we now reconsider the example I proposed earlier about the connection between being seen as working-class and voting Democrat, it is clear that the kind of detailed sequence I suggested as filling in the gap between cause and effect is in fact a sequence of reasons for action. For if it is a man's aim to secure his best interest as he sees it, he obviously has a good reason for voting for the party which will better his lot; (22) what we do when we fill in the details here is show how, in the light of the agent's beliefs, a *rational* step towards securing his best interests is to vote the way he does. Now, we may want to say even so that this was an *improper* reason for voting for a party, and appeal, perhaps to Burke's account of the high moral purpose of political parties. (23) Thus we can both agree that, given a certain aim,

117

a man would have a good reason for behaving the way he does, and yet still claim that this was an improper reason, because the goal itself was improper. From the point of view of the agent this reflects on a second important point about the difference between reasons and mechanical causes, namely that a person who makes a decision is not engaged in a causal inquiry into his own motives — a point which goes some way to explain the difference which was pointed out earlier in this chapter between the first-person knowledge of psychological events and the observer's knowledge. (24) A man making up his mind may well inquire into the causal factors which lead him to assess things as he does; he may, for example wonder whether it is only the result of feeling so tired that he thinks it right to vote for a zoning ordinance which would secure peace and quiet for the area in which he lives. But such causal inquiries are not basic to our making decisions, for in general what we are doing is wondering *what is the right thing to do*, not wondering what the possible causal explanation can be of why we make up our minds in the way we do. Indeed, it is obviously the case that a man who asked only causal questions about his own behaviour would never be able to make a move at all, since he would never *decide* on anything, only learn about the antecedents of possible decisions. (25) It is certainly true that an observer may inquire into the causal antecedents of my decisions, though even here it is an impossibility that dealings between him and me should entirely consist of this, for if he always regards my decisions as events to be causally explained, and never as proposals to be rationally evaluted, it must either be the case that he regards them all as pathological symptoms to be treated causally, or else that for some other reason he has decided that he and I should not enter into normal human relationships. (26) Normally, the agent's view of himself and the observer's view of him are integrated in the sense that we adopt the same perspective on decisions, choices or whatever; and where we do not, it is usually because the process of 'stepping back' and asking causal questions reflects our belief that there is something quite amiss with the agent's behaviour. A third point which is explained by this is how it is often unclear in the social sciences what status is accorded to our everyday first-person accounts of our actions, and the reasons

118

for them. For, of course, it follows from the above that we have a choice of taking the proffered reasons at face value, and thus giving an account of what happens which reflects what the actors think and say about it, or else of giving an account which undercuts theirs by trying to explain their accounts as the results of some underlying causal process, unknown to them, and not featuring among their reasons. I have already mentioned Durkheim's attitude to the explanation of religious behaviour as an instance of this; (27) but, of course, there are many other instances, and ordinary speech yields plenty of examples, both of plainly under-cutting accounts and also of borderlines cases. This is not surprising, since it is obviously difficult to draw a clear line between one kind of case and the other, if easy enough to point to some clear examples. We should all regard the 'reason' offered by a subject under post-hypnotic suggestion as a rationalisation − if he had been told to open a window in a room which was barely warm enough in any case, and yet said that he thought it was terribly hot, we should not regard this as properly a reason, but only as a rationalisation. The equal but opposite case where a man enters a room which is stiflingly hot, and asks to open a window because it is so hot would be a case where only under very special circumstances would we think this was a rationalisation. But it is easy enough to think of cases on the borderline, say where there is no obvious need to open a window, but the man decides to, saying he feels hot; if he is a nervous kind of man, we may regard his window-opening as a more or less characteristic display of nerves, without exactly wishing to say that he had no reason to open the window and was therefore merely rationalising. (28) Two conclusions follow from this brief account. The first is that if *causal* acounts of human action are of necessity 'third-person' accounts of our behaviour, then we have an asymmetry between the view of the agent and the view of the spectator which is at odds with ordinary social interaction and quite without parallel in the natural sciences − where, of course, the phenomena are not credited with any view at all. It is literally impossible to say how we should integrate a fully developed, physiologically founded psychology into our everday view of ourselves; all that is obvious is that its development, should it follow the

119

lines suggested earlier in this chapter, would necessarily have a considerable dislocating effect on our pre-scientific notions about ourselves. The second is that the empiricist programme cannot claim the plausibility it tried to borrow from our everyday use of psychological explanation, for the attempt to place such explanations in the causal framework common to the natural sciences distorts them in striking ways. Thus this programme has to rest on the actual successes of the behavioural sciences themselves, and not on appeals to the supposed common sense of mankind. (29)

The other major aspect in which a causal analysis of human action might be thought to be alarming is in its implications for the view of human choice on which everyday conceptions or moral and political assessment rest. Until recently, empiricist philosophers have not only claimed that their assumptions about the ubiquity of causal determination were compatible with our everyday views about moral responsibility, but have claimed these assumptions were actually required by these views. The argument was essentially that predictability was presupposed by such practices as punishment – for obviously no one would defend punishing a man whose behaviour was so unpredictable that he might be affected in any way or none by punishment. But what was ignored by such arguments was the notion of *desert*, which does not seem to be causally analysable; to say that a man is responsible for an action in the sense that we think he is deserving of blame (or praise) for what he did does not look forward to its effects on him, so much as backwards to the choice he made. This is obvious enough – we punish people for things they have already done, and equally we praise them for things they have already done, and these are different things from our attempting to discourage them from doing something in future or our attempting to encourage them. In holding that a person deserves praise or blame, we assume that he had a choice of action at the point where he did whatever it is we are praising or blaming him for. This means, in brief, that we think he could have done something other than what he did, and that he chose not to. But if we think back to what we earlier saw as the essentials of causal explanation, it seemed then that we wanted a causal explanation to show that what

120

happened was the only possible event, given the antecedents. On the face of it a causal explanation of choice seems therefore to deny that it *was* a choice, since it assimilates the choice to one of the events in a sequence in which none of the events could have come out any way other than it did. (30)

This crux has been battled over for a considerable period of time, and various solutions proposed, none of them gaining general acceptance. What is important here, however, is to see that there are practical consequences at stake. If we do suppose that adequate causal explanations of behaviour are available, in principle, then it seems that our understanding of moral and legal speech will have to change drastically. There are writers who accept such a conclusion perfectly happily: for example, Lady Wootton in 'Social Science and Social Pathology' (31) is quite prepared to dispense with the notion of responsibility, and to turn what we know as punishment into one among other instruments of social treatment. Praise and blame, punishment and reward, become essentially forward-looking notions, instruments of a manipulative social technique; and, on Lady Wootton's view, this is a step forward and a step out of superstition and barbarism. Now, this is a plausible view at first sight, and it is certainly more intellectually respectable than supposing that no changes at all would be wrought by changing our beliefs about the nature of choice. Even so, there are two sorts of difficulties it leaves untouched. The first we have seen already, that, as agents, we simply do not, and apparently cannot, dispense with the notion of choice as applied to our own actions, and it seems to be a source of both moral and logical disquiet to treat other people in a way in which we could not possibly treat ourselves. The second kind of difficulty is the moral doubt which is raised by dispensing with the notion of responsibility. So long as we see people as responsible agents, such methods of social control as punishment have the defence that they allow people to choose between conformity and, at a price, non-conformity; that they allow people to remain untouched by the law, no matter what they think, until they actually do those things forbidden by the law; but on the view put forward by Lady Wootton, what now appears as the evil of punishment inflicted without anyone having committed a crime could

121

come out as 'preventive medicine' and injustice be rewritten as progress; again, the distinction between the pathological criminal who cannot help himself and the conscientious objector who chooses punishment as a form of moral protest seems also to disappear. We can hardly let the cry of 'progress' quell our doubts about such apparently illiberal developments. (32)

We thus arrive at what is patently an unsatisfying situation. The model of science with which we began yields us a coherent account of the goals of explanation, and the usefulness of theory; and it offers us a programme for the social sciences which rests on the attractive basis of the causal explanation of individual human behaviour. But on closer inspection, it seems that the programme runs into unsuspected difficulties; not only does it reveal internal incoherences and ambiguities about the envisaged psychological science, but it also clashes in crucial ways with our everyday, pre-scientific understanding of ourselves, and evidently threatens some practical consequences of a profoundly disturbing sort. There are two possible responses to this conclusion. The first is to declare an agnostic position about the future, to await the sophistication of computer analogies of human behaviour, to see how linguistics and other aspects of cognitive psychology progress, and await the conceptual reshuffle which such progress will force upon us. So far as the progress of psychology goes, this is, I think, the proper view. (33) But it is wholly unsatisfactory on another plane, for it does nothing to help us to elucidate the actual practice of the social sciences in the absence of these yet-to-be achieved advances. We must, then, turn to the second position, which amounts to the argument that our understanding of social life, and of individual behaviour in a social context is different in kind from that which the methods and concepts of the natural sciences allow us to achieve, and that the difficulties brought out by this chapter are the expected results of trying to assimilate these radically different kinds of understanding. The most cogent argument to this effect has been produced by Professor Winch's 'The Idea of a Social Science', and it is to this argument that we now turn.

NOTES

1. B. F. Skinner, 'Walden Two' (Collier-Macmillan, 1962).

2. Brodbeck, in 'Minnesota Studies', iii 231-2.

3. Mill, 'Logic', bk vi, ch. i, sec. 2.

4. T. Hobbes, 'Leviathan', bk i.

5. Chomsky, John Locke lectures.

6. D. E. Broadbent, 'Behaviour' (Methuen, 1968) pp. 187-8.

7. W. Grey Walter, 'The Living Brain' (Penguin, n.i. 1968) pp. 113-19.

8. Ryle, 'Concept of Mind', pp. 35 ff.

9. Peters, 'Concept of Motivation', pp. 12-14.

10. Chomsky, 'Language and Mind', ch. iii.

11. Lord Robbins, 'The Nature and Significance of Economic Science', 2nd ed. (Macmillan, 1935).

12. J. S. Mill, 'The Definition of Political Economy', 'Collected Works', iv 309-39.

13. Ryle, 'Concept of Mind', pp. 62-9.

14. D. Hume, 'A Treatise on Human Nature', bk i, sec. xiv (Selby-Bigge ed., pp. 155 f.).

15. Popper, 'Poverty', pp. 149 f.

16. A. MacIntyre, 'The Antecedents of Action', in A. Montefiore and B. Williams (eds), 'British Analytical Philosophy' (Routledge, 1966) p. 221.

17. C. Johnson, 'Revolutionary Change' (Little, Brown, Boston, Mass., 1966) pp. 59 ff.

18. Nadel, 'Theory of Social Structure', ch. 1.

19. Broadbent, Behaviour', p. 194.

20. Ibid., pp. 186-8.

21. Cf. Peters, 'Concept of Motivation', pp. 3-16.

22. Downs, 'Economic Theory', pp. 36 ff.

23. Edmund Burke: quoted in 'The Philosophy of Edmund Burke', ed. L. Bredfold and R. Ross (University of Michigan Press, 1960) p. 134.

24. S. N. Hampshire, 'Thought and Action' (Chatto & Windus, 1959) ch. 2.

25. Ibid., pp. 109 f.

26. P. F. Strawson, 'Freedom and Resentment', 'Proc. Brit. Acad.' (1962).

27. Cf. Ch. 1, n. 6.

28. A. MacIntyre, 'The Idea of a Social Science', 'Supp. Proc. Arist. Soc.' (1967) 100 f.

29. A. J. Ayer, 'Man as a Subject for Science', in P. Laslett and W. Runciman (eds), 'Philosophy, Politics and Society' (Blackwell, Oxford, 1956-67) vol. III, p. 29.

30. G. E. Moore, 'Ethics', 2nd ed. (Oxford University Press, 1966) pp. 119 ff.

31. B. Wootton, 'Social Science and Social Pathology' (Allen & Unwin, 1959) ch. 8.

32. H. L. A. Hart, 'Punishment and the Elimination of Responsibility' (Hobhouse Memorial Trust lecture, 1963).

33. Ayer, in 'Philosophy, Politics and Society', p. 29.

6 Is the Science of Social Life a Science?

The difficulties which the last chapter showed up, and which seem inherent in any attempt to assimilate the explanation of human action to the causal explanation of non-human phenomena, lead us now to consider the view outlined in the opening chapter which holds that between the natural sciences and social science there is a difference not of degree of complexity, but of kind. Until now we have considered the difficulties involved in trying to assimilate the social and natural sciences only insofar as they were problems raised by trying to give an adequate explanation in any field whatever. But now we must turn to the claim that the difficulties which have beset us, especially those which were apparent by the end of the last chapter, are the result of a deepseated confusion about the nature of explanation. The argument, briefly, is that the programme of integrating the social sciences as one or several branches of a unified science of nature is in principle mistaken. The social 'sciences' are not, and cannot hope to become, sciences at all.

Such a claim might seem on the face of it absurd, and so obviously contradicted by the evidence of what sociologists, economists, historians, anthropologists, political scientists and the like do and say that no one could take it seriously. Certainly the assumptions of the authors of most sociological texts would lead us to dismiss the claim out of hand. Professor Martindale's monumental work on 'The Nature and Types of Sociological Theory', (1) to take one example only, would lead us in this direction. It begins its account of modern sociological theories with discussions of their roots in philosophy, and it pays a good deal of attention to the ideological uses to which sociological theory has often been put. Yet it treats the lines between philosophy. ideology and social science as clear-cut and unarguable: and it locates contemporary sociological theory firmly within the bracket of science, noting with regret such lapses into philosophical speculation or ideological persuasion as may creep in. The story we are told by such a textbook is that sociology became a respectable university discipline in the first two decades of this century, and in so doing it became a genuine science.

More important than the fact that writers of textbooks *claim* that what is done is science, is the day to day practice of social scientists in their empirical research. And this evidence is, on the face of it, overwhelming. Social scientists like all scientists employ complex computing machinery, with the assorted equipment of card punches, tape-readers and the rest that goes with it; teams of research workers are assembled to work the machinery and help evaluate the results; work of this sort is co-operative, with data banks being established in order to allow other scientists to use the data once collected; it is sophisticated in the use of novel statistical techniques for the evaluation of results; it is even experimental, with observation rooms being utilised for experiments with small groups, and 'simulation' exercises being run, so that events which will not recur in the real world — the Six Days War between Israel and the Arab States, or the Cuban Missile Crisis of 1962 — can be recreated in essentials and analysed accurately. Surely we can take it for granted that this is indeed a scientific activity that we are watching; what more could we ask for?

There are several things to be said in reply. The first is that even if we were convinced that what we were looking for was a natural science of human behaviour, we might remain very sceptical about the success of that science so far. One ground for such scepticism would be that the social sciences have so far been theoretically underdeveloped, and that the immense enthusiasm for statistical techniques is largely a response to this theoretical weakness. Such a view is plausibly developed by Professor Chomsky, whose 'Language and Mind' argues that the so-called behavioural sciences have only contrived to mimic the surface features of the physical sciences; (2) they can detect the regularities of outward behaviour, but cannot account for its interior logic and organisation. This view I shall say no more about, although some of the discussion in Chapter 8 bears upon the problem of understanding what

126

kind of theory social theory is. The chief reason for this reticence is that Chomsky's own work is concerned with language-learning and the associated branches of cognitive psychology, and that it is as yet quite unclear what its implications are for sociological or anthropological theory. We have from Professor Chomsky himself no more than some doubts about the efforts of so-called 'structuralism' to uncover a syntax or grammar in totemic and mythic behaviour. (3)

The major point, however, is that such an appeal to the actual practice of social scientists does nothing to settle the doubts of the real sceptic. So far as he is concerned, the machinery is misunderstood, and its results mistakenly categorised. Let us think again of our imagined atheist contemplating a highly developed religion: such a religion may require the elaborate computation of astronomical phenomena in order to work out which days are holy days, and which days require special dietary observance; it may, moreover, question people about the piety of their lives, and interrogate them about their hearing of divine messages – in short, this religion employs all the apparatus associated with the social sciences in its elaboration both of its theology and its rites. Yet it is clear that this will leave the atheist unmoved: there is no God, so religion cannot be put upon a scientific basis. The whole exercise, in his eyes, is an exercise in self-deception. One question, therefore, which we must answer in this chapter is whether the suggestion that the social sciences are not part of a natural science corpus amounts to the kind of claim made by the atheist above, and if not, in what ways it differs. And this leads into the argument which the atheist is most likely to use. He need not deny that the scientific theologians had found out *something* with all their enquiries, their statistics and their astronomy; all he needs to deny is that what they have done is produce a scientifically validated account of man's relations with God. In other words, what he denies is that their interpretation of their results is the correct one. This, I think, is the claim now under consideration. What a writer such as Professor Winch in 'The Idea of a Social Science', is doing is claiming that social scientists are prone to misunderstand their own practice; they think, but mistakenly, that the kinds of explanation they are

127

concerned to give are exactly like those which natural scientists are concerned to give. (4) Their apparatus and their techniques are certainly useful, but not for the reasons they suppose; and when they give illuminating and logically proper explanations, they are likely to do so without quite realising it. Thus we need to rephrase our old questions about whether the social sciences are really sciences, since in this form they will not receive an answer, and ask instead what are the dissimilarities between the behaviour of human beings and that of objects in the natural world, and what are the consequences of these dissimilarities for the attempt to model social science on the natural sciences.

The claim which so to speak permeates Winch's argument is that social behaviour is to be understood as *rule-following* behaviour, and not as *causally regular* behaviour. It is the object of this chapter to elucidate this distinction and explore some of its consequences. In the next chapter I shall turn more to criticism in estimating its implications for the day to day practice of social science. But here we ought to notice one preliminary point. The conception of men as essentially rule-following creatures is taken by Winch from the later philosophy of Wittgenstein, in whose 'Philosophical Investigations' there is a great deal of talk about rules and rule-governed action; (5) but it would be a great mistake to associate the idea only with Wittgenstein and recent writers. It is a central conception of the great theorists of the past. Durkheim's explanation of anomic suicide, to take a famous example, rests heavily on the view that men are so basically rule-following creatures that where there are no rules or an excessive conflict of rules, there may seem no way out but death. (6) And such examples could be multiplied in the writings of Weber or Talcott Parsons. It is clear, therefore, that Winch's arguments have their sources within the practice of social science and the reflections of its practitioners.

Winch develops his case by opposition to the methodology stemming from Mill's 'System of Logic', the methodology which in its more current formulation is essentially that which we have hitherto been describing. On the view made famous by Mill, the goal of a social science is to produce explanations conforming to the canons of the hypothetico-deductive ideal; and such explanations require above everything else that we should find and validate causal generalisations, from which, in their role of major premisses to our deductions, we can derive causal explanations. As we saw, such generalisations are usually thought of as expressing *de facto* — i.e. contingent - uniformities in the way that natural phenomena are found together and in sequence. Thus a statement like 'Jones was ruined because he sold all his shares the day after the market broke' hangs on a generalisation to the effect that selling shares after the market breaks invariably precedes the loss of a great deal of money. Such statements of natural uniformities are commonly described as statements of 'constant conjunction'. Now, leaving on one side the doubts we raised as to whether this analysis of causation is adequate, there is one as yet only mentioned consequence of this analysis that becomes very important. This is, that causal generalisations assert contingent or *de facto* connections only, which in turn means that in any causal explanation the causal antecedents and consequents must be identifiable independently of each other — for, as we saw before, it is this requirement which distinguishes causal connections from connections of meaning. Where this requirement is breached, the connection will seemingly become a definitional connection, and the causal argument, therefore, circular. Thus if someone asserts: 'Campus demonstrations are always caused by excessive displays of force on the part of university administrators', and means us to take it as a causal generalisation, he must be able to offer some way of identifying demonstrations independently of identifying excessive displays of force. It may be difficult to provide such criteria; but in their absence there will be the danger that demonstrations may be defined in terms of what provokes them, hence that the causal generalisation will turn into a logical or conceptual statement instead. If this were to happen, what we are left with is likely to be nothing more than 'campus demonstrations are caused by whatever causes campus demonstrations', or else the stipulative definition that 'campus demonstrations are those mass actions on campus which are preceded by excessive displays of force by university authorities' — a definition which may have some use, though it seems at first sight unlikely.

Now, what is assumed by philosophers of science who

think that the goal of explanation is the production of causal generalisations is that it is always possible to describe any fact or event in the natural order in such a way that its description is logically independent of the description of any other fact or event. (7) This is not to say that all descriptions commonly in use meet such a requirement, for most do not; but it is to claim that they can always be replaced by descriptions which do meet the requirement for the case in hand. A simple example will illustrate the point. A bottle of cough mixture of known efficacy may be referred to around the house as the mixture that cures Johnny's colds'. In this description, some of the causal consequences of the medicine's use are already implied; thus we cannot produce as a contingent proposition, 'the mixture that cures Johnny's colds cures Johnny's colds'. But of course we do believe that there is a causal connection between Johnny's taking the mixture and being cured; and we can state this by redescribing the mixture in such a way as omits the causal implications formerly present. Thus if we employ its trade name, we can say: 'Spasphagene cures Johnny's colds' without any logical qualms, for it is a perfectly good causal — i.e. contingent — statement. Or we could equally well have used the chemical analysis of the mixture, and asserted a causal connection in this way; and it is plausible to suppose that we could in principle always manage some such redescription.

The importance of this assumption for behavioural science is brought out by Charles Taylor's 'The Explanation of Behaviour'. only if we can describe all events, especially those events which are human actions in social situations, in such a way that they are not logically or conceptually linked to any other events, could we begin to establish mechanical causal laws of human behaviour. A causal psychology of the kind envisaged in the last chapter thus requires us to be able to identify the components of action in such a way that they acquire the necessary logical independence, and thus permit us to establish causal connections between them. And essentially, what Winch argues is that we cannot do this without the total loss of the very subject-matter we set out to investigate in the first place. What Winch claims is that the connections which hold between actions are *conceptual* connections, and that the terminology which we employ in

130

talking about actions is indispensable to our identifying actions *as* actions – rather than mere bodily happenings, physiological events. (8) Human actions, on this view, are meaningful, and meaning is not a category open to causal analysis; thus, so long as meaningful actions form the subject-matter of social inquiry, the most important category for our understanding of social life will not be that of cause and effect, but that of meaningfulness and rule-guidedness. Two things ought to be said before we advance to explain Winch's case. The first is that this initial stand is very reminiscent of Weber's definition of the object of social inquiry as the meanings attached to their actions by human agents, (9) and hence that it is a stand which can sympathetically assimilate one important strand of the actual practice of social science. The other is that we must not assume too quickly that Winch is here telling us to abandon our slide-rules and computers; at the very most, he is telling us what sort of connections our data can uncover, not that the data is either unnecessary or illusory.

As we should expect from the stress on connections of meaning, the argument for an irreducible logical gap between human actions and mere events in the natural order hinges on certain properties that seem essential to language and to quasi-linguistic behaviour. One major property of language-using, and of the behaviour that goes with it, is that these are so to speak performances which can be done well or badly, correctly or incorrectly; and the assessment of behaviour along such lines requires that there should be a set of socially maintained rules which embody the criteria of correct and incorrect performance. These rules will include the criteria for the correct and incorrect application of a word, as well as rules of a different scope concerned with the appropriate and inappropriate occasions for its use, and the same goes for actions also. A more obvious kind of rule, and much scrutinised by sociologists, is that which lays down a norm of some kind, such as the legal rule which forbids dangerous overtaking, or the moral rule which insists on minimum levels of kindness in family dealings, or the professional rule which won't allow a lawyer to defend a man he knows is guilty. But precisely because of their obviousness, these rules can be ignored, and our attention concentrated on the first two

131

kinds of rule. So close is the link between language-learning and rule-guided behaviour that Winch devotes a good deal of effort to arguing that it is *in principle* (and not, as we should all be bound to agree, impossible as a matter of fact) impossible that a human being should learn a language outside a human society. (10) The commonsense view would seem to be that while, of course, we cannot imagine that as a matter of fact anyone actually would develop a language in isolation, nonetheless we can perfectly well tell a logically coherent story about what sort of process this would be. Surely, we might say, a man might develop a set of labelling expressions for phenomena which attracted his attention, and repeat them every time the phenomena recurred, producing so to speak the same response whenever the same stimulus came along. In time, this might enable him to form the notion of the right wɔrd for an object, so that he would be able, if he uttered the wrong word to correct himself, and recall that what he had seen was, say, not a crow, but a thrush. It is no doubt an important fact about the way human beings actually behave that they are brought up in society, where they learn a language from other human beings who correct their mistakes and teach them the conventions of that society. Nonetheless, this is not necessary to the very concept of having a language at all; it just happens to be the way we learn the languages we do. And the stimulus-response account of language which we are offered by such psychologists as Professor Skinner (11) is simply the development of these commonsense assumptions. In all of them, the common element is that we ought to be able to account for the rules which govern language and social behaviour in terms of habits which are themselves causally explicable. Hence, of course, it is important to show either that language is essentially causal, and only happens to require the particular cause and effect relationships existing in societies, if one is defending a stimulus-response account, or else that language is essentially social and rule-governed and that this is its most basic characteristic, if one is setting out to defend a position like Professor Winch's.

So much of human behaviour involves language and language-like capacities that a blow to the causal analysis of language is plainly a considerable blow to any kind of causal

132

analysis of human action. Consider, for example, how much of political behaviour is linguistic: people listen to arguments and produce counter-arguments, they look at newspaper accounts of current events, hear the news on the radio, talk to friends, relations and candidates. It could be said, and quite properly, that all these things are causal influences on the way people behave in political matters — what people do depends on what they hear, read and so on; nonetheless, this does not mean that the *meaning* of what they hear and read can be causally explained. Indeed, to try to do so is precisely to put the cart before the horse, since the causal relationship is parasitic upon the meaning of the words heard or read. Suppose the newspaper calls the incumbent prime minister a fool: this may well make a supporter of the ruling party angry, and make an opponent of that party laugh heartily; in that sense the words will have had an effect. But their having that effect depends on the readers of the newspaper recognising the meaning of the words in the first place. If, for example, the report had been in a foreign tongue, then no effect at all would have been achieved, and yet the words would have differed only in that their readers failed to recognise their meaning. We cannot explain the meaning of words in terms of causation because it appears that social causation hangs upon people recognising the meaning of utterances and behaviour, that social causation rests upon a prior identification of conceptual connections. (12) And, of course, there are areas of social life where this is strikingly true, namely those areas where we have verbal formulae for the performance of certain acts — like promising, declaring allegiance, giving verdicts and the many other examples scrutinised in J. L. Austin's 'How to Do Things with Words'. (13) In such cases, saying *is* doing; the jury which says via its foreman 'We find the defendant guilty' is thereby finding the defendant guilty. In such cases, the relationship between the meaning of what is said and the consequences of saying it is uniquely tight.

What Winch insists, then, is that as the above indicates, we cannot analyse meaning in causal terms, but only in terms of rules, and that rules are necessarily social, and cannot sensibly be seen as the possession of individuals. The basic argument for the latter position is that the social maintenance of a rule is essential to the concepts both of getting the performance of an act or a speech-act right and of making a mistake. If a man is to be said to understand a word or to employ it meaningfully, he must be able to correctly reapply the term; that is, he must be able to identify an identical case — and thus to employ a judgement like 'this is the same thing as before'. But to say that something is the same as something else — as when we say that a man is the same person we saw two weeks ago in Leeds, or that a tree is the same sort of tree we saw in Italy last summer — we must employ criteria of identity, in virtue of which we can claim to have identified it, and by reference to which someone else can tell us that we have misidentified it. The reason is simple enough: things are the same or different in certain respects, and what we need is rules which pick out the respects in question. Winch claims that these rules must be public because otherwise there is no distinction between one's applying the rules correctly, and one's merely thinking one has applied them correctly. (14) The publicity of rules implies that they are embodied in the behaviour of people beyond oneself, and thus that their actions afford a test of one's own. Indeed, it is this publicity of rules which shows in what sense a person can be said to be using private rules, and that this is a sense which is parasitic upon their public status. Suppose I invent a private game of adding 'eenie' to everything said by a foolish aunt; this then is the rule of the game, and a move in the game is defined and assessed by reference to whether it complies with the rule or not. Moreover, to invent such a rule is implicitly to graft it onto the stock of public, i.e. social rules, since the only terms on which I can make sense of what I am doing for myself are precisely those on which I can make sense of my actions for others; and this means that their authority is as good as my own on the issue of whether I am following 'my' own rules. That this is true is readily seen; if some friends were puzzled by my laughing whenever my aunt spoke, I might render this intelligible to them by telling them what I was doing; and it logically follows that they can now play exactly the same game. If, however, I were now to start adding some other suffix, or none, they could complain that I was no longer following the rule; and if my actions were sufficiently arbitrary could complain that the only rule I seemed to

134

observe was that of saying something which would frustrate their attempt to guess the rule I was following. From this it follows that learning a language is learning to share rules with others in a community, and equally that the meaning which my own thoughts, words and deeds bear for me is integrally the same as they bear for other people. This is not to deny the possibility of eccentricity or innovation either in language or behaviour; it is, however, to say that innovation has to be grafted onto an existing stock of common practices if it is to be understood even by the innovator; the language of all societies is full of neologisms but it makes no sense to think that language could be all neologisms; and equally, all sorts of commonplace behaviour once began as novelties, but it makes no sense to think we might start again with total novelty in all meaningful behaviour. (15)

The consequences of the rule-guidedness of meaningful behaviour are numerous. One dimension worth exploring further is that of correctness and incorrectness, not least because it shows up the great complexity of what sociologists often investigate under the heading of normative constraints. It will be recalled that so far we have argued that unlike stimuli which are or are not causally effective (and nothing more), rules can be followed or broken. But there are different ways in which this can be done. We distinguished above between rules at the level of establishing criteria for what was or was not a case of the given sort, rules which laid down the appropriateness or otherwise of what was said, and rules which laid down the permissibility or otherwise of the views or action in question. Such lines of distinction are not adequate to detailed sociological or philosophical inquiry, but they do serve a useful purpose in sorting out the kinds of conventions we look at in sociology and elsewhere. Thus if a man were suddenly to announce 'I have got all my usual clothes on during lunch in a crowded restaurant, and he was to our knowledge a perfectly ordinary respectable kind of man who had never behaved like this before, we should assess his behaviour in various ways. At the first level, what he says is both meaningful and correct — i.e. he is telling the truth about the fact that he has got clothes on, the words are applied correctly to the situation; but at the second level, they are not, for what he says is quite out of place. The convention he breaks is difficult to characterise, but it is something like a rule to the effect that we must not say what there is absolutely no point in saying — and here there is no possible question of his *not* having all his clothes on; since no question is raised, the utterance is odd, and beside the point. Hence it offends against rules of appropriateness. On the level of norms and their enforcement, it is dubious whether such behaviour raises normative issues — we might, perhaps, think it ill-mannered to behave so strangely in a public place. On the other hand, context is all important; we might secretly applaud the behaviour, knowing it to be a sociological investigation according to the canons of Professor Garfinkel. (16)

Rules have long been a central concern to all those sociologists and anthropologists who have been concerned to chart exactly the roles which a given society recognises, and the rules which govern role-behaviour; and this is an aspect of the subject to which the arguments of Winch give due prominence. An example of this concern lies in an area of obvious interest to political scientists, namely voting. (17) Round about the act of voting cluster a variety of rules, specifying how to vote in the sense of how to do what counts as voting at all and also in the sense of how to make what would amount to a rational choice of candidate or policy. And, of course, there are rules which tie in voting to the other political behaviour of citizens and their rulers — rules about what authority is conferred by success at the polls, rules about what sort of canvassing is legitimate, rules about how the votes are to be scrutinised and counted. We are in everyday speech quite prone to slide together the various kinds of rules, so that we might say of a man who had cast a particularly thoughtless vote that 'he could scarcely be said to have voted at all'; or we might criticise the rules which define what counts as a vote in the light of the goals which legitimate the rules about what counts as winning — we might, for instance, object that when we transfer British practices of universal adult suffrage to a country with 90 per cent illiteracy, what we end up with is hardly voting — the rules which define the role of the citizen seem to have so little point in the altered context. But, of course, we can distinguish readily enough rules of recognition and rules of

136

assessment. Thus the man who stands in the street outside the polling station and shouts his preferences does not succeed in voting at all; he certainly displays his political preferences, and he may even exercise political influence by persuading or dissuading people from voting in some desired direction; nonetheless, what he does *does not count as* voting. But, of course, he may vote correctly in the sense that what he does counts as voting, by fulfilling all the requirements for casting a valid vote, but still fail to cast a sensible vote, by voting for an obvious incompetent or a crook, or without thinking at all what the results of his action will be. The point, however, is simple enough: the sociological concern with rules, as also with the roles which they govern, is a concern with forms of behaviour which can be assessed as correct and incorrect performances; this correctness or incorrectness can be assessed at a variety of levels, and in the light of a variety of rules. But the point remains that it is only in the light of rules, and by the standards they provide, that we can intelligibly call behaviour correct or incorrect at all. Where we ceased to talk in the context of rules, we should necessarily cease to talk in a context where it made sense to think of 'getting it right' or 'getting it wrong' at all: for Winch, this is tantamount to saying we cease to talk of human actions at all. (18)

This can be elucidated rather rapidly if we revert to what was earlier said about the relationship between rule-following and making behaviour intelligible even to oneself. It was claimed that the only terms on which we can understand ourselves are those on which other people can also understand us. (19) It is a consequence of this that a person can only set out to do those things for which there are avaiable standards of success and failure. This, to take an example of some contemporary force, it is required of any citizen of the U.S.A. who applies for a passport that he should take an oath of allegiance first, before being given the passport. This is a performance which can misfire in all sorts of ways — one might get the words wrong, or say them in front of an unauthorised person, or in the wrong place; and it is a generally valid hint for sociologists that the way to see what the rules are which we obey is to see how many such dangers an action is exposed to. There are equally a lot of borderline

137

situations; it is not clear whether it matters if one mutters the oath, or says it very rapidly, and so on. But it is abundantly clear that the situation is vitally different from that of trying to renounce citizenship, where there is no procedure to be followed. It would be futile to look for an authorised person to hear one's renunciation or a proper place in which to utter it; and equally no one could object that one hadn't got it right, since there would be nothing in the way of conceivable success to contrast with it. Of course, one might embark on all sorts of activities which we could loosely describe as 'renouncing citizenship', from emigration to starting on a life of crime; and any one of these things could be efficiently managed. Yet the cluster of rules which go to creating the act of swearing allegiance have no counterpart in an act of renouncing it, and this is a significant aspect of the dealings of American citizens with their government. Differences of this sort within societies, and more especially between societies, form the subject-matter for sociologists and anthropologists, for these rules give us the logical skeleton of possible lives and activities in our own and other societies, and show us the essence of differences between one culture and another. No student of the literature can fail to be impressed with the recurrence of the emphasis on the related notions of rules, norms and roles, and the equal emphasis on the way in which these form the scaffolding both of social life and the individual career. (20)

I have so far argued that Winch's concern with rules at any rate fits in with a major concern of sociologists and anthropologists, and we have seen no reason as yet to qualify acceptance both of the view that it is only in the light of rules that actions can be said to be correctly or incorrectly performed and the view that it is only in a social context that such rules can be maintained. It is time to move on to consider three issues stemming from this. The first is the question of the relationship between rules and regularities, especially in terms of the kinds of understanding which each is said to yield. This issue leads on inevitably to the consideration of the fact that social science is distinguished from the natural sciences by the unique property of its subject-matter - that it entertains beliefs about its own behaviour, and thus presents us with the problem that the beliefs of the

138

sociologist or anthropologist *about* the persons who make up the society under investigation have to take account of the beliefs of those persons about the very same facts; this involves an ambiguity in the notion of social theory which preoccupies not only Winch. Finally, this leads us to ask whether the kind of understanding appropriate to social theory is not more like philosophical reflection than it is like scientific knowledge of causal connections.

On the first issue, it is worth noting straightaway that our recognition in the last chapter that human behaviour displays regularities is indeed the starting point of much sociological and anthropological research. But in the light of our discussion of rules, it is also worth noting that regularities are by most anthropologists used as *evidence for* the existence of a rule in the society in question. Thus Professor Nadel argues that when we try to discover the rules governing a society — in his case, the interest is in charting the norms governing the roles recognised in that society — we rely on statistical evidence about the frequency with which certain kinds of behaviour occur, evidence which is supplemented, and in fortunate cases supplanted by explicit statements of the members of the society, and by their reactions in the way of sanctions and rewards to deviance and conformity. (21) In other words, where there is a regularity, we seek for a rule underlying it; and this suggests that social scientists do *not* think that the proper procedure is to try to reduce rule-guided behaviour to causal regularity; and this in turn suggests that the role of regularities in social science explanation is by no means as basic as it is in the natural sciences. So true does this seem to be of the practice of sociologists that the presence of a well-attested regularity is more than likely to lead to the guess that there is in operation some rule or other, even where those who are actually following it may deny it, and may even be sincere in their denials. In other words, we do not seem to be willing to stop at discovering regularities; we go on to look for a covert *meaning* to action. And this amounts to saying that in the case of human beings

and not in the case of the rest of the natural order — we have a form of understanding in terms of how the agent perceives the matter, such that the regularities we initially discover are only the external appearance of what we can

139

understand from the inside.

The relationship between the internal, rule-guided aspect and the external, merely regular aspect of social behaviour is well brought out by an example in Professor Hart's 'The Concept of Law'. (22) A stream of traffic controlled by traffic lights certainly displays a great degree of regularity in its behaviour. Regarded purely as a causal sequence, it yields us correlations between red lights and an absence of movement and between green lights and movement. In this way we might account for movement and its absence in terms of the effects of green and red lights, though we should be hard put to it to think what kind of causal connections were at work. But at this level, we should not know what we do as a matter of fact know, that there are regulations about traffic such that a light's turning red is not a mechanical cause of the car's coming to a standstill, but is taken by the driver as a reason (in the light of the traffic regulations) for bringing the car to a halt. The connection between the lights turning red and the cars stopping is thus a conceptual connection, for in terms of the rules governing our behaviour on the road a red light *means* stop. And it is plain that this meaning is not causally analysable, in the sense that the explanation of the way in which a red light means stop is not at all like that of the way in which clouds 'mean' rain — i.e. that they are a causally connected sign of rain; the explanation of the meaning of red lights is like the explanation of the meaning of words and other conventional symbols. Thus the regular causal sequence has an 'inside' to it, namely the conceptual, rule-governed sequence. This is an important point, for it explains the sense in which we have a better understanding of human behaviour than of any other natural phenomena; when Greek philosophers such as Aristotle defended explanations in teleological, purposive terms they were not merely naïve, for it is plainly the case that with human beings we are in the unique situation that they can tell us what they are up to. The fact that natural phenomena of other kinds do not behave like this means that we have to settle for causal sequences only, i.e. for regularities externally observed; and indeed it makes no sense to suppose it could be otherwise. But the fact that physics or chemistry explain their subject-matter only in terms of causal sequences of this sort is no

140

reason for supposing that we ought to limit the explanation of human behaviour to such categories; to do so would be a self-destructive and deliberate impoverishment of the subject. Thus we can conclude that understanding human behaviour, both 'individual' and 'social', in rule-guided terms gives us an insight which would be unavailable where the events in question displayed *only* regular sequence. (23)

The fact, however, that in the social sciences we can rely upon the accounts of their activities which are offered by the agents brings with it some complications for the notion of social theory. To see what these are, we must begin by reflecting on the distinction between the external and internal aspect of rule-following. If we think about some simple piece of physics, say the working out of the direction a body will move in under the influence of two forces at an angle to each other, our task is only to work out the sums involved in that particular triangle of forces. And if our answer fails to square with the facts, there is only one thing to be said – we have made a mistake in our sums; and it necessarily is *our* mistake, since there can be no question of the body getting it right or wrong. But in the case of the traffic at the lights, a failure on our part to predict the action of the man who 'jumps the lights' when they are at red is a very different matter. It is true that we have made a false prediction, but *our* getting it wrong rests on *his* behaving wrongly. A causal generalisation has only one task to fulfil, namely telling us what will and will not happen under particular conditions; irregularities are thus falsifying counter-examples to the causal law. But rules are not falsifiable in any simple way – except of course that it may be false to say that there is a rule – and breaches of a rule are errors on the part of those whose behaviour is governed by it. We can thus be perfectly correct in saying that there is a rule governing the behaviour of traffic at traffic lights, and yet admit that people sometimes or even often break those rules. (24) Once again, reflection on sociological research shows how true this is – the whole study of deviance rests precisely on the recognition that there are rules governing most people's actions which are systematically or casually broken by 'deviants'. And rules are followed or broken by people who are aware of what the rules are, and who thus model their behaviour on them –

141

even if only in the backhanded sense that they try to avoid detection when they break them. This is plainly a major difference from the physical sciences, where there can be no such question; there our theories are determined by behaviour which in itself is meaningless — there is no question of the electron being uncertain whether to comply with Heisenberg's uncertainty principle.

The problem this raises for social theory is the following. As Kuhn points out, the scientific community is defined by the theories it accepts, which in a sense prescribe the norms and rules governing acceptable research and acceptable solutions to scientific problems. A scientist becomes 'socialised' into the scientific community by accepting the rules about e.g. what counts as an experiment, and what as an explanatory hypothesis; learning the current 'paradigms' is learning the rules of scientific life. Now for the physical scientist there is only one socialisation process, that whereby he joins the scientific community, and it is the vocabulary of this community which defines the subject-matter of his inquiries and the proper mode of conducting those inquiries. But this is just what makes the natural sciences unlike the social sciences. Consider the electron again: there is no question of the electron characterising its own behaviour in some way or other which antedates the arrival of the physicist; and thus there can be no room for us to *mis*characterise the behaviour of the electron as the result of failing to understand the logic of *its* own characterisation. (25) But this danger is just what social scientists are exposed to as soon as they venture beyond the mere cataloguing of what people say about their activities. For there are here what it is not too fanciful to describe as two levels of theory — the level of the scientists' theories about the phenomena, and the level of theories which are held by the phenomena themselves. Since the 'phenomena' here are social beings they already have an account of what they are doing and why, and an elaborate, if not necessarily very explicit, set of beliefs about why this makes sense. In this sense they already entertain theories about their behaviour, theories which serve both to explain and to direct their activities. Thus the social scientist must undergo two socialisation processes rather than one. One is analogous to that of the natural scientist who is socialised

142

into the community of natural scientists; the other is *dis*analogous, namely socialisation into the rules of the community being studied. The importance of this latter process is obviously a good deal easier to see in anthropology, where field workers consciously and explicitly set out to learn how to live among the Nuer or the Barotse, and where they do see the process very explicitly as one of learning both the language and a multiplicity of social conventions.

If we follow Winch's interpretation of the consequences of this fact, the major consequence is that our subject-matter is defined by *its* criteria of significance and not by our own; and thus what we discover is the logic of the social order in question, and not an order which we impose on events ourselves. One thing that this entails is that the mode of understanding employed by the investigator must be that employed by the people whom he is studying; and this means that the usual account of such concepts as *Verstehen*, namely that imaginative understanding of the agents' point of view is a useful heuristic device, is quite inadequate. For example, to have no artistic appreciation makes it not merely more difficult to write the history of art; it renders it *logically impossible*, because it means that the proffered account cannot be a history of art *as* art, but only, let us say, one of artistic objects as a form of commercial property. (26) Merely to employ *Verstehen* as a psychologically useful first step towards a scientific understanding of events is to totally miss the point. For the point is that the identification of the events to be understood necessarily depends on understanding the rules which make them count as events of whatever kind it may be. Thus when we describe a set of actions as *praying*, this necessarily is to employ *religious* criteria; when we describe an act as that of *voting* this necessarily is to employ *political* criteria. (27) It ought to be said at once that Winch does not forbid us to go on from there; we can analyse religion, politics, art or whatever else, in a way that the participants do not. (28) The claim is not one which dictates where our inquiries shall end, but one which says where they can logically be said to start; and the claim is that whatever we may go on to say, we must root our story in that which is told by the agents themselves. This claim has some implications for sociological and anthropological practice, for it does of course rule out some kinds of explanation even in principle. The kind of analysis excluded in this way is exemplified by Frazer's picture of primitive religion in 'The Golden Bough'; as a rationalist and a Victorian, Frazer saw primitive religion as a peculiar kind of failed technology; since it was obvious to him that there could not be gods such as the primitives worshipped, it was necessary to find some explanation of what went on when they sang, chanted, danced and sacrificed as they planted their crops; to Frazer the only possible explanation was that they were trying to make the crops grow better. But the crops grew no better, and hence the technology was manifestly no good. Compared with the use of decent ploughs, chemical fertilisers and effective irrigation, primitive religion is agriculturally a total failure. In effect what Frazer did was impose Victorian and English standards of agricultural technology onto a primitive society, and then complain that in those terms primitive religion was more or less perverse and unintelligible. But, as the whole anthropological world has pointed out since, such questions as Frazer asks get us off on quite the wrong foot. What we have to do is begin by recognising that such behaviour is religious ritual, not amateur farming, and thus that an understanding of it has to be gained in terms of the logic of ritual, not in terms of a strangely non-rational technology. Of course, we may well ask in some other terms why it is that agricultural technology has not developed in some given society, but this is a different question, and one whose answer will scarcely be found by misidentifying the phenomena of religious life. (29)

And this central aspect of the nature of social theory leads us back to a reconsideration of the relationship between social science and philosophy. For a second result of the facts noted above is that the social sciences are characteristically in search of a philosophical understanding of their subject-matter. This is widely thought to be a rather shocking conclusion — as in the light of our initial account of philosophy as essentially a second-order subject it is — so it deserves close scrutiny. The argument is simply this: individual or group behaviour in a social context is to be explained through the medium of explicating the *concepts* of their own behaviour which the agents utilise. This is a widely

144

recognised sociological truth to which such traditional concerns as that with 'the definition of the situation' have always paid homage. The concepts which individuals possess are simply the mirror-image of the rules which shape their lives in their society. And this point can be illustrated as Winch illustrates it by taking the consequences of a new concept for social life. (30) When diseases come to be accounted for in terms of the 'germ theory', this is a social matter; the medical 'way of life' changes very drastically as a result of the new theory — and indeed what it means for there to be a new medical theory can only be made sense of in terms of the ways doctors now treat patients, what they now count as the same diseases and so on. Thus when we elucidate concepts we are elucidating the possibilities of social life, and conversely when we explain social life we elucidate the concepts available to members of that society. When we began our account of philosophical argument we described it as essentially a conceptual study. Now we see that the social sciences are permeated by conceptual considerations; for on this chapter's account, it is the task of social science to reflect on the concepts with which we make social life intelligible, to show how we are able to assess our behaviour, make plans, give reasons, and so on, and also to show what would be lost, were certain key concepts not available. But this activity is much like that of philosophy through the centuries, where thinkers have been inquiring into how it would be if we saw the world in ways other than those we usually employ, what we could go on doing unchanged, and what would be radically altered — one example being in the area of last chapter's questions, where we ask what would be the result of abandoning the concept of 'choice'. And if this characterisation is correct, it is a common preoccupation of both philosophy and social science to inquire into the rationality of life understood in terms of various conceptual schemes. None of this implies — to repeat what we have before asserted — that the facts do not matter, or that philosophers would do a better job than properly field-trained anthropologists when it comes to collecting ethnographic data. What it implies is more modest — that the inquiry into the kind of significance possessed by the data thus collected is more like the inquiries of philosophers than it is like the inquiries of chemists or physicists.

Before we go on in the next chapter to ask whether such an account as this is plausible when applied to economics rather than anthropology, and whether it has internal ambiguities which weaken its overall attraction, there is one obvious issue we should settle. This is the question of whether the acceptance of the arguments of this chapter does irreparable damage to the arguments of the first four chapters concerning the demands of scientific explanation, and the assumption of those chapters that these demands applied also within the social sciences. The answer seems to me to be that it is only in certain rather superficial respects that our earlier arguments have been damaged. Obviously the one claim that has to be resisted is that we should hope to develop a unified science of the whole natural order, both human and non-human. The discontinuities to which this chapter and its predecessor have pointed make such a claim impossible to sustain. It should be remembered, though, that this claim was in any case part of a propagandist programme for a certain view of science, and not a central logical tenet of the account of explanation which we defended earlier. In other respects the model seems unimpaired. The importance of causal histories remains as great as ever, once it is recognised that in human action we usually employ the concept of cause as equivalent to that of having good reasons: (31) we still want to follow events made intelligible by showing how under the circumstances one thing rather than another was the thing to do — and thus the thing to be expected. The importance of deductive relationships is as great as ever; only if we know that a rule covers all of a given class of cases, and that all of a given group of persons follow that rule can we move towards deductively certified prediction of their actions; equally, the importance of consistency and inconsistency are undiminished, when we consider that neither we nor the people we study can persist in following what are seen to be inconsistent rules. And our commitment to theoretical realism is now better founded than ever, for in the case of human beings alone can we have our assertions about the rules governing the phenomena confirmed by the testimony of the phenomena themselves. The logical properties and the

146

ontological presuppositions made by explanations thus seem to be unchanged, even if the social sciences aim at the elucidation of rules rather than the establishment of regularities only, and at the unravelling of conceptual rather than contingent relationships. To this extent we can say that the form of the inquiry may remain unchanged even when its content is seen to be so radically different; and thus we can to this extent allow Professor Winch's views to give us pause about the content of social science, without weakening anything we have said about the formal requirements of scientific explanation.

NOTES

1. D. Martindale, 'The Nature and Types of Sociological Theory' (Routledge, 1962) chs 3, 7, 9.
2. Chomsky, 'Language and Mind', pp. 58 ff.
3. Ibid., p. 65.
4. Winch, 'Idea', pp. 40-4.
5. Ibid., pp. 24-33.
6. Durkheim, 'Suicide', ch. v.
7. C. Taylor, 'The Explanation of Behaviour' (Routledge, 1964) pp. 10-17.
8. Peters, 'Concept of Motivation', pp. 12-14.
9. M. Weber, 'Theory of Social and Economic Organization' (Free Press, Chicago, 1957) p. 88.
10. Winch, 'Idea', pp. 33-9.
11. B. F. Skinner, 'Verbal Behaviour' (Appleton-Century-Crofts, New York, 1957) but see Chomsky's review in 'Language' (1959) 26-58.
12. B. M. Barry, 'Political Argument' (Routledge, 1965) pp. 17 f.
13. J. L. Austin, 'How to Do Things with Words' (Oxford University Press, 1962) pp. 4-7.
14. Winch, 'Idea', pp. 37-9.
15. R. M. Hare, in 'Jnl of Phil.' (1957) 748.
16. H. Garfinkel, 'Essays in Ethnomethodology' (Prentice-Hall, 1967).
17. Winch, 'Idea', pp. 50 f.

18. Ibid., pp. 57-65.

19. Ibid., pp. 33 ff.

20. See the massive account in T. Parsons, 'The Structure of Social Action', 2nd ed. (Free Press, Chicago, 1958).

21. Nadel, 'Theory of Social Structure', p. 25.

22. H. L. A. Hart, 'The Concept of Law', (Oxford University Press, 1961) pp. 87 ff.

23. Von Hayek, in 'Economica' (1942) 289-90.

24. Hart, 'Concept of Law', p. 88.

25. Winch, 'Idea', pp. 86 ff.

26. Ibid., p. 88.

27. Ibid.

28. Ibid., pp. 89 ff.

29. Ibid., pp. 113 f.

30. Ibid., pp. 121 f.

31. Cf. Popper, 'Poverty', p. 149.

7 The Social Sciences as Sciences

It is now time to turn to the scrutiny of the arguments presented in the last chapter. In outline, the tactics here adopted are to ask whether the views put forward by Winch are so restrictive that they rule out of court what is plainly good practice by social scientists, or whether on the other hand they are so loosely framed that they cannot be readily used to decide the logical propriety or impropriety of an offered explanation. It is plain that these are the dangers of such an account as Winch's — that it will rule out too much, or else that it will rule out too little. There is one preliminary which ought to be mentioned. It is clear from the literature that the implications of the case outlined in the last chapter are not altogether obvious, for the literature is full of different interpretations of them; it is also clear that we cannot take for granted the assurances of their author as to the implications of these views, for an author is only an authority on what he *thinks* are the implications of his views, not on what the implications actually *are*. The unavoidable consequence is that in what follows we are forced to take a fairly independent line, and not much time will be spent defending this interpretation of Winch's views against rival interpretations — justice will be done them in the bibliographical note, however. (1) The only other point to make now is that most of the conclusions of this chapter are negative in the sense that they are conclusions about the limited methodological consequences of the arguments of the last chapter.

Let us begin with this last point. We have mentioned already the image of social science which I labelled 'Hobbesian', and we saw that this was one of Winch's targets. It was argued that if Hobbes intended to convert social science into a sub-department of physics — as Comte seemed to want to turn sociology into a department of physiology —

he would have been sadly mistaken. For analysing social life merely in terms of 'matter in motion' would be self-defeating in that the distinctively social aspect of social life would vanish in the process. It might be true — if Hobbes's notions about physics had been more adequate — that we could obtain physical accounts of the actions and interaction of complex physical systems; but what we should lack is exactly what we now possess, the understanding of social life as social life. Now this argument is not novel; it has in previous times been employed by biologists who argued that attempts to wholly explain the behaviour of living organisms in chemical terms was conceptually erroneous, in that those new properties which were characteristically those of *living* organisms emerged at a given stage of chemical complexity — hence the usual name of the doctrine of 'emergence' — but were not reducible to complex chemical properties. (2) And within the discipline of sociology, many writers have held that what was distinctive about social life could not be reduced to some other kind of property, but must be understood in social terms — and they have appealed to the biological example in their support. However, the argument has two weaknesses. The first is that it leaves it very unclear as to what it is that makes two sorts of property not like each other, and hence leaves it unclear as to when we could say that we had explained one in terms of the other. More importantly, it is also a very thin argument; in any plausible formulation, it is rather uninteresting. For consider the exactly similar situation in the parallel accounts of a phenomenon which might be offered by physics and chemistry: the chemist discovers that he can mix hydrogen and oxygen in proportions of two to one, ignite the mixture and produce water; the physicist can in principle describe this process in terms which make no reference at all to hydrogen, oxygen or water — that is, in the terminology of mechanics. Now, the language of mechanics or 'matter in motion' is certainly logically distinct from the language which we should ordinarily call the language of chemistry, and between such statements as 'the mixture becomes water' and the associated physical descriptions, we need bridging statements which show how we are to map events described in the one conceptual scheme onto events described in the other. (3)

150

But the requirement of translation in this way does not show that there can be no such subject as physical chemistry; given the flourishing state of that discipline, any argument which tried to rule it out of existence would rightly be thrown out at once. All the argument can possibly show is that the criteria employed for the identification and explanation of events by one discipline are logically distinct from those employed in another discipline. As to whether results in chemistry can significantly affect results in physics and vice versa, the argument is necessarily silent. And this is surely the same situation as prevails in the social sciences. If the 'socialness' of social phenomena is lost when the description of these events is translated into some other conceptual scheme, why should this matter any more than the fact that the 'chemicalness' of chemical phenomena is lost if they are redescribed in the language of atomic physics? If this is the extent of the difficulty, then nothing has been done to show that Hobbes or Comte was mistaken *conceptually* or *in principle*. Of course, I do not suggest for a moment that we seriously reconsider their contributions to social theory; but what is true is that their deficiencies stem from their weakness in describing social life, not from a mistake of principle about the possible explanations they are allowed to give. It might, of course, be retorted that this is to underestimate the power of Winch's argument, and certainly it is not for me to say that this account is the only possible one. What we can reasonably claim, however, is that there is a valid general lesson to be learned about the caution with which we should draw methodological conclusions from philosophical claims. (4)

And the same point can be illustrated by looking at a second claim, namely that when we identify and explain social phenomena we are bound to employ the criteria which the agents themselves employ. As we have already seen, this implies that when we look at politics we employ political criteria, and when we look at religion we employ religious criteria; thus we are much more nearly participants in the events than could ever be the case in the natural sciences. I now want to show that one methodological conclusion of some importance does follow from this, and that one other does not. Let us begin with what does not follow. It does not follow, and Winch is ready to agree on this point, that we have to stop at the level of understanding which the participants themselves enjoy. (5) A particularly simple and clear-cut case which shows this is the day to day practice of economics. A man who is engaged in selling some good or other employs a vocabulary which describes economic activity, and which yet fails to overlap significantly with that of the professional economist. The trader may experience pleasure when he has a lot of ready cash available, and he may congratulate himself on the ability this gives him to either purchase goods that happen to catch his eye or to sit out a particular bad period of trading; he may notice some of the things with which the economist is professionally concerned, as for example that when they have bought a number of his wares, people seem less anxious to purchase more; or again that when a major employer of labour in the area takes on more hands into his business, the general prosperity of the whole area rises. It is, of course, highly probable that he will notice these things, and in some way take account of them. But, it is the economist rather than the trader who spends his time thinking about 'liquidity preference' or 'diminishing marginal utility' or 'the multiplier effect' — and it is not by any means true that the economist is thereby enabled to be a better trader than the trader who lacks such a vocabulary. In everyday life, the people who engage in day to day economic activity do not thus analyse and explain their own behaviour; yet at the level of trying to explain and control the economic problems which confront whole societies, the theoretical framework which incorporates such a vocabulary is quite indispensable. Only if we can begin to assign values to the multiplier, for instance, can we begin to predict and control booms and slumps, achieve a steady growth rate and the like. In so doing, we are of course abstracting from the concrete detail of what everyday life looks like to the participants and conceptually organising their world in quite other terms than theirs. Since such a process is quite essential to such a science as economics, it would obviously be a defect of Winch's arguments if they led to the conclusion that this process was impossible or illogical. Yet they do not seem to lead so far; for all he demands is that the account given by the economist should be based on,

152

or rooted in that of the actors themselves. There can be no logical objection to concepts like that of the 'multiplier' of that of 'diminishing marginal utility'; for such concepts plainly get their meaning from what buyers and sellers themselves would say about their activities. The assertion that this is what gives them their meaning seems plainly true when we recall that the way in which we distinguish between a piece of pure geometry and that geometry applied to the representation of economic theory relies on our being able to translate the graphical relationships into descriptions of the effects brought about by people engaged in what they themselves would describe as economic activity. (6)

What, however, does seem to follow, and to be meant to follow, from Winch's arguments is the apparent inevitability of a 'culture-bound' sociology and anthropology. It has been argued, for example by Professor MacIntyre, (7) that on Winch's account, it would be impossible for a primitive to understand statements about civilised societies and equally impossible for a civilised man to understand statements about primitive societies; and Professor MacIntyre appears to take this as a knock-down refutation of Winch's position. However, a view which almost amounts to this has been put forward by anthropologists, such as Levy-Bruhl, (8) and is certainly susceptible of a less absurd interpretation than this. The key point is that the classification of activity as activity of a certain kind essentially relies on an appeal to its significant features; and the claim is that their significance is lent them by the social organisation of the community from which the investigator comes. Thus we identify some actions as being those involved in economic exchange, others as those involved in political participation and so on. This identification amounts to placing the actions in a context of social rules which endow them with a point and a purpose. Such an account was given by Weber, for example, and it certainly fits in well with Winch's views; and it does much to explain why the sociologist's understanding is a participant understanding. But it leads to one obvious difficulty, that if we are investigating an activity which is very alien to anything we have done, it may be impossible to describe it in terms that are not seriously misleading, simply because it may be impossible to locate it within the framework of our own culture; it is not

153

just a matter of finding informants who will tell us what they are doing, it is also a matter of our being able to make sense of what we are told — and between an account of what *we* would be doing in their shoes and an account of what they in their shoes *say* they are doing, there seems no room for a simple, objective, culture-neutral account of what *as a matter of fact* they are doing. That two cultures might therefore be literally unintelligible to each other seems beyond the bounds of logical possibility, in that there are a good many *a priori* constraints on what a language could be like, and hence on what human beings could have to communicate to each other, (9) so that it seems that we need have no such doubts as Professor MacIntyre pours scorn on. Yet at the level where we begin to organise our knowledge of the social world theoretically, the dangers seem very real.

Consider, for instance, the theoretical framework for the understanding of politics which is offered by Gabriel Almond's 'The Politics of the Developing Areas'. (10) This suggests that in all societies politics involves a process of articulating and aggregating interests, and it so interprets the notion of politics that all societies may properly be said to have a political system, and to have political processes going on within them. It is, of course, not suggested that all societies define political roles so clearly as do countries like Great Britain or the U.S.A.; for the framework is an abstraction from the actual political behaviour of all societies in order to give us the means of describing all societies in similar terms. But it is arguable that the framework is nothing like abstract enough. The notion of an 'interest' raises no problems at all within the political context of Britain or the United States, where people explicitly create interest groups with the avowed aim of securing the interests of their members, and where politicians see it as one of their major concerns to satisfy these interests as far as possible. In the context of the American and British political culture it is indeed difficult to see how politics could be carried on at all, save in some such fashion, and it is difficult to see how we should fare in the absence of 'secondary groups' which acted as go-betweens to make the views of the public known to politicians and to gain benefits for their clients. (11) But this is very much a cultural matter; it is the politics of the

154

advanced, industrialised world which we thus describe. Does the framework really do justice to the priestly government of ancient Egypt, or to clan organisation among the Tikopia? It would obviously be false to suppose that hierocratic politics was in any obvious way concerned with the satisfaction of group interests, and plainly false to suppose that it would have been better for hierocratic politics had there been flourishing pressure groups; yet if we do not commit ourselves to such falsehoods, what is left of the notion of 'interests' in our analysis of politics, for we do not genuinely explain anything merely by using the same word ambiguously in two different contexts? If the notion of an interest is adjusted to the politics of ancient Egypt it seems to cease to be our notion of an interest; if it is not, it seems terribly out of place. No doubt it is true that there are identities between the practice of government in ancient Egypt and modern Britain which have gone unnoticed; and no doubt it is true that we have only recently come to appreciate just how complex is social life in so-called 'simple' societies. But this scarcely amounts to an argument for the view that the politics of ancient Egypt will readily submit to analysis in terms of the interest group theory applied to contemporary Britain. Insofar as sociology and political science are perennially prone to couch their explanations in terms of organising concepts only properly at home in the societies which have evolved their authors, we may guess that we have been stepping off on the wrong foot more often than not. Given that these are the so-called 'policy sciences', the implications of organising our experience of foreign cultures in terms which represent their activities as merely peculiar or inefficient versions of our own are plainly practically as well as intellectually alarming. If there are to be theoretical frameworks which will equally encompass the behaviour of people in our own and vastly different cultures, it is clear that the level of abstraction at which they will have to be pitched vastly exceeds that suggested by Professor Almond.

We are now in a position to examine more closely the claim made in the last chapter to the effect that the social sciences aim at a philosophical understanding of their subject-matter. We have already agreed that this is not to turn such matters as the prediction of how people will vote over

155

to the armchair thinker; only the field work displayed in 'Voting' (12) or 'The American Voter' (13) will achieve this kind of result. We must, however, go on to characterise the claim a little more fully than we did at the end of the last chapter, for only in so doing can we see how the claim is much more plausible in some fields than others — and hence, of course, how the general theory on which the last chapter rested is more applicable to some social sciences than others. The claim, it was said, amounts to saying that we must know how the agents conceive of their own activities, and in so doing we are coming to understand conceptual links in their behaviour — a point which explains why it was so hard in Chapter 5 to make sense of human actions as simple cause and effect sequences. The nature of the claim is made clearer by example; and in the process, we can see why it was that at the end of the last chapter I stood by the view that we look for causal sequences in human behaviour, even though these are not characterised as mere causal regularities. Suppose we consider the life of a criminal who commits a crime, is caught, tried, sentenced and punished; here we have a sequence in which (as in other causal sequences) the earlier events explain the later. If we ask why Jones is being arrested by the police, we are told it is because he is thought to have committed a crime; if we ask why Jones is in prison, we are told it is because the judge sentenced him to imprisonment. The earlier events lead to the later events, and thus form a causal sequence. But it is a causal sequence with a difference. For in this case the events are also conceptually linked; they are logically interdependent in that the concept of punishment logically implies that of crime — punishment is, as a matter of logic, punishment-for-a-crime — and where it cannot be said that a person has committed a crime, it cannot be straightforwardly said that he has been punished. (14) Equally, the behaviour of a 'defendant' vis-a-vis a 'judge' is conceptually underpinned; to play one such role, it is necessary that others should play logically related roles. In this way explaining what one person is doing implies a host of conceptually related activities on the part of other people, and in explaining even one person's behaviour, we necessarily elaborate a shared conceptual scheme. This does not for one moment diminish the importance of factual inquiry in social

156

science: to analyse the internal logic of 'criminality' brings us not one inch nearer knowing how many people commit what kinds of crime; to find that out, we obviously hav• to go and look at the data. And again, although the workings of a legal system imply that there is what we might call a legal logic to the behaviour of those who participate in that system, it remains a solidly factual matter as to *how* any particular society organises its legal system, and *what* conceptualisation of their roles its 'judicial' officers have. Analogously, the practice of voting can only come to be assessed, not as a process which merely precedes some person or group taking decisions, but as one which is designed to *entitle* them to take decisions; and equally with the rules governing what counts as winning, the connection between getting most votes and winning is not one of regular concomitance, but a matter of how the rules of a given political order lay down criteria for victory. Getting most votes just *is* winning under some rules; but of course nothing but factual inquiry will tell us *who* has won, by how much, and by what methods. (15)

But once more the conclusion turns out to be rather less striking than it looks. Indeed, the claim turns out to be relatively well-accepted, in that the practice of social scientists scarcely calls it in question. The apparent paradox of suggesting that social scientists seek a philosophical understanding of their subject-matter still remains; but its roots can be seen to be nothing more than the tendency to think that all the social sciences answer the same questions. For it is plainly true that certain kinds of anthropology are much more obviously dominated by the kind of concerns described by Winch than is, say, econometrics, where the conceptual problems are taken as solved, and the attempt then made to understand the regularities which appear in economic activity by seeing what mathematical relationships hold between crucial variables. Winch's argument appeals quite explicitly to anthropological examples; he says that the student of a strange tribe trying to make sense of their activities is much like the philosopher who tries to distance himself from our own conceptual scheme to see what kind of sense our everyday thinking and acting makes. (16) Some sociology clearly falls into this category, too; Professor Goffman's work in 'Asylums' (17) is a case in point. The aim

157

there is always to make sense of the activities of such unlikely rule-followers as the inmates of the back wards of mental hospitals and their nurses. By drawing a series of analogies between the medically conceptualised world and the prison world of punishment and reward, Goffman illuminates coherences which we should not otherwise perceive. (18) But this is not all that sociologists do, and Winch's account would have rather little relevance to the work of the demographer, say. For he, like the economist, takes for granted the conceptualisation of the world employed by the people whose behaviour he is studying, and seeks to elicit the consequences of their behaviour which they generally neither forsee nor exercise any control over. Although it is true that population trends, like the growth rate of the Gross National Product, have their roots in the intended behaviour of individual people, it is not the case that they are themselves intended, and for the most part they can be studied without attending to the intentions of anyone. It is worth noting that one of the most popular labels for the social sciences has been 'the study of the unintended results of human actions' (19) -- a label which does justice precisely to what Winch does not, and which fails to do justice precisely to what he does justice to.

The claim that much of social science is concerned with the results of action, rather than the intentions embodied in that action obviously weakens the assimilation of sociological and philosophical understanding considerably, though it suggests that sociologists would be unwise to see this assimilation as more than the recognition of what they mostly take for granted. However, it does raise some further questions. The first is that of how we elucidate the internal logic of ways of life, and the second that of how the accounts of those who merely live a particular way of life have to mesh with the accounts of their observers. Asking these two questions is a preliminary to defending my own view that the importance of causality in social science is untouched by Winch's arguments. The final question will be whether arguments along the lines of Winch's rule out so-called 'functionalist' accounts of social life, and this will serve as introduction to the next chapter's discussion of such 'holistic forms of explanation.

158

One of the claims seemingly made by Winch is that human behaviour makes sense both to agents and observers only within some way of life, but that all ways of life make equally good sense. This raises two obvious problems, the first whether it really is true that we always act for reasons — i.e. in such a way as to make sense to ourselves and others, and the second whether we cannot say of entire ways of life that they are irrational. It is worth remembering that practical sociological, perhaps also political consequences hang on this. Writers such as R. D. Laing have argued that even the so-called insane act in a way which makes sense, and moreover that they can only be treated as human if we act towards them on the assumption that their behaviour does make sense; (20) although it is not true that the acceptance of Winch's argument entails that we accept Laing's as well, it is certainly true that to give Laing's case a sympathetic hearing, we must believe some such case as Winch's. The argument underpinning the two assertions above is simple enough. If we are to say of a person that he *did* something, as opposed merely to having had something happen to him, he is said to be acting for reasons which make sense in a context, a way of life. Such reasons are *only* intelligible within a conception of reality offered by a given conceptual scheme, and since there is no such thing as a super-conceptual scheme embracing all others and allowing us to evalute them, it seems that all conceptual schemes are on a level. The first part of this claim is both alarming and eventually quite unclear. Its alarming quality is the following. We often say of ourselves that we did something 'for no reason', or that someone acted irrationally. If Winch-like arguments rule out such assertions, then such arguments must be wrong, for it is obvious that assertions like these are perfectly proper. But there is really no such conflict. The point which Winch is making is that there is always some correct and recognised description of his action that both the agent and his fellows can accept, such that it makes it possible to say or deny that *that* was what he did. It has been said that even this is false, for example because there is no right or wrong way to go for an afternoon stroll — to borrow an instance from Professor MacIntyre. (21) But this objection overweights Winch's case; all that this requires is that a man who says that he is going for a stroll must meet

159

certain conditions as to his goals, motives and subsequent intentions — he cannot maintain that he is out strolling if he is setting off at a great pace to catch a train. And in this limited sense it is plain that Winch is right; even an 'aimless' stroll has aims. But once again, it looks as if such a weak thesis places few restrictions on what sociologists may find about the way in which people do and do not act for reasons. If we consider Weber's famous thesis that rationalisation is a comparatively recent and fairly restricted phenomenon, (22) it is apparent that it meets the logical requirements set out above. For it is not the case that Weber claims, and Winch denies, that until recently people acted for absolutely no reason at all. Rather, Weber is claiming that the conscious shaping of means to ends is a comparatively recent phenomenon, and this claim certainly *could* be true — whether or not it *is* — quite compatibly with anything said by Winch. And even the statement, which we often make, that we acted for no reason falls inside the boundary of sense, for all we mean by such a statement is that our action was not done as part of a plan involving it as a means to some further end. We certainly do not mean that it was unintelligible and unintended. For we draw a clear line between actions which are unpuzzling, even though done for no reason, and those which are puzzling, because we simply do not know why we did them.

The thesis of the last paragraph has, however, been regarded as infinitely less shocking than the view that we cannot describe entire ways of life as irrational. This claim has led to a very warm debate indeed. For Winch claimed that because everyone's criteria for reality are embedded in a way of life we cannot make negative existential claims of the sort exemplified by 'The Azande believe in witches, but of course there aren't really any such things'. (23) This claim has an ancient and famous antecedent in Tertullian's Paradox, the claim that to understand Christianity it was necessary to believe in its truth — with the logically disagreeable consequence that there were no unbelievers, only misunderstanders. (24) But it has another consequence, disagreeable for believers, too, which is that the argument is reiterable for other faiths, even for faiths which are incompatible with Christianity. In this case, we are faced

160

either with suspending the law of non-contradiction (and our earlier remarks about the importance of consistency show what a curious step this would be) or else assert that contrary to the appearances, the various faiths are not incompatible. It seems equally paradoxical to claim that we cannot say that there are no such things as witches, and hence that Azande witchcraft cults are irrational and unfounded. Certainly, this is one case where the claim is in flat contradiction with the work of the anthropologists. When Nadel discusses roles, he says that some roles are 'mythical', and by this he means that it is impossible that anyone should actually possess the attributes required for those roles — and the example he gives is that of the witch's role. (25) In other words, there really aren't such beings as witches. Moreover, it appears on closer inspection that even Frazer emerges less badly than it seemed. While it is certainly true that the connections between the practices he observed were religious and ritual connections, it was plainly a proper question to inquire whether they did any good, even if his notions about the kind of good which a practice may do were too limited. For what is clear now is that the concept on which this whole account has been hung, that of a 'way of life', will not bear the weight. Only if 'ways of life' were logically separate in a much more rigid way than we can plausibly suppose them to be, would there be an absolute gap between the logic of belief and the logic of farming; given the implausibility of this assumption, it emerges as perfectly proper to ask why religion flourishes, when there is on the face of it more need for farming. It may, of course, be immensely difficult to understand why people believe in witchcraft, and immensely difficult to give any coherent account of what people gain from prayer. But once we have discovered what the agents themselves believe the point of their activities to be, we can certainly go on to ask whether the world is so constructed that their accounts are plausible or implausible, and hence whether their behaviour is rational or not. We can do this because ways of life overlap and compete, share assumptions and serve different purposes; it is plain from the entire history of human thought that societies have radically revised their intellectual assumptions as the result of just this kind of overlap and competition. While it is true that there is no

161

single God-like stance from which to evalute these processes, it remains the case that there are various human stances from which to make the evaluation, and make it we do. (26)

Once we have cast doubt upon the claim that we are always concerned to explain the reasons which people have for the actions they perform, and equally upon the claim that these reasons are logically in order as they stand, we can raise another awkward question. This time, it concerns the necessity of attaching our account of the social behaviour of individuals and groups to the account given by the agents themselves. We have seen that this priority of the agents' own accounts has to be stretched to allow us to build on to those accounts the technical vocabulary and the interest in unperceived results of the economist or the demographer. But now it is time to ask the more embarrassing question of whether the claim made by Winch allows us to disbelieve the account of their reasons offered by the agents in question, and thus to substitute an account of our own. It seems on the face of it that any account which claims to go behind the reasons offered and to uncover the *real* reasons of the agents concerned is ruled out as *a priori* impossible. For such an account can hardly be said to be rooted in the agent's own account, when its whole point is to deny that account. It is important to see that this is not just a matter of showing that the agent is lying, and in that sense uncovering his real reasons; rather, we mean accounts which claim that no matter how honest agents may be in telling us their reasons, they will nonetheless be mistaken, they will misdescribe their actions. Examples of such accounts which come to mind are those based on the idea of ideological self-deception, (27) and those which employ the psycho-analytic concept of repression. (28) The existentialist analysis of many moral dilemmas in terms of *mauvaise foi* also hovers on the ambiguous border between mere lying and unconscious self-deception; it is clear, though, that for Sartre and others, this is a case of a continuum rather than a clear-cut line, and thus that they are apparently at odds with Winch's dictum. Winch has rather little to say about this; the Marxism to which he does object is a mechanical kind not currently at issue; and on psycho-analytic explanation he says only that it must be couched in terms of concepts available to the agent — thus

162

the concept of 'father-fixation' would have to take account of the father's role in, say, Trobriand Islands society if we were to apply psycho-analytic concepts to the Trobriand Islanders. (30) It looks, however, as if many of the concepts of ideological or psycho-analytic explanation require a radical break with the conceptualisations of the people whose behaviour is to be explained. Take the explanation of the enthusiasm with which working-class crowds in August 1914 greeted the outbreak of war — a phenomenon of enormous importance, since it defeated the hopes of all those democratic socialists who had supposed that the obvious futility of war would lead to a mass working-class revolt against it. The crowds were no doubt composed of men who would have given numerous different accounts of their actions — perhaps in terms of the patriotic duty to defend one's country, perhaps in rather xenophobic terms of the need to crush the English, French, Germans, Austrians, Russians or whomever; a Marxist might, however, say that they were actually lining the pockets of arms manufacturers, and that that was the single central description of their behaviour, and as for their cheerfulness, that was to be explained as a holiday mood resulting from the cessation of their routinely alienated lives in factories and wherever else they laboured. A Freudian could have explained some part of this behaviour in terms of sexual jealousy, whether that of the fathers sending their sexual rivals away to be killed or that of the young men who were going off to obtain the glory which would make them suitable mates for the objects of their sexual drives. Now, it is an important aspect of such explanations that in a sense the agents *cannot* accept them; that is, they are the kind of reasons for which people do not think they act in general, and a man who came to see his behaviour in these terms would cease to act thus. Hence it seems true to say that the behaviour engaged in by the agents we are studying could only have taken place as it did, so long as they did not conceptualise their world in this way; and thus we seem a long way away from Winch. It must be remembered that we are not concerned to ask whether Marxist or Freudian explanations are *true* accounts, but only whether they are sufficiently logically coherent to get into the competition as explanations at all. And it seems unquestionable that they

163

are — though this is not to deny that there are a great many logical puzzles inherent in both Marxism and psycho-analytic theory. But is it really the case that they clash with Winch's demands? Once again, the answer is ambiguous. Uninterestingly, it is clear that Winch is right in supposing that we initially *identify* our phenomena in the terms used by the agents themselves; but this is accepted by Marxists and Freudians too. But if this claim is extended to mean that even our undercutting explanation of that activity must be couched in terms already available to the agent, then that claim must be ignored. Both the therapeutic effect of psycho-analysis and the political effects of Marxism depend to a large extent precisely on teaching people a new conceptual scheme within which events wear a different significance from what they did before. Any argument which tried to rule out such innovation would plainly be wrong; the fullest extent of the case can be no more than we allowed in the last chapter — that innovatory explanations must, to be intelligible, be attached to what was understood before.

This discussion of the conditions under which we reject the reasons proffered by the agents leads us back into the question of causation again. It does so in the following way: once we have allowed the rejection of the agents' reasons for their behaviour, we are led rather rapidly to ask about the conditions under which people are prone to self-deception. (31) Some such conditions are so well known that generalisations about them could not even be dignified as pieces of science. Nonetheless, they are involved in causal explanations, and thus they are causal laws. Gladstone ascribed one of his election defeats to the influence of the brewers and distillers, and said he had been swept from office on a tide of booze. Now, such an explanation of his defeat — though probably false — appeals to an obviously valid generalisation. Electoral agents, like impatient lovers and sharp businessmen, know that a person who has drunk a good deal is less likely than normal to scrutinise what he agrees to. It would obviously be futile to legislate such causal laws out of social science. Yet if they are let in here, why not elsewhere? We saw above that where we think we have better accounts of the agents' motives and reasons we are prepared to reject the accounts they offer us. But we also want to know what are the conditions which lead people to disguise their real motives even from themselves; and again we want to know what determines the particular disguise which those motives wear. Sociologists and anthropologists have long asked exactly such questions, and they are plainly good questions, and worth asking. It is this which makes it worthwhile to defend Weber's account of 'significance' against Winch's criticism of it; Weber argues that we must back up our accounts of the meaning of actions with causal analysis, and Winch objects to this — properly, so long as he objects only to the assumption that we should causally analyse 'meaning'; (32) but on two counts Weber is certainly in the right. In the first place, as we saw, it is true that if people endow their actions with a certain significance, and thus follow certain social rules, they will necessarily display regularities in their activities, so that the absence of these regularities would mean that our account of the significance of their actions was wrong. And, in the second place, it is also true that people will only endow their lives with certain kinds of significance under particular circumstances. If we claim that people do things which have a certain significance for them, we can also claim that there are causes and effects of their behaving in this manner. Not only can we analyse the internal logic of a way of life, we can ask what the origin and results of its existence are; and thus we restore causality to a central place in social science. For example, we might want to know what the economic and technological causes were behind the sudden springing into existence of the Gothic style in architecture. On Winch's view, it looks as if we cannot ask questions about anything other than the aesthetics and the liturgical merits af Gothic architecture, for it is these which are involved in unravelling its internal logic. But why should we thus restrict ourselves? Why can we not inquire also into the causal preconditions of the style's being available, as well as into the aspects of the medieval view of the world which gave the style its meaning and point? If there are any objections to asking such questions, it can only be the factual difficulties of assembling evidence and assessing its weight which lie behind them, for conceptually the inquiry is plainly in order. Once again, it looks as if Winch's arguments distort our perception of the great *variety*

165

of questions we can ask within the social sciences; of course we must inquire into the aesthetics of aesthetic change, but that does not mean we must not inquire into the economics and technology of it as well.

Before raising my final query about the compatibility of Winch's claims with the kind of explanations offered by 'functionalists , I should say something about the frequent appeals to 'what we can say' — or 'cannot say'. The status of arguments about what is conceptually proper has often been misunderstood for a rather silly reason — the addiction of many philosophers to examples involving visitors from other planets and the like. This has led Professor Rudner among others to criticise arguments invoking Martian visitors as vacuous empirical hypotheses, (33) vacuous because we are in no position to gain evidence about Martian visitors in the absence of any visits, and empirical, because it would be an empirical matter what these creatures understood once they arrived. Now he is clearly right in saying that it is an empirical matter whether Martians could or could not pick up such of our concepts as to enable them to understand our social life; but this is just to miss the point of the examples. For the point about 'what we can say' or what Martians could be said to understand, is that it is not an empirical issue, but a conceptual one. That is, we appeal to what it would make sense to say; and again, we are not interested in what Martians would or would not say as a matter of fact, but rather in what as a matter of logic they would have to say, if we were to say they understood our social life. Given our criteria, it is an empirical matter whether they are satisfied on some occasion — thus it would be an empirical matter whether a Martian so far understood the concept of politeness that he opened doors for ladies; but it is a conceptual matter that 'politeness' is bound up with such things as opening doors, and that behaviour has to satisfy such criteria to be properly called 'polite'. The appeal to Martians is misplaced in the sense that there is a grave risk of the allegory running off with the argument. But we could be much more austere than this. We could e.g. ask whether a being confined to the vocabulary of Humean causality and Newtonian mechanics would be able to generate a vocabulary adequate to the description of social life as we know it. What

166

our examples always do is invite us to reflect on the kind of responses a creature would have to have before we were able to say that it had understood social life; but the example is superfluous in that we always could confine ourselves to asking what would be the minimum vocabulary rich enough to adequately characterise social life.

One problem does remain; it is a central philosophical problem, but there is strikingly little to be said about it. We have all along insisted that philosophical claims were conceptual claims, and that they were clearly distinct from empirical claims. That is, we have described the job of philosophy as reflection on what kinds of demand make sense, not that of trying to bring home the factual data for the sciences. To this we ought to add one qualification, not because it will make any great difference to the argument hereafter, but for the sake of showing that the truth is complicated. From what has been said during the last four chapters, it emerges that theoretical understanding involves in some measure conceptual innovation, and it is equally clear that theoretical changes are up to a point forced upon by the facts, by the evidence. (34) In this sense, conceptual claims do seem vulnerable to factual proof and disproof; new facts may make us change our minds about what it makes sense for us to say about the facts. But, sadly, there seems nothing more than this to be said about the process; if we *cannot say how* we should have to change our minds — which is the essence of the claim that a conceptual shift is involved — then that is all we can say.

Finally, then, we raise the question of whether we can integrate functionalist explanations in social science with the framework offered by Winch. The interest of the question is twofold. In the first place, functional explanations of social phenomena are awkwardly poised between everyday explanations of what we are doing in terms of what we each suppose to be the point of acting as we do, and accounts at a very abstract level of the interacting elements of a 'system'. (35) And in the second place, this ambiguous status is reflected in Winch's rather half-hearted description of functional explanations as 'quasi-causal'. The question is whether we should admit such explanations as logically coherent or not. Winch says of Malinowski's account of

167

Trobriand religion that it does not shed much light on religious forms of behaviour by being cast into a functional mould. (36) But this complaint is as distressingly vague as the account it criticises; the point surely is that if no causal explanations are allowed, then this one also should be ruled out on principle, no matter how feeble the causal explanation it offers. A functionalist might well agree that Malinowski's account failed to shed much light, but object for very different reasons from those of Winch — for example, by claiming that Malinowski misidentified the functions which religion habitually serves. The question thus arises of whether we can make Winch's objections clearer for him. And the point of so doing is to shed a final light on the relationship between the agent s and the observer's accounts of a given piece of behaviour.

Not until the end of the next chapter will we be in a position to say anything very definite about the analysis of functional explanations; and even then we shall not have very high hopes that what we say will apply to more than a proportion of the greatly varied accounts which are labelled 'functional'. But some considerations can be sketched out now. The central one is that since functional explanations are necessarily teleological, they are allied in their logic to the purposive accounts we give of our own actions. Yet the goal that is postulated for actions is often something very different from the achievement of any particular person's wishes, namely some such goal as 'system-maintenance'; and the imagery which goes along with this is either organic or else heavily dependent on the analogy of self-regulating mechanisms equipped with feed-back loops and the like. (37) Now, if we were to accept such imagery whole-heartedly we should plainly break Winch's rules, since it is plainly not true of the parts of a self-regulating mechanism that they know what they are doing in the way that human beings know what they are doing. But, of course, it might be said that functional accounts do not require us to be so whole-hearted, and that they only require us to see that our ordinary accounts of what we are doing can be supplemented by showing how our actions interact with those of other people in an unintended, but non-accidental way. It is for this reason that we employ functional language, for our

168

major concern is to show how 'different' modes of behaviour can still be functionally equivalent – so that noisy ceremonies of rolling apprentices in barrels or occasional wild-cat strikes may each serve the same purpose of breaking up industrial tedium, for instance. And at this point, the question of whether we fulfil the requirements laid down by Winch depends for its answer on deciding how stringently to interpret him. Interpreted as loosely as I have suggested he must be, his requirements will obviously be met if we can produce the same kind of bridge statements between the agents' accounts and the 'functional' account as we can produce in such cases as economics.

The final point to be made is that *some* functional statements are in any case so deeply embedded in our ordinary explanations of social phenomena that it is hard to see them being ruled out in principle, whether or not we regard them as 'quasi-causal'. Thus a native English informant who was totally uninterested in politics could probably vouchsafe the information that the point of people going to the polls was to choose a new government. He would not be telling us what he voted for, because it is quite certain that he would not bother to vote at all; what he tells us is what the point, purpose or function of the social institution of voting is. Given the extent to which we explain our behaviour in purposive terms, it would be very surprising if we did not have ideas about what purposes were served by the social institutions which mediate our activities and assign us our roles. We may be utterly wrong in our beliefs about how well they achieve these ends, and we may have next to no idea about how coherent these various ends are; nonetheless, what we offer are, in this everyday sense, functional explanations. If, as many writers have said, functionalism in social science is nothing more than common sense jargonised, we should not be surprised at the prevalence of these explanations. Nonetheless, it certainly casts doubts on the exclusiveness of Winch's categories of causal and rule-guided explanation. Whether functionalism as a type of holistic explanation of social phenomena can achieve more surprising results than this; and whether it can thus force us to change our whole image of social life; these are the questions we now ought to turn to.

169

NOTES

1. E.g. A. C. MacIntyre and D. R. Bell, 'The Idea of a Social Science', 'Supp. Proc. Arist. Soc.' (1967) 95-132; A. R. Louch, 'The Very Idea of a Social Science', 'Inquiry' (1963) 273-86; R. Rudner, 'The Philosophy of Social Science' (Prentice-Hall, 1966) pp. 80-3.

2. Nagel, 'Structure of Science', pp. 433-5.

3. Hempel, 'Philosophy of Natural Science', ch. 8.

4. P. G. Winch, 'Mr Louch's Idea of a Social Science', 'Inquiry' (1964) 202-3.

5. Winch, 'Idea', pp. 89 f.

6. Ibid., p. 89.

7. MacIntyre, in 'Supp. Proc. Arist. Soc.' (1967) 112-13.

8. J. Cazeneuve, 'Levy-Bruhl', 'Int. Encyc. Soc. Sci.' ix 264.

9. W. V. O. Quine, 'Word and Object' (Wiley, 1960) ch. ii, cf. Chomsky, 'Language and Mind', ch. iii.

10. Almond and Coleman, 'Politics of Developing Areas', ch. i.

11. Ibid., pp. 33-45.

12. Berelson et al., 'Voting'.

13. A Campbell et al., 'The American Voter', abridged ed. (Wiley, 1964).

14. H L. A. Hart, 'Prolegomena to the Principles of Punishment', 'Proc. Arist. Soc.' (1959-60) 1-26.

15. See such studies as D. E. Butler and A. King, 'The British General Election of 1964' (Macmillan, 1965) etc.

16. Winch, 'Idea', p. 114.

17. E. Goffman, 'Asylums' (Doubleday, New York, 1961).

18. Ibid., pp. 304-20.

19. K. R. Popper, 'The Open Society and Its Enemies', 4th ed. (Routledge, 1962) ii 93.

20. R. D. Laing, 'The Divided Self', new ed. (Penguin, 1965) chs 1, 2.

21. MacIntyre, in 'Supp. Proc. Arist. Soc.' (1967) 102.

22. Weber, 'Theory', pp. 158 f.

23. P. G. Winch, 'Understanding a Primitive Society', 'Am. Phil. Qtly' i (1964) 309.

24. B. A. O. Williams, 'Tertullian's Paradox', in A. Flew and A. MacIntyre (eds), 'New Essays in Philosophical

Theology', new ed. (S.C.M. Press, 1963).
25. Nadel, 'Theory of Social Structure', p. 50.
26. See e.g. Evans-Pritchard, Nuer Religion (Oxford University Press, 1956) or 'Witchcraft among the Azande' (Oxford University Press, 1951).
27. K. Marx, 'Selected Writings', ed. T. B. Bottomore and M. Rubel (Penguin, 1963) pp. 89-90.
28. S. Freud, 'The Psychopathology of Everyday Life', new ed. (Benn, 1966).
29. J. P. Sartre, 'Being and Nothingness' (Methuen, 1957) pp. 56-86.
30. Winch, 'Idea', pp. 89-90.
31. MacIntyre, in 'Supp. Proc. Arist. Soc.' (1967) 97-105.
32. Winch, 'Idea', pp. 111-16.
33. Rudner, 'Philosophy of Social Science', pp. 6-7.
34. Kuhn, 'Structure of Scientific Revolutions', pp. 68-70.
35. F. Cancian, 'Functionalism', 'Int. Encyc. Soc. Sci.' vi 40-1.
36. Winch, 'Idea', p. 131.
37. Brown, 'Explanation in Social Science', pp. 110-12.

8 Wholes, Parts, Purposes and Functions

The aim of this chapter is to tackle two issues simultaneously, in the hope that each will shed some light on the other. The first issue is that of the relationship between 'holistic' and 'individualistic' explanations in social science, in particular that of evaluating the rival claims firstly that all explanations in terms of 'social wholes' must be reduced to explanations in terms of individual behaviour and its consequences and secondly that explanations in terms of individual goals, aims and purposes are necessarily out of place in social science, which should only concern itself with the behaviour of social, that is holistic, phenomena. (1) The second issue is whether sociology and anthropology employ a special kind of explanation, namely *functional* explanation. The obvious connection between these two problems rests on the following consideration: one major reason why there has been a recurrent enthusiasm for functional explanation in social science has been the perception that in many social groups, both large and small, there are regularities of behaviour which do not seem accounted for by what individuals do or intend; yet these regularities seem to serve some purpose in maintaining the activities of the group as a whole, and tempt us to explain their persistence in terms of their contribution to these goals. (2) Thus we have a form of explanation seemingly irreducible to individual goals, couched in terms of the properties of a social 'whole' of some kind. Conversely, it is precisely because holistic explanations seem so often to be predicated on the 'needs' of a group, and couched in terms of the group's actions in satisfying those needs, that the objection is raised that holistic explanations ascribe purposes, goals and intentions to entities such as clans, families, organisations of a limited sort and even whole societies, which logically cannot possess them; such ascriptions of purpose as *are* permissible are said to be

172

derivative from ascriptions to their proper objects, namely individuals: the tendency to extend them from this kind of object to whole social groups leads in too many cases to a belief in the supernatural purposes which God or Manifest Destiny is said to have in mind for societies. The most determined critic of 'holism', Professor Popper, traces this superstition from its Greek origins in Plato's analogies between the human character and the 'soul' of the state right through to Stalinism and Fascism in the mid-twentieth century. (3)

In view of the vast literature on these topics, our need to select only a few issues is more acute than ever. Accordingly, we shall adopt the following strategy. In view of the argument of the past two chapters about the relations between the agents' accounts of their behaviour and the observers' theories about this behaviour, we begin by exploring the reasons behind the rival claims that holistic explanation or individualistic explanation are alternatively vital or fatal to sociology. I shall argue that this is largely a sham battle in the sense that the fight has been between alternative, not exclusive, accounts of a common sociological enterprise. We can then see that arguments about the 'reduction' of one kind of explanation to another have confused several different senses of reduction, and that provided these are kept distinct, there is not much reason for alarm. Nonetheless, we shall also see that there is one kind of explanation which really would cause serious conceptual difficulties, and that this is teleological explanation, which would raise difficulties in accounting for the relationship between an individual's explanation of his own actions in terms of his own goals or purposes, and the holistic explanation of these actions in terms of the society's goals or purposes. Teleological explanation, it will be argued, is necessarily holistic and causal, and is not — in spite of the claim of current orthodoxies — reducible in principle to explanation by mechanical causation. Functional explanation, to be taken seriously, must put itself forward as a form of teleological explanation; and we shall have to turn to see whether functional explanations of social phenomena are at all common. It may seem that the existence of a school of 'structural-functionalists' makes this inquiry quite ludicrously unnecessary; but it will emerge that not only are non-functionalists sceptical about the existence of genuinely functional explanations, it is also the case that eminent functionalists equally disclaim any distinctiveness for their explanations. In concluding by showing what kind of evidence we should need before functional explanations became acceptable, we can show why this reticence is justified. On the way to this conclusion, enough should emerge about the relationship between what are usually described as functionalist explanations and our everyday accounts of motivation, intention and the like to show that most such explanations easily meet our requirements about their roots in everyday, first-person accounts of our behaviour.

The claims of holism are founded on two main considerations. The first of these is the feeling that sociology ought to have a distinctive subject-matter. It is worth noticing, incidentally, that this is not peculiarly a trait of writers such as Durkheim in the late nineteenth century; (4) it was a consideration for Plato, when he asked what the proper concern of political skill was, and concluded that it had to be the management of the state *as a whole*. (5) It has always seemed that the study of the motives, values, cognitive capacities and skills of individuals belongs to individual psychology, so that it must be the properties of social wholes, not the properties of their parts, which were of concern to sociology. This was the view of Durkheim when he claimed as one of the rules of sociological method that social effects must always be traced to social causes and that the introduction of psychological facts or theory was necessarily an error. (6) The second consideration lies in the phenomena themselves. There are regularities and constancies in the behaviour of groups of people which allow us to talk about groups having a stable structure in spite of a fluctuating membership, and about the existence of social roles which can be filled by different people at different points in time. A particular football team preserves its group identity in spite of changes in personnel; it may preserve something we can call its character over long periods; and we can talk at an even greater level of abstraction, not just about the role structure of a football team, but about the role

174

structures of teams in general. In addition to this kind of constancy, there are those regularities which are not, as it were, part of the evident logic of the group, but which nevertheless arise from its activities, and thus seem to be persistent and non-accidental. In the middle of the nineteenth century, the statistics produced by Quetelet and Guerry concerning criminal acts committed over a period of years gave rise to a good deal of speculation about how such extraordinarily regular figures as theirs could have orginated in the fluctuating and transitory motivation of individual criminals. A common feeling was that it must be in the facts about groups of men, and not in the facts about individuals that the causes of such regularities must lie. (7) Again, the reactions of groups of different sorts to their environment seemed to manifest a steady drive towards equilibrium not apparently recognised or intended by the members of that group. Clans in some societies have been seen to maintain a steady size by amalgamation in periods when they have declined in numbers, and by splitting up when their numbers grew. (8) It looks on the face of it as if this tendency is a holistic property of a self-regulating system, and one to be explained in terms appropriate to such a system. The sociologist is thus concerned to explain the causal relations obtaining between holistic qualities, in discovering for instance what kinds of organisation can coexist and which cannot, what structuring of roles is compatible with what role performances and so on. If causal generalisations of such a kind can be discovered, not resting on evidence about the individual traits of the members of a given group, but on its recurrent roles and the norms governing role performances, then the sociologist and anthropologist seemingly ignores individual psychology, and even ignores the history of any particular group and its members: he moves to the science of social groups. Given the establishment of the laws which we hope will emerge about the nature of groups, we can, as Durkheim wished, go on to explain how an individual will have to behave if it falls to him to play some particular role — or, as the discussion of *anomie* shows, if he is unlucky enough to find himself without a role to fill. But this explanation is essentially derivative.

Now, the above is a weak argument in that it pulls apart individual aims and group results in a misleading — and ultimately artificial — way. For one thing, we ought to distinguish carefully between the constancies arising from role performances, and the regularities which merely happen to result from what people do. As Nadel points out, the language of roles and the norms associated with roles is very much the language of everyday life, that in which people already do describe and explain their actions; and norms are consciously appealed to in explanation and justification by the actors in social situations. (9) If our so-called 'holistic' accounts involve accounting for the structure of groups in terms of roles and their associated norms, then there is no contrast with the explanation of individual behaviour in psychological terms, though there is of course a great difference of emphasis. And it is certainly true that what the group does is quite easily analysed as what the individuals in that group do. If, on the other hand, what the group does is something quite other than what is intended by individuals — as the given murder rate is not intended by anyone, but is a shorthand summary of the results of the various decisions and non-decisions taken by individuals — then there is a good deal of difficulty about ascribing this to the group as something it *does* rather than as a by-product of the things it does. Of course, the point of trying to explain murder rates, or suicide rates, as something which a society does is obvious enough: the aim is to assimilate their production to the production of those things which people consciously aim at producing. But to show that this assimilation is proper, we need to be able to demonstrate conclusively its intended — if only covertly intended — character. (10)

The other fatal ambiguity lies in the notion of the 'individual' in whose life we are said not to be interested. For there is all too frequently a confusion between *actual* and *typical* individuals. It is of course true that at a given point in time a given group is made up of actual — nameable — individuals. Thus the group 'British members of parliament in 1965' contains all those persons who can be said to have been members of parliament in Britain in 1965. Now, in this sense of individual, we can obviously talk about groups without talking about named members of those groups; we can discuss, for example, the qualifications needed to become a British member of parliament, and certainly not mean the

176

qualifications required to become some particular member of parliament. But in *that* sense of individual, it is equally true that individual psychology is not about individuals either, save in the sense that it is the psychological theory applicable to them. We have innumerable expressions which refer to 'individuals', but only as typical individuals. Thus we might say 'The American President cannot be a member of Congress', and here we certainly do not refer to any particular president, nor to any particular congressman; the statement amounts to saying: 'the rule governing the role of president forbids its being filled by anyone concurrently occupying a congressional role' or even 'the American political system is so structured that presidential and congressional roles are mutually exclusive'. And what that equivalence shows is that where 'individuals' are typical, not actual, statements about groups and about individuals are logically interchangeable. (11)

But even this would be to concede too much to 'holism' for the purposes of some 'methodological individualists'. Unfortunately, just as the 'holistic' argument suffered from ambiguities about what kind of individuals were being ruled out, so does methodological individualism suffer from ambiguity about what kinds of individual to rule in. It is much too late in the day to try to legislate as to who is entitled to the umbrella of the doctrine; what is clear is that there are too many people for it to comfortably cover. Moreover, the moral and political arguments with which Professor Popper's attacks on holism have been so much enlivened do not do much to clarify the methodological problems at issue: for Popper, the great wickedness of holism is that it goes along with a Fascist or Communist belief in group destiny, a belief which enables self-styled beneficiaries of this destiny to trample on the rights of the weak with an easier conscience. The difficulty is that while it may be true, as a matter of fact, that believers in destiny are dangerous men, this is not the same thing as explaining what the logic of individualist explanation is. (12) Seemingly, the positive doctrine is that we should explain the actions of particular people in terms of the 'logic of the situation'; that is, when faced with Caesar at the Rubicon, we explain his decision to cross over into Italy in terms of the logic of the situation of an ambitious man

177

with an army at his back and unprepared enemies in front of him; and the actions of whole groups of people should be explained in terms of the outcomes of the actions undertaken by the individuals who go to compose those groups. Now, it is at once clear that the term 'individual' is doing too much work. So far as the explanation of the actions of named individuals is concerned, as when we explain Julius Caesar's actions, the account is in outline so obviously right as to be quite unexceptionable; even someone who wished to account more 'ultimately' for Caesar's actions in terms of their place in some historical process would still agree that we begin by explaining how, being what he was and where he was, the logical thing to do was what he did. But it is the status of explanations of recurrent social phenomena which present more interesting problems. For instance, what is the sense in which we explain economic phenomena by way of individuals? Certainly, we do not usually want to know about named individual shopkeepers or named individual consumers — that is, we do not primarily want to know about such people, though we can of course apply such economic theory as we possess to explaining their activities, as when we might be writing a biography of Carnegie or Rockefeller, and have to explain why they acted as they did, and why their moves were successful in achieving their aims. Normally it is agreed, economics is not about individuals in this sense; in fact when it is said to rest on what we know about individuals' behaviour at all, this is always agreed to be the behaviour of 'typical' individuals in a certain kind of situation, namely the market situation. It is in this sense that J. W. N. Watkins, for example, explains his adherence to the tenets of method-ological individualism, and there is no doubt that such an account makes excellent sense of both classical and Keynesian economics. (13) But it has the disturbing effect of closing the logical gap between institutional and individual oriented explanations — as we saw before. The 'logic of the situation' to the typical individual in an economic context covers to all intents and purposes exactly the same ground as the notions of norm and role outlined above. A typical individual is simply anyone happening to occupy a role, and the logic of the situation is what is laid down by the norms governing that role. The distinction marked here between wholes and parts is no more significant than that marked by talking of the play and its *dramatis personae*; in this sense, the *dramatis personae* are individuals, and they outline the parts which any particular and actual person who takes part in a particular performance of the play will have to fill. But we can talk about the play without talking about actual performances, and we can talk about the parts without talking about the way in which particular actors play those parts. Moreover, we can concentrate on some individual part and follow its course through the play. So what we are saying is that the argument between holists and individualists is no more to the point in principle than is a debate about whether in principle to study the play or its parts: they are two sides of the same activity. Thus we cannot be surprised that two such writers as Weber and Durkheim turn out in the end to be doing much more nearly identical things than their initial methodological claims would lead us to expect. Proof of the case we have argued could be obtained exhaustingly in the same way it was obtained in the periodical literature on this issue: Professors Goldstein and Watkins ended their debate after six years less certain than ever what it had been about. (14)

What, in part, underlies this strange state of affairs is an ambiguity in the kinds of 'reduction' that have been proclaimed sometimes as goal and sometimes as objects of anathema. In view of the complexity of the topic, this is not surprising; it does, however, mean that here we shall have to concentrate on two or three points only, and leave the rest to extrapolation. The first kind of reduction argued over is, as we mentioned above, the reduction of sociological generalisations to psychological ones. The characteristic muddle here is to suppose that if the truth of sociological statements can be shown to depend on the truth of psychological statements this means that the former are logically equivalent to the latter, i.e. can be reduced to the latter. Thus in his essay on 'Bringing Men Back In' George Homans argues that general sociological theory relies on the existence of psychological theory, and infers that sociological explanation thus employs psychological generalisations, and hence that it is the same thing as psychological explanation. (15) Now, this is muddled in the following sense; the fact that certain kinds of socio-

179

logical generalisation would not be true if there were not various corresponding truths of psychology simply cannot show that the meaning of the one kind of proposition is identical with that of the other. We saw earlier that this kind of argument would not hold up for the proposed 'reduction' of psychological to physiological phenomena; and of course it is no more plausible here. Suppose that the proffered holistic sociological statement is one to the effect that a capitalist economic system needs an adequately enforced normative structure of universalistic and achievement oriented attitudes, and that capitalism's continued existence in the United States can be explained in terms of this need of the system being met. The psychological generalisations corresponding to such an explanation would not make mention of such things as the 'needs' of the 'system' but would presumably refer to the impossibility of an individual having the disposition to do those things which are essential to capitalist behaviour unless he also has the various goals and aims which are summed up as his possessing universalistic values and being achievement oriented. The sociological truth — if it *is* one — rests on, but is not identical with, the psychological truths — if they *are* such. A second kind of fear which sometimes seems to assail sociologists is that sociology will be reduced to history, in the sense that sociological generalisations will be reduced to genetic accounts of the origins of some institution or other. Indeed, it has been said that one of the virtues of 'functionalism' is that when we concentrate on the functions of, say, incest taboos, we are more certain to avoid being misled into asking the non-sociological question of how incest taboos originated, either in some particular society, or in all the societies in which they appear. (16) But this worry is obviously pretty groundless, though it points to something important. Its groundlessness is simply that there is plenty of room both for the discovery of generalisations and their application to particular historical sequences of events — in other words that there is plenty of room both for sociological generalisation and historical application of such generalisation. But it is clearly important that we should distinguish between the statement of generalisations, and their application in the explanation of particular events; or to put it more simply, we ought always to be clear *what* we are

180

trying to explain. Do we want to know what occasioned the acceptance of an incest taboo in this particular society; or do we want to know what, given that there already exists an incest taboo in that society, makes people go on adhering to it; or do we want to know if there are general causes disposing all societies to produce something resembling the incest taboo in some respect? All these are possible questions, but they need vastly different kinds of evidence if they are to be satisfactorily answered. It is plain that we can go on asking very different kinds of question, so long as we are clear which kind we are asking on any particular occasion. In particular, it is obviously vital to recall that the explanation of some particular event requires us to be able to bring to bear on it a variety of generalisations, but that this explanation does not render these generalisations proven. Fears that the proper subject-matter of sociology might vanish are obviously silly; to worry over whether a book like Smelser's 'Social Change in the Industrial Revolution' (17) is history or sociology is plainly wrong — insofar as it applies sociological insights to the explanation of historical events it makes good history, and insofar as it uses the evidence of these events to illuminate sociological theory, it makes good sociology. The final kind of reduction which worries students more than it ought is more or less 'metaphysical', for it is the old problem of whether and in what sense wholes can be said to be more than the sum of their parts. That a whole is not *merely* the sum of its parts is clear as soon as one reflects on the difference between a motor which is assembled and ready to run and a motor which is stacked in components on a shelf; sociologically, the difference is equally valid if one thinks of the difference between an army organised and equipped and that same army, perhaps still equipped, but confused by mistaken orders. The same parts form two wholes of very different properties depending on how they are put together; and this certainly means that there are 'holistic' or structural properties which can sensibly be said to belong to the whole and not to any of the parts. But it is equally true that a whole is no more than the sum of its parts in the sense that if we dismantle a motor what we are left with is simply the parts of that motor, not them and some mysterious property which formerly held the whole thing together. And if we can

181

borrow a little further from the example of the motor, we can reinforce our earlier argument that the debate about the relative merits of talking about wholes and parts was misdirected. For here also, we can equally well talk of either. We can talk of the 'parts' of a motor in typical terms, terms which refer only to the jobs they do in the process of converting fuel into energy at the flywheel — words like 'valve' are very obviously functional terms, used in such a connection. And, of course, we can talk about the way in which particular parts do the jobs that have to be done — and in so doing we call on the evidence of such sciences as metallurgy to tell us how well a valve made of a given metal would perform, for example. (18) No more in this case than any other is reduction a serious issue: metallurgy underpins, but is not identical with mechanical engineering, much as psychology underpins but is not identical with sociology.

But now we ought to turn to one kind of holistic explanation which would cause us conceptual difficulties if it were seriously advanced — and this is functional explanation. It is a commonplace in the literature that the term 'function' is variously used, and almost all discussions list several such uses. (19) The point of the listing is simple enough; 'function' is generally synonymous with 'job' or 'purpose' or 'point', and is thus employed properly either when we have purposive action to explain, or else when we have events dependent upon purposive action. Thus if we are discussing the functions of a good secretary, we almost certainly mean the jobs which whoever employs the secretary wants her to perform; when we refer to the function of a switch on an instrument panel we refer to the job which it has been designed by us or someone else to do — in this sense, an enormous amount of human vocabulary is functional, simply because a great part of our environment has been moulded by human beings for human purposes; words like 'knife', 'hammer' and the like are functional words, since they refer to the purposes for which these objects are commonly used; and many social labels equally refer to the jobs which people are employed in — 'soldier', 'clerk' whatever it may be. If in sociological explanation nothing had ever been meant more than that people had been employed, or that institutions had been designed — or that in the opinion

182

of the observer they *ought* to be employed, or *ought* to be designed — for certain purposes, then references to function would have been quite harmless. It is true that only references to people's actual purposes would actually have any explanatory power — people would be explained as behaving the way they did because they had been employed to behave that way, and were carrying out their instructions, or institutions would be explained as having the effects they did because people had set them up to bring about precisely those effects, and they had succeeded. It is also true that no one would have felt any alarm about such explanations, since the intentions and the standing purposes of human beings are quite acceptable causal antecedents of events. Explanations in terms of the goals which people and institutions *ought* to be achieving are, of course, non-starters, and universally recognised as such: to say that we *ought* to do something does not explain why we do — or do not do — it. To explain our acts or abstentions, we should have to refer again to people's beliefs about what they ought to do, and this is again to refer to their intentions. (20)

The problem about functional explanation now becomes clear: it is that we are left to explain in what sense functional explanations can be in place if we are *not* talking about deliberate human contrivance or results of such contrivance. In what sense can we *explain* the occurrence of some event(s) by the invocation of function? It is clear that the right answer to this question is that functional explanations are only in place where an event or a series of events is explained by showing that it was required for some goal or other, *and* that this fact is a sufficient condition of the event's occurrence. In other words, teleological explanation is what we are concerned with. Now, this alone is quite enough to frighten away many sociologists who believe that teleological explanation is necessarily fallacious, in that it involves making effects precede their causes; it is this which leads Marion Levy, a noted structural-functionalist, to insist that he is not 'committing teleology'. (21) However, it is impossible to assail the proposition that functional explanation is teleological explanation; and thus it follows that non-teleological explanation is also non-functional explanation. If the teleology on which all talk of functions depends is not that

183

of human purposes, and if functionalists refuse to allow any other kind of purposes into the argument, the functionalists do not give functional explanations at all. This conclusion is by no means so shocking as it might at first sight appear; it is indeed a conclusion to which more than one functionalist has recently come. (22)

Let us see why this is so. To explain an event teleologically is to explain its occurrence on the grounds that it is contributory to a goal or end-state, and to imply one essential thing — that the goal or end-state is *sought* or *maintained* by the system in which the event takes place. What this last requirement amounts to is that the system in question has to possess some kind of negative feed-back characteristics, in the sense that a movement away from its goal is compensated for by some kind of correcting mechanism. In recent years, the engineering of such goal-directed systems has been one of the most fertile branches of engineering, and hence there has been a great deal of interest in the theory of self-regulating mechanisms and their role as models for much of human and animal behaviour. But the humble central heating system illustrates perfectly adequately for our needs what is involved in such a system, and what the role of functional explanation is in this context. Such a system is usually set to maintain a steady temperature, say 65 °F; it contains a thermostat, a device that operates a throttle controlling the supply of fuel to the boiler, such that when the temperature falls much below 65 °F the supply of fuel to the burner is increased, and when the temperature rises above 65 °F the supply is decreased. The important point about this system is that the *simplest* causal law governing its behaviour is one which relates the events taking place — increases and decreases of fuel supplied — to the achievement of an end-state; in other words, we say that fuel is supplied in such quantities as will tend to maintain the temperature at 65°F; fuel is added in order to bring the temperature up, or diminished in order to bring the temperature down — and the use of synonyms for *in order to* shows that it is a teleological explanation at issue. (23)

That this suggestion of goal-directedness is essential to the explanation is evident from the consideration of Professors Hempel (24) and Nagel's (25) mistakes about it. On their

184

analysis, to say 'X occurs for the sake of Y' is to say either that X is a sufficient or else that it is a necessary condition for Y. That is, either we are saying X will bring about Y, or else we are saying that Y will not occur without X. This means that we are simply uttering in misleading language causal explanations of a mechanical kind; for if X is a sufficient condition of Y, it is the occurrence of Y that we are explaining by adducing the occurrence of X as its cause; on the other hand, if X is only a necessary condition of Y, then we are explaining the occurrence of X, but only by pointing to the occurrence of Y — and not as the cause of X either, but simply on the grounds that since Y could not occur without X, its occurrence means that X must have occurred. But it is evident at a glance that these are not equivalents at all. For one thing, the direction of causal implication is quite wrong; if we say X causes Y, the implication is that an alteration in X will cause an alteration in Y, but where we assert that X occurs for the sake of Y, the implication is reversed, namely that an alteration in Y will bring about an alteration in X. (26) The truth of this can be seen in the case of the central heating system — if we want to save fuel, we lower the temperature we set out to achieve, i.e. we alter the end-state, and by altering the goal, we alter the behaviour of the system. Equally, the proffered reformulation asserts, what the original explanation did not, that the goal was achieved, for it asserts that X brings about Y; but it may well be the case that X does not. Suppose the weather is cold, or the fuel of poor quality; it may be the case that an increase of fuel supplied to the burner does not succeed in getting the temperature up to 65 °F. It still remains true that the function of the increase was to bring about this result. And the third point is that the focus of interest is quite wrong in the translation; *we* want to explain the occurrence of X, *it* explains the occurrence of Y. Hempel's formulation in terms of the analysis of X as a necessary condition of Y does no better. He says that to explain X's occurrence by the occurrence of Y is a mistake, where X is thought of as a sufficient condition of Y — and that is certainly true, *except* where X and Y are parts of a self-regulating process, a condition which Hempel steadfastly refuses to allow to make any difference. It is for this reason that Hempel argues that if X is to be explained by Y, it must be because X is a necessary condition of Y. There is some plausibility in this argument: we do certainly think of antecedents as necessary conditions of goals, and that they are brought about accordingly, as when we say that more fuel *had to be* fed to the burner to bring the temperature up. And as with necessary conditions, we are happy to infer backwards from the increase in warmth to there having been an adequate increase in fuel supplied. But what remains implied in our teleological explanation, and omitted from Hempel's reformulation, is that the fact that X is necessary for Y is part of the explanation of the occurrence of X; and this points to the fatal flaw in Hempel's translation: it is not a blow to the teleological explanation of the occurrence of X that Y is never attained, but it is fatal to an explanation of X by way of its being a necessary condition of Y. Certainly we can say, *if* Y occurs, that X as one of its necessary conditions must also have occurred; but if Y does not occur, no such inference is possible. But if X occurred, and Y did not, we can still explain X's occurrence as needed by Y — saying that it is this which explains X's occurrence just is what is involved in saying that we are dealing with a goal-directed system. And it is thus clear that teleological explanation is not mechanical explanation phrased peculiarly, but a different kind of explanation. (27)

Nonetheless, this does not mean that we ought necessarily to be content with teleological laws and teleological explanations; indeed, everything I have said so far about our inclination to look for hidden mechanisms and to inquire into the workings of systems suggests that teleological explanations are very much our first thoughts, not our last. In the case of our central heating system, it is clear that we can talk about the mechanical causal connections between the parts just as readily as we can talk about the goal-seeking activities of the whole system. We can explain the end-state in terms of the way a switch is set in the control box, and we can explain quite simply how increases and decreases in temperature turn the switch on or off; a simple system contains little more than a pump, a switch and a thermally sensitive contact, so we can explain the goal-seeking of the system in the mechanical terms of the pump being switched on or off at various temperatures, and the fuel flowing in greater or lesser quantities in consequence. In this sense, our teleological laws are not the most basic laws of the system, for underlying our account of the behaviour of the whole, there is an account of mechanical causal connections. It is this which really motivates the analyses of Hempel and Nagel, for they are less concerned to offer an analysis of teleological statements than to insist that all teleologically explained systems can also be explained in mechanical terms, a different and more contentious matter which happily does not occupy us here. (28)

The advantage of the teleological laws in the above example rested in their greater simplicity in explaining the way the system operated when successful; on the other hand, they would be of much less explanatory value if something were to go wrong with the system so that it was no longer a functioning whole. For the repair man, the connections which matter are the mechanical, step by step connections from thermostat to pump to burner. And this now raises the issues for functionalism in sociology or anthropology. Is functionalism committed to saying that societies are systems with negative feedback properties which maintain or try to maintain some kind of end-state — and how could functionalists know they were right to say this? If functionalism is thus committed, are societies such that teleological or functional explanations are irreducible or reducible — i.e. are societies such that it is only possible to explain them *at all* in teleological terms, or are teleological laws no more than the simplest kind of causal laws we have to explain their behaviour with? If it is said that they are the simplest laws, but not irreducible, how credible is this? But if it is said that they are irreducible, what is the relationship between what individuals say about their behaviour, and the functional explanation of that behaviour?

Since there is nothing resembling unanimity about the answers to be given to these questions, we cannot do more than show what some of the difficulties are. An obvious point of departure is Malinowski's brand of functionalism (29) — though it ought to be remembered how much hostility his self-assumed leadership of the 'functionalist school' aroused in other functionalists. Malinowski

187

distinguishes between the 'charter' and the 'functions' of institutions. The charter covers the avowed goals of the institutions and its participants, and functions are thus left to cover something other than conscious intentions — so that we are apparently outside the area of what we saw as quite unproblematic. But as every critic of Malinowski has said, at this point everything becomes unclear. For Malinowski veers between regarding institutions as functional-for-individuals and regarding them as functional-for-society-as-a-whole; and he does not take the plunge into what really would be teleological explanation, the assertion that certain kinds of behaviour appeared *in order to* satisfy societal needs. The result is that Malinowski faces several, not very similar problems. For if the claim is that institutions are functional for individuals, this amounts to no more than saying that they have results which people like, even though these results are not the stated motives for the individuals' behaviour — it does not explain the origin or the continuation of the institutions as it stands. Any problems about using the fact as part of an explanation are nothing to do with problems of teleological explanation; for — if we are going to explain either the origin or continuation of, say, religious practices in terms of the covert satisfactions of individuals — our explanation will be couched in terms of people's choices and goals and intentions; and our problems will be concerned with such notions as 'unconscious' wishes, or with identifying the 'basic human needs' which people are said to be satisfying. On the other hand, when we claim that religious rituals are functional for social adaptation, we do have troubles in plenty. We may simply mean that as a matter of fact religious ritual has certain effects on the extent to which people feel at ease in society or some such thing; but this is not to explain religious ritual, merely to talk about its effects; and it says nothing as to its 'functions'. In Malinowski's case, the argument tended to be trivialised in one of two directions. Either it was assumed that religious rituals would not have kept going unless they were useful in some way or other, so the assumption of social needs simply becomes a catch-all for whatever it is that keeps religious ritual going in a community; or alternatively, the goal of system adaptation or whatever it is becomes so loosely defined that every element

188

in the status quo becomes functional, just because it *is* an element in the status quo, and in this quite tautological sense necessary to it. Moreover, none of this shows — what is the crucial thing to be able to show — that societies have such goals as require them to generate religious rituals or their equivalent, independently of what particular beliefs are held by individuals. To show this, we should be able to show (*a*) what goal religion serves, (*b*) that wherever religion declines, some other forms of behaviour functionally equivalent to it appear, (*c*) that there is a process of feedback between the inability of the social system to meet whatever goal it is and its developing the substitute for religion. We might add the requirement (*d*) that such an explanation should be the simplest available. The consensus among social theorists is that not merely does Malinowski fail to meet such requirements, but that even the most careful attempts since his day fare little better. (30)

The same troubles plague more recent work. There is a justly famous essay by Robert Merton on 'Manifest and Latent Functions' in which he repeats practically all of Malinowski's errors. (31) Once he has rejected teleological explanation as logically unsound, he has no room to regard 'manifest functions' as anything other than intended useful consequences, and 'latent functions' as unintended useful consequences. The only reason that he can have for using the expression 'latent function' is that it emphasises that the good results he is looking at are not those which gratify the actors, but those which gratify other people. For example, Merton refers to the latent functions of machine politics, and shows, both interestingly and convincingly, that the corrupt politics of city-bossism which offend all good liberal thinkers actually achieved all kinds of useful results in acclimatising immigrants to American life at a time when their welfare certainly would not have been looked after by a non-existent welfare state. (32) This is an important insight, and it explains many things — such as the inability of the Democratic party to clean up machine politics; it would be folly to expect the beneficiaries of machine politics who provide the Democrat rank and file vote to go out and smash the source of their own good fortune. It is also a useful warning that unless we want people to suffer a good deal of misery, it is no

189

use setting out simply to eliminate corruption without creating welfare services that will serve the same purposes. But none of this amounts to functionally explaining anything at all. It certainly does not set out to explain why city bosses appeared — though it would suggest some explanations; at most it is an explanation of why city bosses will be hard to remove, not couched in functional terms at all, but in terms of the benefits which city-bossism confers on the people who would have to be persuaded to remove it, and this is an explanation couched in the ordinary idiom of rewards and costs to individuals. We might, just, use the explanation as evidence of self-regulating behaviour on the part of 'the American political system' if we were prepared to argue that the system goal of low levels of societal conflict had spawned the adaptive mechanism of the city boss. But this would offend rather drastically against our requirement that the teleological explanation should be the simplest explanation available, since it would be much harder to establish this explanation in any satisfactory form than it would be to establish the so to speak mechanical underpinning that the rewards available to city bosses and their clients were such as to provide entrepreneurial openings which vigorous and not too scrupulous men could step into and fill, and that their doing this had such useful side effects for other people that these latter had no good reason to intervene to suppress corruption. Unlike the central heating system, in which we begin with the system as the most easily understood unit, and its purposes and goals laid down by ourselves in advance, here we begin with an intimate causal knowledge of the behaviour of the 'parts'. It seems perverse to ignore the fact. And indeed in Merton's work, the term 'function' serves no purpose at all, save to make a nod to those who believe in the autonomy of sociology, and to decorate the word 'consequences', indicating that Merton was impressed with the unlooked-for goodness of the consequences of much social life in America. And it is this equation of 'function' with 'good consequence:' which dominates the sociological literature of recent years, as a glance at such a journal as 'The American Sociological Review' illustrates: articles on such topics as 'Some Social Functions of Ignorance' turn out to be articles on 'Some Unthought-of Good Effects that Ignorance

190

Produces for Almost Everyone'. The reader who doubts this is recommended to verify it for himself. (33)

A recognition of the difficulties, and a sophisticated response to them is met with in Talcott Parsons's methodological views. For Parsons's view is that what he terms structural-functional analysis is a method of second best. (34) The ideal would be a mathematised social science whose logical structure was analogous to that of analytical mechanics: states of the system at any given time, and changes in those states could be analysed by the same kind of simultaneous equation employed by the physicist in the analysis of physical systems. This goal, however, is far out of reach, and we must for the time being employ functional analysis, by looking at social systems as wholes and seeing what their elements are, and how these elements contribute to the whole. This certainly indicates that Parsons expects teleological or functional laws to be the most available causal laws of social life, and that he holds that they are not irreducible; this certainly is what a functionalist ought on our earlier account to be committed to. The obvious analogy on which such a position rests is the organic analogy: there we may begin with a functional analysis of the various systems and sub-systems which go to make up an organism, while still hoping that in the end we shall be able to proffer a physico -chemical analysis of the various causal mechanisms by which the organism operates. It is not surprising that Parsons himself appeals to precisely such an analogy.

But its force is not great. In the case of organisms, it is clear that there are very obvious, often simple feedback processes which are immediately observed, and in our own cases experienced; and hence it is so to speak an immediate observation that goal-directed activities are occurring. In social life, this situation hardly seems to hold good. Of course, it would be madness to deny that social life is full of goal-directed activities: there are innumerable institutions contrived and manned for various purposes, seeking goals of one kind and another; there are innumerable individual actors adapting their actions to the various goals they are set on achieving. In all this, social life is plainly full of goal-directed activity. But what of purposes which are not reducible to those of people, what kinds of 'goals' can the social system

191

be said to be pursuing, what end-states is it trying to maintain, and within what limits? There is no need here for us to argue the extreme case that such questions cannot be informatively answered: textbooks on sociological theory are rightly concerned with the substantive answers that are returned to such queries. All that is appropriate for the philosophical elucidation of the problem is to point out that if the claim for functionalist explanation is that it is simpler than the alternatives, this claim is enormously weakened by the fact that there is so little agreement on the answers to these questions, and by the obvious inability to identify the processes of feedback, correction and stabilisation. In the one area where 'system' has always been obvious, and processes of feedback identifable, namely economics, no one would dream of employing functional explanations — we do not, for instance, believe that a price drops in order to clear the market of a glut; we know that the mechanism at work is one which involves the wishes of sellers to get something for their wares, and it is on this that our explanations are founded. Why should not this be the model, rather than the model of the organism? (35)

Curiously enough, all the strictures of the previous pages are not regarded as such by one of the leading exponents of structural-functional analysis, Professor Marion Levy. In the 'International Encyclopedia of Social Science', Levy claims that the methods of structural functionalism are only those of science generally. (36) In all sciences we ask how one thing is related to another, how one event brings about another, what patterns of events are discernible. Levy dismisses teleological explanation as inherently improper, and agrees that any form of functional explanation must be couched in terms of sufficient and necessary conditions. Now at this point, the only reasonable response would be to drop the term 'functional' from our vocabulary altogether, and talk simply of explanation. But a hint as to Levy's reluctance to do this emerges when he discusses what he calls 'functional prerequisites', and in so doing shows how powerful is the image of 'a job to be done' which we mentioned earlier. For Levy characterises functionalists as being concerned to take a social system as a going concern and to ask of it what kind of jobs have to be done if it is to go on as a going concern; and

192

he rightly distinguishes this question from another which also much interests functionalists, namely what jobs have to be done if such a concern is to be started up — for obviously what has to be done to keep an industrialised society going is very different from what has to be done to get a backward country industrialised in the first place. But, to repeat our complaint, none of this rests on anything we could describe as functional *explanation*; if the word functional were dropped and we talked only of prerequisites we should be no worse off than at present. If what we want to know is what kinds of beliefs, values, technical information and social organisation people have to have if they are to launch an industrial revolution, we have enough of a problem on our hands without plunging it into verbal obscurity.

But if the scepticism of the past pages is warranted, one last task remains, that of explaining why we regard societies as systems and why we slip so easily into talking about the needs of such systems, and the tasks that confront them. The explanation is in a sense strikingly simple. It is a necessary truth that self-regulating systems have numerous analogies with societies, for the notion of self-regulation is initially derived from the paradigm of human beings organising themselves in groups, laying down rules to be followed, and modifying the instructions later in the light of experience. Objects other than groups of men are regarded as systems by analogy with such groups; so it is scarcely to be wondered at that such notions as information feedback and flexible control should be at home in social life, when that was the source from which they were initially taken. To apply cybernetics to the understanding of society is almost a joke, when it is remembered that the term 'cybernetics' comes from the word which designated a human controller. (37) In this sense the political scientists who earnestly offer us a system or functionalist analysis of political life can plausibly be accused of dressing up the familiar in unfamiliar language.

To be impressed by functionalist claims it is probably necessary to be impressed by the apparently organic nature of social life, and this means to be impressed by a seeming wisdom in the whole that does not stem from any of its members singly. There are signs that Durkheim thought we should uncover such a collective intelligence informing social

193

life; though the notion of collective representations may not have to bear so much weight. (38) But this does raise a logical problem. We might, for instance, talk in teleological terms about society adapting to changed conditions, say that we accounted for an increase in popular education in the late nineteenth century in terms of the need to reduce the number of people competing for jobs in a stagnant economy. This is teleological in the sense that we explain current changes as produced to avoid future dangers. But we can unpick the explanation in simple ways: what we mean by the need to reduce competition can be analysed out into individual fears of coming hardship, with lower rewards for workers, so that parents were more willing than before to let children stay at school, and employers put less pressure on them to start work early. In this way we unpick teleological explanations into intentionally based ones. Now, what we should have to believe if we were really impressed with organic analogies is that we could not always do this; and to believe this would be to believe that the relation of individuals to the social organism was exactly like that of the organs of an animal to the whole animal. And this is a very odd belief for anyone to hold. It is conceivable, though only barely, that some evidence could begin to make us believe that this relationship really does characterise the dealings between individuals and their societies; it is true that some theorists showed signs of hoping that it could be made to hold. But it is surely clear that there is absolutely no reason to suppose such evidence will appear, or that such aims are well-founded. Homans's plea to 'bring men back in' is hardly needed, for without a perverse effort of the imagination, it is difficult to lose sight of them in the first place; the weaknesses of the functionalist attempt to do so show us just how difficult.

NOTES

1. Contrast Popper, 'Open Society', ii 91 with Durkheim, 'Rules', ch. i.
2. Homans, 'The Human Group', pp. 268-72.
3. Popper, 'Open Society', and see 'Poverty' dedication.

4. Durkheim, 'Rules', pp. xxvii-lviii.

5. Plato, 'The Republic', ed. F. M. Cornford (Oxford University Press) pp. 40-140.

6. Durkheim, 'Rules', p. 104.

7. Radzinowicz, 'Ideology and Crime', ch. 2.

8. Nadel, 'Theory of Social Structure', p. 18.

9. Ibid., p. 20.

10. Radzinowicz, 'Ideology and Crime', pp. 72-4.

11. S. M. Lukes, 'Methodological Individualism Reconsidered', 'Brit. Jnl of Soc.' (June 1968) 119-22.

12. Popper, 'Open Society', ii 269-80.

13. J. W. N. Watkins, 'Brit. Jnl for Phil. Sci.' (1952-3) 34-6.

14. See J. Goldstein, 'Brit. Jnl for Phil. Sci.' (1959) 240-1 and Watkins, ibid., 242-4.

15. Homans, 'Amer. Soc. Rev.' (1964) 815-18.

16. K. Davis, 'Amer. Soc. Rev.' (1959) 768-71.

17. N. Smelser, 'Social Change in the Industrial Revolution' (Routledge, 1959).

18. J. Fodor, in M. Brodbeck (ed.), 'Readings in the Philosophy of Social Science' (Collier-Macmillan, 1968) pp. 236-8.

19. Rudner, 'Philosophy of Social Science', pp. 106-7.

20. Homans, 'Amer. Soc. Rev.' (1964) 816-18.

21. M. Levy, 'Functionalism', 'Int. Encyc. Soc. Sci.' vi 21 ff.

22. Ibid., p. 22.

23. R. B. Braithwaite, 'Scientific Explanation' (Cambridge University Press, 1953) pp. 322 ff.

24. C. G. Hempel, 'The Logic of Functional Analysis', in 'Symposium on Sociological Theory', pp. 282-4.

25. E. Nagel, 'Teleological Explanation and Teleological Systems', in H. Feigl and M. Brodbeck (eds), 'Readings in the Philosophy of Science' (Appleton-Century-Crofts, New York, 1953) pp. 537-58.

26. Taylor, 'Explanation of Behaviour', pp. 10-17.

27. Ibid., pp. 17-21.

28. But see ibid., ch. i generally.

29. J. Rex, 'Key Problems of Sociological Theory', 2nd ed. (Routledge, 1963) pp. 67 ff.

30. Cancian, in 'Int. Encyc. Soc. Sci.' vi 30-4.

31. R. K. Merton, 'Social Theory and Social Structure', rev. ed. (Free Press, Chicago, 1957) ch. iii.

32. F. Greenstein, 'The American Party System and the American People' (Prentice-Hall, 1963) pp. 38-41.

33. W. E. Moore and E. E. Tumin, 'Some Social Functions of Ignorance', 'Amer. Soc. Rev.' (1949) 787-95.

34. Parsons, 'Essays in Sociological Theory', pp. 215-18.

35. Brown, 'Explanation in Social Science', p. 131.

36. Levy, in 'Int. Encyc. Soc. Sci.' vi 22.

37. 'Cybernetics', 'Oxford English Dictionary'.

38. Durkheim, 'Rules', ch. iii.

9 Prediction as a Goal of
   Social Science

Up to this point, we have examined the two major and rival theses regarding the nature of the social sciences that were outlined in the opening chapter of this book. We have seen that although there are some deeply disturbing anomalies in the claim that there are *no* important differences between the human sciences and the natural sciences, these anomalies do not eliminate inquiries into the causes and effects of social activities, and they do not much impinge on our initial account of satisfactory causal explanation. In these two last chapters, we shall try to justify the concerns of the third thesis we mentioned, that which stresses the social causes and effects of social theory. In this chapter we shall explore the implications of the long-standing view that the aim of developed social science is to produce the prediction of large-scale social changes, and that its maturity as science can be estimated by the yield of such predictions; in the final chapter we shall raise some of the problems of 'objectivity' in the social sciences, and briefly discuss the topic of ideology. What provides a common link between these chapters is the fact that the social sciences are preeminently 'policy sciences'; (1) that is, they have been developed by and for men who have wanted to use the knowledge they could gain to bring about changes of one or another kind. Equally importantly, they may well have policy effects, even where they are not developed for policy purposes — just as any other science may spawn technologically relevant side-effects, though research was not initiated for technological reasons. For in the case of the social sciences, one important consideration is that how people act in society depends on what they believe about society: if they come to believe a different story, they will also come to behave differently. This fact was as well-known by Burke, who as a conservative wished to limit social speculation, as by Marx, who as a revolutionary wished to harness it to the cause of revolution.

In this chapter then, we shall consider three issues. The first is the validity of the claim that explanation and prediction are logically identical, merely two faces of the same knowledge, with the apparent implication that successful explanation must entail an increased ability to predict future events. The second problem begins at this point, for it is that of the feasibility in principle of projects for large-scale sociological prediction; and the final question again stems from this problem, for — in the light of such current phenomena as committees set up to predict what will happen over the next thirty years — we must distinguish between law-based and trend-based predictions, and evaluate Professor Popper's claim that the neglect of this distinction has been fatal to much sociology. (2) In the course of discussing these issues, we shall be able to see rather further than before into the distinction between logical and methodological considerations, and also to see how these are — and are not — related to substantial claims about the real world.

The claim that explanation and prediction are logically 'isomorphic' — that is, the claim that they are formally identical — rests essentially on a simple logical point, made earlier in our account of deductive explanation. According to the deductive view of explanation, as we then described it, explanations when completely spelled out are deductive arguments. To explain a particular occurrence, we have to be able to deduce the statement that this occurrence took place as and when it did from the general law covering that class of case together with some statement(s) about the holding of the initial conditions for the occurrence. In the terminology of causal connection, we assert the dependence of the event to be explained on its causal antecedents in the light of an underlying causal generalisation. Thus we could explain the way in which Thomas Jones voted in the British general election of 1966 by pointing to the fact that he had been a staunch supporter of the National Union of Mineworkers for the past thirty years. We know, now, that such an account is not straightforwardly an explanation, by the rigorous standards of such 'deductivists' as Professor Hempel: it is rather an 'explanation sketch', (3) the outlines of what could, were there any chance of people being misled, be trans-

198

formed into a 'complete' explanation. Moreover, we also know by now that to cite membership of the N.U.M. as a *causal* antecedent is subject to the qualifications we made about the role of reasons as the causes of human action — membership of the N.U.M. is a shorthand indication of the kind of reasons for voting which will move Thomas Jones. Still, these *are* only qualifications; and the important point remains the deductive mould into which we can put such explanations. And in the case of this explanation, there is no difficulty about doing just that. With the backing generalisation that 'All staunch, long-standing members of the N.U.M. vote Labour' and the initial condition that 'Thomas Jones is a staunch, long-standing member of the N.U.M.' we can infer that 'Thomas Jones votes Labour'. The key element in all this is the backing generalisation, for it is on this that the identity of explanation and prediction hangs. It will be recalled from our earlier discussion that a general statement of the form 'All X are Y' is not to be analysed as a conjunction of singular statements about all the Xs which happen also to be Ys, but is rather to be read as a hypothetical statement to the effect that 'If anything is an X, then it is a Y', and as such a statement it is said to be strictly speaking tenseless, and to have no particular spatio-temporal reference. Thus 'All long-standing, staunch members of the N.U.M. vote Labour' is to be read as 'If there is someone who is a staunch, long-standing member of the N.U.M., then he votes Labour'; and as we saw, the formulation of such statements in the predicate calculus as statements of the form $(x) (Fx \rightarrow Gx)$ is designed to do justice to the logical structure hidden beneath the grammatical surface. It is important to be clear about how we read a symbol such as ' $\rightarrow$ ', as 'if . . . then'; for it is equally about past, present, future and hypothetical cases, so that 'All X are Y' is to be read not just as 'If anything is an X it is also a Y', but equally as 'If anything was an X, then it was also a Y', 'If anything is (in future) an X, it will be a Y', 'If anything were to be an X, then it would be a Y'. (4) This, it is plain, means that not merely are explanation and prediction logically isomorphic, but so equally are explanation and retrodiction, and explanation and hypothetical prediction. That is to say that the generalisation about the relationship between membership of the N.U.M. and voting

Labour equally governs such statements as 'Thomas Evans was a long-standing and staunch member of the N.U.M., so he must have voted Labour' or 'If Thomas Evans had been a staunch, long-standing member of the N.U.M., he would have voted Labour'. It goes almost without saying that this feature of explanation is noticeable in day to day life, where we are very frequently called on to take advantage of it — especially where we are concerned to reproach someone. Parents are often to be heard telling their children 'If you had grown up in the kind of household we did, you would take more notice of what your father tells you', a counterfactual utterance clearly predicated on the assumption that the children have *not* grown up in such a house, and do not take much notice of what father says. Radicals reproach conservatives in such terms as 'If you were a Bolivian peasant, you would regard Che Guevara as a hero', which again is predicated exactly on the belief that the person addressed is neither a Bolivian peasant nor an admirer of Che Guevara. And, of course, prediction and explanation run everywhere hand in hand: parents are likely to tell their children 'If you bring up your children as permissively as we've brought you up, you'll be sorry'; and the conservative is likely to tell the radical 'When you reach my age, and know more about the world, you'll see it's not so easy to change things for the better'. Now, what all this means is that the only differences between explanation and prediction lie in whereabouts in the deductive argument we begin. With the case of explanation, we begin with the event to be explained, i.e. with the conclusion of the argument, and look for the appropriate generalisations and initial conditions from which to deduce this conclusion. In the case of prediction, we begin with the generalisation and the initial conditions and then go on to forecast the coming occurrence. And in the case of our hypothetical inferences, we simply suppose the initial conditions, and then draw the inference as to the consequences of this supposition. And one illumination which this sheds on a contentious point is worth noting. The social sciences are often said to suffer drastically from their inability to engage in controlled experiment; but this charge is also often said to be nothing more than a practical inconvenience, shared with such strikingly successful sciences as astronomy, and thus not in any sense a logical handicap. (5) The grounds for this charge and rebuttal are now clear. If we are concerned with the testing of explanations, and especially of the underlying generalisations on which they rest, experiment will be extremely useful, in that we can *produce* the initial conditions and see whether the conclusion holds. Obviously, such a process gives us a degree of control over science that is otherwise difficult to obtain. But it is not *logically* necessary, in that we can wait until nature provides our experimental situations for us, or we can infer with care from the situations we do observe in nature to those which we cannot observe or create, but can at least envisage.

But this is a merely practical consideration. It is plain that as a matter of logic, the identity of explanation and prediction is unshakeable. (6) However, this by no means entails that the goal of science is to try to produce wide-ranging predictions in practice. Two considerations come into play at this point. The first concerns the kind of generalisations available. We saw earlier that valid deductive arguments required universal generalisations as their general premisses, and that where we have not got such laws, we often offer explanations as the best available, without claiming that they are conclusive. The second concerns the consequences of the hypothetical analysis of causal generalisations. A statement to the effect that '*If* anything is an X it will also be a Y' does not tell us whether anything ever *will* be an X — and hence cannot tell us whether anything *will* be a Y. A generalisation such as 'All trades unionists vote for radical parties', if it is really meant as a causal law — and we shouldn't forget that it may not be, that it may be no more than a summary of the behaviour of trades unionists at the present day — does not tell us anything about voters for radical parties in, say, 1983. Unless we have such singular statements as 'there will be at least 750,000 trades unionists in 1983', we have no prediction at all; in short, we need statements about initial conditions if we are to utilise hypothetical generalisation for positive predictions. Now, it is not a matter of logic whether we can in fact produce either appropriately universal generalisations or secured statements about initial conditions; it is a matter of how the world is actually constructed that determines whether such statements and such generalisations can be established. Methodological claims about what a

201

developed science *ought* to aim at thus depend both upon assumptions about the logical requirements of explanation and upon reasoned guesses as to what the world is like. What will not do — and what has tended to happen — is to project onto the world the image of strict deductive argument and pass that off as the methodological aspirations of social science, just as it will not do to project the present weakness of social science explanations back onto logic and claim that they invalidate deductive reasoning. Two questions dominate this issue. The first is whether the social sciences can produce anything other than approximate laws and generalisations, and produce genuinely universal laws with an adequate spatio-temporal range of applicability. The second is whether we can make the necessary singular predictions about initial conditions, such as would enable us to draw from our generalisations predictions of a positive kind. The two issues are connected in that predictive success and failure feed on themselves: if we possessed strictly universal, non-probabilistic generalisations, then we should be able to predict with accuracy the states of affairs which form the causal antecedents of those states of affairs which are the subject-matter of more distant prediction. And, equally, if we cannot predict with exactitude what will happen in the near future our guesses as to the farther future will become rapidly no more than guesses.

Now, it has been argued by some writers that the supposed isomorphism between explanation and prediction defended above is mythical, since there are successful and developed branches of the physical sciences where we can explain in general what is going on, but cannot predict particular occurrences. Professor Hanson argued this for the case of quantum mechanics, (7) where we cannot predict single quantum jumps, and it could be extended to genetics, where we can tell after the event why a successful mutation survives — in terms of the theory of natural selection — but we cannot predict before the event why a particular mutant should appear. Now, the obvious retort to the claim that here we have explanation without the possibility of prediction is that this rests on an ambiguity about *what* is explained. In neither of these cases is there any claim that we can explain the single event which we cannot predict; that is, we can explain

202

the mutation's survival, but we cannot explain its initial appearance, and it is this, and this only, which we cannot predict. Or we can explain the probability of cases of quantum jumps, but we cannot explain why one jump occurs — and it is this that we cannot predict. In other words, what we cannot explain we cannot predict, and conversely. (8) Here as elsewhere, there is nothing to be gained by quarrelling over the application of the label 'explanation' to some particular theory. But what can be said is this: where we have the result — after careful and prolonged scientific investigation — that no determinate laws are discovered, and we also have a general theory which explains why this should be so, then methodologically it is a futile occupation to bemoan their absence. In social science it is presently the case that we are quite well equipped, but with approximate and not very far-reaching generalisations about how people behave in given situations. Thus we have rather a good idea of what motivated voters in Britain during the 1950s, but the explanation of why the Conservative Party remained so consistently in power would be extremely hard to extrapolate to the United States of the 1950s, or to Britain in the 1960s, let alone to more remote societies and times. (9) Such generalisations thus offer us little in the way of backing for detailed prediction, though they may be invaluable in providing us with day to day help in assessing our situation. The other great problem for the social sciences is establishing before the event rather than after which causal antecedents are the important ones. This is obvious enough, in the light of the need for initial conditions in causal explanation. But there is a less obvious point relevant here. We have argued so far that explanations of human affairs rest, directly or indirectly, on what people have reasons for believing and intending under the situations they are in; and this is ineluctably to introduce into the initial conditions of social events the beliefs and feelings of the social actors *about* those initial conditions. Reasons are only effective reasons in the light of beliefs and attitudes; but beliefs and attitudes are also subject to more or less conscious reappraisal. Whether or not this is a vital difference in the logic of explanation of human affairs is momentarily beside the point; what is certainly true is that (in any situation other than one where there is complete

203

control over what people can believe) it is as a matter of fact much easier to reconstruct from hindsight what a person or a group must have believed and wanted than it is to predict this in advance of their acting at all.

If the only evidence about the possibility of prediction were culled from our experience of everyday explanation and explanation in the social sciences, it is doubtful that anyone would have thought that scocial scientists *ought* to aim at establishing long-term predictions. The image which seems for so long to have dominated the intellectual scene, however, is that of astronomy with its predictive triumphs dating back so far as the Babylonians. There has indeed been a debate since antiquity couched almost in the same terms that Plato and Aristotle gave it; the former, impressed with astronomy, and believing that a uniform natural order must operate on uniform principles throughout, put forward astronomical theories about the cycles of change and decay and growth in social life; (10) Aristotle, judicious, impressed by the multiplicity of different natural phenomena, insisted that we ought only to aim at the kind of exactness which the particular subject—matter permitted, and that it was folly to erect anything grandiose on the weak foundations of our social knowledge. (11)

But the attractions of a predictively successful social science are obvious enough. The belief that there is a 'pattern' in history is one of the most widespread of human beliefs; Stone Age tribes have their myths, and contemporary states their generally accepted accounts of their history which are often as mythical. There is not a great leap from believing that there has been a pattern in what has happened in the past to believing that this should provide evidence about what can be expected to happen in the future. Of course there has usually been a good deal of ambiguity about whether the guide is to what *will* happen, or whether it is a guide to what *ought* to happen; but this ambiguity is grounded in our own doubts about how much of our future is under our control, and is as common in sociological theory as in earlier theological and mythological accounts of history. So obvious is this kinship between the theological systems evident in Judaism, in such works as St Augustine's 'City of God', (12) or in Plato's account of the 'Golden Year', that

204

more than one writer has argued that an allegedly sociological system ought to be analysed as in reality a theological system because of the needs it fulfils in this way. Thus Professor Tucker argues that Marx was a covertly religious thinker, and that the sociological mask worn by his work is largely delusive. (13) But it is equally true that many of the founders of the contemporary sociological tradition happily accepted that what they were doing was, so far as its social purpose went, a similar undertaking to that of the great religious systems of the past. Saint-Simon, for instance, proposed to found a New Christianity on Newton's law of universal gravitation, a cornerstone to replace the old Christian claim that God is love; and Saint-Simon's (14) ambitions rubbed off on his greatest disciple, Auguste Comte, who gave a good deal more than merely the word 'sociology' to the subject. Comte shared with many other nineteenth-century thinkers the belief that the sociological and cosmological theories associated with Christianity were played out, and that they no longer gave people the sense of where they had come from and where they were going to which all societies needed if they were not to be overtaken by anarchy. Sociology, and especially a sociological account of history, together with predictions about the way society would go on developing, was intended to fill the gap left by scepticism and secularisation. Even those nineteenth-century thinkers to whom Comte's mature, and bizarre, attempts to reformulate medieval Catholicism and its hold on social life held no appeal at all, saw that he grasped a point of great importance: they agreed that there was a need for a scientifically respectable account of how modern society had come about, what its problems were, how it was solving them or failing to solve them, and what means were available for the improvement of the future it faced. (15) De Tocqueville, Marx, Durkheim and Weber all faced up to this need in their different ways.

It is, however, necessary at this point to reiterate what we have already said, that the aspiration to this kind of predictive social science was not an aspiration which anyone could have contracted from a consideration of its existing achievements. Rather, it was culled from the apparent need for the kind of doctrines which traditionally religion had provided and was now failing to provide, and from an assumption,

205

largely fed by the success of the natural sciences, that the social universe was predictable in the same way as the rest of the natural world. The less a thinker felt this homogeneity between the social order and the remainder of nature, the less likely he was to aspire to prediction in sociology. Comte, Mill and Marx all emerge as more inclined in this direction than were, say, Weber or Durkheim. The assumption which dominates Mill's picture of the goals of social science is the Newtonian assumption that the universe is a determinist order; what this means is that it is in principle possible to predict every state of the universe from a consideration of any other state together with a full knowledge of the causal laws operating at that time. What is true of the universe in gross is true in detail of any subsystem within the universe which is sufficiently isolated to be studied on its own. From a consideration of the system at any time, we ought to be able to predict (or retrodict) its state at any other time. Writers like Mill were explicit about the origins of their assumptions, and references to 'celestial mechanics' and to hopes of a 'mécanique morale' are frequent. (16) The sociological implication is that since societies are also determinist systems, a full knowledge of any society at a particular point, together with a knowledge of the causal laws operating on it, should allow us to predict its state at any other time. Of course, everyone agreed that the actual computation of these predictions was quite impossible. The aim was to gain agreement on the principles involved.

However, it is apparent after a moment's thought that this is a much less plausible programme than it appears at first sight. In exploring the doubts we must have, we can answer the question posed in Chapter 1 as to whether the kind of determinism and indeterminism in social science is like that in the natural sciences, and also enforce the lesson we have already received about the need to distinguish between the demands of logic and the possibilities allowed us by the phenomena. The first problem we need to raise is the ambiguity we earlier touched on, as to whether religious, mythic or sociological predictions tell us what *will* happen or what *ought* to happen. The problem is this. Ordinarily we have a practical motive for wishing to know what will happen next; we are not motivated by idle curiosity about what will happen to our society. Rather, we want to be able to act: we want to ensure that favourable trends will continue, and that unfavourable trends will be stopped, or where this is impossible that we shall circumvent their ill-effects. But now we face the problem we raised in Chapter 1 about the inter-action of the prediction and the behaviour predicted. The initial puzzle is that if the prediction is meant as a prediction of what will happen no matter what we do, then it is no use as a guide to action. We can only utter an unconditional or categorical prediction — what Popper calls a 'prophecy' — when we are sure that no action of ours will materially affect the outcome. (17) Thus once the Wall Street crash of 1929 was well under way, we could have predicted that prices would slump all the way down, because we knew that in a free market for securities, a panic once it has begun cannot be terminated by the deliberate actions of buyers and sellers in that market. This is analogous to predicting of a man who has fallen from the top of the Eiffel Tower that he will fall to the bottom — once started, there is absolutely nothing he can do to stop himself. But unlike the case of a man falling from the Eiffel Tower, the Wall Street crash prediction is likely to be unrepeatable. For men learn from their mistakes, and thus come to modify their future behaviour. Thus once it emerges that the predictability of the Wall Street crash depends on the fact that a freely operating stock market of the 1929 variety does not allow for co-operative efforts to slow down or avert disasters, the natural result is a modification of the system, and hence a falsification of attempts to repeat the success of the previous prediction; and this, of course, is a major point of difference between the kind of events which form what we term the Wall Street crash and those which form the sequence of someone's falling from the Eiffel Tower. It remains true that as a matter of logic, there is predictability in the sense that *if* the same circumstances and antecedents appeared again, and *if* the same causal laws operate, then the same effects will occur. But methodologi-cally, there is no room for the pursuit of prediction in this sense, since we know that as a matter of fact the same laws will not operate in future and the same initial conditions will not recur. This, then, is one of the ways in which long-run predictions will run into trouble; and it must be noted that it is not analogous to anything at all in the case of the natural sciences. For in the example we have chosen, the reason why the prediction itself alters the future circumstances depends upon people coming to understand why that prediction would have been successful; that is, the prediction alters subsequent behaviour, not in virtue of an independent status as a causal antecedent, but because people come to understand the prediction, and it then affords them reasons for behaving differently. This can only be the case where the phenomena in question have theories about their own actions and can sensibly be said to understand explanations of their own behaviour; and the only such phenomena of which we have any knowledge are human beings. The importance of this point will emerge a little later when we discuss self-validating and self-defeating predictions.

Since it seems that predictions offered as accounts of what will happen no matter what are of no use as guides to action, or else are used as guides to action at the cost of their status as unconditional predictions, what of those conditional predictions which are used to tell us what *would* happen if no one intervened? It is plain that at an everyday level, we employ such predictions incessantly and essentially — though it should be noted that their scope is usually limited. (18) Thus we warn each other that the house will fall down about us unless we get the roof fixed, or that we will run down the little old lady on the crossing unless we slow down at once; and generally, economists, public health officials and a thousand and one inspectors and advisers tell families, governments and private persons what causal sequences are in train, precisely so that they will be able to intervene in them. More and more detailed knowledge of such causal sequences makes us more and more able to intervene successfully in them, and thus brings events increasingly under our control. But it makes a considerable hole in the ambition to predict changes far into the future, since the causal sequences laid out in such 'predictions' tend to be wide open to human frustration and modification. If what we learn is thus almost always what is happening, and what will happen *if* no one intervenes, we obviously learn rather little about what *will* happen, interventions and all. This conclusion, though a blow to a determinist picture of social life, is in no way destructive

208

of our account of the need in explanation for the production of such causal sequences; nothing in that account required that such sequences should be shown to hold far into the future, nor that they should be immune to future intervention by human beings. This intervention is no matter for logical disquiet.

It is, in principle, possible to stick to one's determinist guns, and argue that long-range prediction is not in principle impossible, even though it may be very difficult to achieve, for all that is required is that we should be able to predict the interventions as well as the initial sequences, and to assess the effects of such interventions. Logically, this is obviously the correct response, even though it raises the problems we came across in Chapter 5 about giving a determinist analysis of choice. For if we are to make such predictions, they must be predictions of what will happen no matter what, only one of the events which will happen no matter what will be our own interventions. But this analysis of intervention is most disturbing, since it is so at odds with precisely what is usually thought to distinguish interventions, namely that they are a matter of choice. (19) In what sense can intervention be a matter of choice on this analysis? If what a prediction 'no matter what' achieves is to rule out intervention to frustrate the course of events predicted, we seem to plunge into very deep water if we rule out our intervention in our own interventions. Such a move could only be made by a very committed fatalist who was prepared to abandon the whole concept of choice as a muddle. And such a fatalist would plainly not share the practical aims which I have suggested as the common motive behind an attempt to offer such predictions. It is thus apparent that both as a practical matter and an intellectually plausible goal, the attempt to rival astronomy with the production of a predictive social science is of dubious value.

Of course, none of this rules out predictions at short range, and it should be said at once that almost all contemporary social science does restrict itself precisely to this kind of prediction — and as we shall later see, to the establishment of trends of recognisedly limited predictive scope. But in connection with such short-range predictions arises one of the interesting differences between the social and the natural sciences. It is one of the features of social life that some persons are in a position of so to speak intellectual authority, in that their word on the state of affairs obtaining or about to obtain tends to be accepted as the truth; their say-so gives people a good reason for believing that what they say is true. Now, an effect of this which has been noticed by many writers, and christened 'the self-fulfilling prophecy' by Professor Merton, (20) is that the assertion by such authorities that something will happen may *make* it happen. The converse case of the self-defeating or suicidal prophecy amounts to the case discussed above, where the utterance of the prediction gives people a strong motive for making sure that it comes false. The kind of example to which the notion of the self-fulfilling prophecy appeals is the following: a man who is regarded as a reputable financial expert may say that a share will rise in price, and his word that this will happen is enough to set in train that rush of buyers which will actually bring about the rise in price which he has forecast. (21) Again, it is a generally recognised duty of members of a government to lie about the likelihood of devaluation, when there are rumours of devaluation in the air; the reason is that the statement of an official that devaluation was to take place would start such a stampede out of the currency in question as to bring about an inevitable devaluation. Now, it is important to notice that in these cases, the way in which the statement of the prediction would bring about the events predicted is very different from the case raised in Chapter 1, where a loud shout that an avalanche is coming is enough to actually bring on the avalanche. The difference is that in the case of human agents, the agents themselves have to both understand what the prediction means and to believe it before it can have any effect on their actions. It is only because they believe what is said that they can use it as grounds for the decisions which add up to the prediction's being fulfilled. The prediction, in Popper's terms, gives the situation a certain logic to human agents. But in the case where I simply shout loudly enough to set off an avalanche, it is only the noise of my uttering the prediction that is at issue. *What* was predicted is neither here nor there; it only happens to be the case that the noise in question was the noise of my uttering a prediction; any other noise of equal

210

loudness would have been just as causally effective. Equally, it follows that the prediction would *not* have had any effect on the avalanche, had it been only written or had it been whispered; but in the case where human agents are involved, it is plain that any mode of diffusing the prediction would be equally effective as a causal agency, so long as the one condition is fulfilled that people understand what is said and believe it to be true. For in the case of prediction in human affairs, it is the meaning of the prediction that matters and not its status as a physical occurrence; (22) and it does not just happen that the prediction is causally effective, in the way it just happens that a loud noise will start an avalanche, rather it is only in the light of what the prediction means that it is logically possible for it to give someone a reason for behaving one way rather than another. As we saw in Chapter 6, what we are elaborating here is in large part a conceptual connection.

We have said enough to indicate the logical problems associated with the idea that determinism reigns in social matters and that long-term prediction is the goal of social science. But before leaving the matter, I should like to illustrate very briefly the practical consequence of these difficulties. The Marxist socialists of the German Social-Democratic party – the S.P.D. – before the First World War had grave intellectual, logical, ideological and policy troubles as the result of their ambivalence about the proper interpretation of Marx's predictions of revolutionary historical change. In principle, the S.P.D. was committed to bringing about the revolutionary transformation of capitalist Germany into a socialist society; but the question that baffled many of the party's leaders was that of their role in this change. If Marx had been right in saying that the changes were inevitably on their way, it seemed to many of them that their role could not be to promote violent upheavals but rather to wait for the coming of socialism in the fullness of time, and to prepare themselves to be socialists in the new socialist order. Plainly, no one leading a mass working-class party like the S.P.D. was going to propose a policy of total inactivity as the only logical consequence of Marxian determinism; nonetheless, a book like Professor Gay's 'The Dilemma of Democratic Socialism' (23) shows just how much the leaders

211

of the party felt themselves in a cleft stick. Were they to try to stir up a working class which, on all the available evidence, did not want a violent revolution, but was happy to make steady progress under the Bismarckian welfare state? Or were they to press through parliament and the organisations of the working class for the limited reforms of the status quo which the working class did want, in the hope that these would somehow cumulatively become the revolutionary transformation predicted by Marx and Engels? Of course, the dilemma of policy is that faced by all socialist parties in industrialised countries, and there is no easy solution of it. But that is not the point. The point is rather that the sociological beliefs of the S.P.D. made the resolution of the dilemma impossible, since they seemed to rule out a policy which could fulfil the incompatible requirements of being revolutionary enough — i.e. activist enough — to be plausible as a policy, and yet fatalist enough — i.e. inactivist enough — to meet the logical requirements of a determinist Marxism. It can, of course, be said that this logical hiatus is not a sociologically adequate explanation of the S.P.D.'s failure, since plenty of people have been moved to action precisely by believing such logically incompatible things as that the victory of their cause was quite inevitable, and also that their fullest efforts were essential to its triumph. This is (up to a point) true, but it is a truth of less importance once a party or a group of any sort is committed to a policy which supposedly relies not on messianic faith but on a scientific assessment of the possibilities of social and political life. For in such a situation, and this was the S.P.D.'s situation, intelligent, secular politicians will find themselves in a dilemma over policy. And no one who reflects on the contributory role of the S.P.D.'s weaknesses in allowing the collapse of the Weimar Republic and the subsequent accession of Nazism to power is likely to think its policy dilemmas unimportant.

Thus far we have been sceptical about the goal of long-term prediction in social science. Yet of course there are examples of highly successful short-run predictions — predicting election results from pre-election polls, (24) predicting crime rates for short periods ahead, or birth rates and the like. A certain amount of economic forecasting and planning runs along similar lines, though, logically, it tends to

212

be a mixture of reported intentions, extrapolation of present trends, and statements of an exhortatory kind as well. But what we ought to notice about such short-run predictions is that in a great many cases they are not susceptible of much in the way of causal explanation, and rely not on causal laws — at least in our present state of understanding — but on the mere extrapolation of trends. Once we have made clear this distinction between trends and laws we can see whether there is any substance in Popper's claim that the addiction of many philosophers, historians and social scientists to the goal of large-scale prediction rests on confusing laws and trends. (25) The existence of unexplained but successful predictions is common knowledge. We have mentioned already the nineteenth-century discovery of the remarkably steady incidence of crime in France, made by two separate observers. The discovery was thought at first to be the beginnings of a truly scientific criminology; although, no doubt, individual criminals acted for all sorts of reasons, nonetheless, the results of these all but random events could be forecast with considerable accuracy. But the delusiveness of these hopes was soon realised, for it was seen that such uniformities in how many people committed crimes brought one no nearer discovering *why* people committed crimes, and thus no nearer knowing the causes of crime; all one had found out about was the rate of incidence of the effects. Such attempts as Lombroso's to explain criminal behaviour in terms of genetic defect and racial throwbacks were no doubt mistaken about the facts, but they were at any rate along the right logical lines in looking for the causal generalisations which would analyse the trends thrown up by Quetelet and Guerry as the outcome of the causal factors involved, operating in the circumstances of the nineteenth century. What criminologists need to know is what motivates criminal behaviour, what sort of upbringing makes a person vulnerable to temptation and so on. With this information to hand, they would be in a position to explain both the trends that existed at any particular time and changes in them, because they could explain both the causation of individual criminal actions and that of the gross statistical regularities resulting from these particular acts. (26) It is only by being able to understand the causal processes that underlie trends

213

that we are in a position to know how safely we can extrapolate a trend into the future. For a trend is not a statement of a lawlike kind at all; it is logically on a level with singular statements, and is indeed simply equivalent to a summary of singular statements: to say, for example, that the trend in petty theft is steadily upwards is only to say that over the period in question more crimes of petty theft were committed in period $t_n \ldots t_{n+1}$ than in the period $t_{n-1} \ldots t_n$. To plan a long way ahead on the basis of such a trend is plainly foolish in the absence of any understanding of the underlying causes. Economists and businessmen alike realise how very unwise it is to estimate future income on nothing more substantial than an unanalysed trend; and where they refer to trends in economic life, it is almost always with a suggestion that they wish to be committed for no great length of time ahead. In recent years the trends in population growth have offered some spectacular examples of the dangers of extrapolation, partly because the nature of birth rates is such that relatively small changes in the current birth rate will extrapolate to remarkable changes in future population over the long run, in just the same way as small changes in compound interest rates will make spectacular differences to one's savings over a long enough period. But it is notorious that birth rates change suddenly, and in the present state of our ignorance inexplicably. In fact when the ceremony to mark the birth of the 200 millionth American was held recently, it was estimated in various quarters that the true figure was some two million less; the trend on which the planners of the ceremony had relied, and on the basis of which the computer counting the babies to the 200 millionth American had been programmed, had reversed itself some time before the ceremony. (27) At a more domestic level, everyone who has been tempted to stake his earnings on a horse knows that there is a great difference between relying on a horse's winning streak — which is betting on a trend — and knowing about its form, breeding, condition and so on — which is betting on a set of causal sequences. If, for example, he could discover that the horse was light on its feet and thus particularly good in wet going, he would hesitate to risk his all if the weather became warm and dry. Similarly with birth rates, if we knew that the desire to have more children was a

214

response to increased well-being, rather than a response to absolute levels of well-being, we should not expect a high birth rate to persist either into a slump or into a long period of settled prosperity. In other words, we can rely on trends for predictive purposes only where we can explain how the trend is caused, and thus estimate its reliability. And this again explains why it is that we can safely rely on unexplained trends only over rather short periods — it is only over short periods that it is at all safe to assume that the causes of which we are ignorant have not altered in any significant way.

But are we to believe that this not very problematic distinction between trends and laws was overlooked by those who are rightly regarded as the founders of the modern social sciences? There is no place here for a review of the enormous nineteenth-century output of work on the trends then visible in the fields of economic, political and social change; and such a survey would in any case be superfluous, since sociology today is quite sufficiently concerned with its origins in the responses of these theorists to the rapid social changes which took place before their own eyes. What, however, we can simply enough do here is explain what the argument hangs on. If it was possible to see in the work of Marx, Mill, Comte, Durkheim or Weber an uncritical projection into the far future of the changes visible in 1840, or 1860, or 1880, then there might be grounds for thinking that such confusion had taken place. For it might then be thought that they had failed to recognise the difference between saying that such and such changes have been taking place, and saying that whenever such and such a change occurs it has such and such consequences. For only this latter causal law would allow any kind of prediction — given that our earlier requirements as to the law's universality and the prediction of the initial conditions could be met. We may agree that these thinkers get into difficulties of one kind and another, but see these difficulties as the result of their doubts about what causes were really operating at the time they wrote, or how reliable the future operation of these causes was, and how profitable would be attempts to control their operation. For if they were well enough able to make the distinction between laws and trends, they were equally able to make the distinction between modifiable and unmodifiable causal sequences — and thus between the trends we can readily reverse and those which we cannot. It is obvious that in everyday life we use these distinctions quite unselfconsciously. For example, we may with many contemporary sociologists see that our lives are becoming increasingly suburban, and that the distinctions formerly existing between urban and rural life are melting equally into suburbanism: this is to talk of a trend; it is a trend which can be partly explained in terms of our desire for fresh air, for living space and ease of movement for our children and so on; thus explained, we know that it is a trend which *could* in principle be reversed if we were able to forgo these desires, but we see that we are not likely to do so, and thus that the suburban trend is likely to go on. In this there is nothing very logically complex.

And in essence, such a commonsense account is exactly what Mill for one offers in his essay on 'Civilisation' (28) — and the same defence can be made of the writings of Marx and Comte, though with allowances for the latter's curious beliefs about *which* causes were at work; while writers such as Weber and Durkheim were methodologically intensely cautious about prognosis. When Mill accounts for the tendency of masses to predominate over individuals and for uniformity of manners to permeate society, both geographically and through the class structure, he explicity claims that he is describing a trend. For in analysing the causes of this trend he inquires what we should have to do to reverse it or at any rate modify it. Since the causes seem to lie in the features of life which have also caused the industrial revolution and its attendant changes, Mill offers little hope for a substantial reversal of the trend; but this is not because it is a universal causal law, which it makes no sense to try to alter, but simply because the costs of trying to alter a trend so bound up with the increasing prosperity of the age would be immensely high, and it would thus be foolish to try to reverse the trend. It is not that no matter what, the processes of industrialisation and the like must continue, but that their reversal would be intolerably expensive; but Mill insists as firmly as he can that while major reversals may be out of the question, it is quite possible to modify the side-effects of the

216

trend, and he encourages us to do this.

Much the same analysis can be given of the seemingly more awkward case of Marx's insistence on the inevitability of the end of capitalism. (29) What Marx shows is simply that both intervention and non-intervention will equally bring to an end nineteenth-century capitalism of a pure and unregulated kind. In some ways, Marx's case is almost too much a matter of common sense. For often it boils down to saying that if capitalism is allowed to continue under no government surveillance, then increasingly violent booms and slumps will equally continue unchecked, for reasons which any classical economist would be forced to agree with. If this process goes on unchecked, then chaos and revolution will follow. But if there is to be intervention on a scale commensurate with the problem, this will require such a degree of government control and regulation as to amount in its turn to the revolutionary overthrow of capitalism from a different direction. Thus capitalism was caught in a cleft stick, and in that sense its end was inevitable – though its endings might be very different. It is of course quite likely that Marx was wrong about the processes at work, and that he oversimplified the range of alternatives open in the latter part of the nineteenth century; but this is to say that he relied on causal generalisations that turned out eventually to be false; and this is a totally different charge from saying that he mistook the logical framework of a correct explanation. It would be no comfort to a confirmed Marxist to have Marx saved from charges of logical confusion only to have him condemned on charges of factual error; but this is immaterial here, for we are not concerned with the latter charges at all. All we are concerned to ask is whether it is those charges that are appropriate rather than the charges of logical error; and on the face of it, the logic of his account is impeccable. As we have said all along, if the goal of prediction fails, it does so because the facts of social life defeat it; this would be enough to account for any failures of which Marx may be accused; the charge of philosophical confusion here is both implausible and beside the point. The desire to predict the future might well have led Marx, as it has led many other writers, to overestimate the importance of the facts which he particularly had concentrated on, to the neglect of others

217

more influential than he believed — but this is to do a possible job less than perfectly, not to set out to do an impossible job. In view of the immense difficulties under which sociologists have always laboured, it ought to be plainly said that were they at all times totally committed to observing the distinction between the extrapolation of trends and the establishment of causal laws, they would inevitably make plenty of errors both in the one task and in the other.

NOTES

1. H. D. Lasswell and D. Lerner (eds), 'The Policy Sciences' (Stanford University Press, 1951).

2. Popper, 'Poverty', pp. 105-30.

3. Hempel, in 'Readings in Philosophical Analysis', p. 465.

4. Strawson, 'Logical Theory', pp. 82-90.

5. Nagel, 'Structure of Science', pp. 450-9.

6. Hempel, in 'Readings in Philosophical Analysis', p. 462.

7. N. Hanson, 'On the Symmetry between Explanation and Prediction', 'Phil. Rev.' (1959).

8. Brown, 'Explanation in Social Science', pp. 158-60.

9. D. E. Butler and D. Stokes, 'Political Change in Britain' (Macmillan, 1969).

10. Plato, 'Republic' p. 263.

11. Aristotle, 'Nicomachaean Ethics', (Oxford University Press) sec. 3.

12. St Augustine, 'City of God'.

13. R. C. Tucker, 'Philosophy and Myth in Karl Marx' (Cambridge University Press, 1961) pp. 21-7.

14. Saint-Simon, 'Selected Writings', ed. F. Markham (Blackwell, Oxford, 1952) p. 18.

15. J. S. Mill, 'Auguste Comte and Positivism' (University of Michigan Press, 1961).

16. Mill, 'Logic', bk vi, ch. ix.

17. Popper, 'Poverty', p. 43.

18. MacIntyre, in 'British Analytical Philosophy', p. 223.

19. Popper, 'Poverty', pp. 43-4.

20. Merton, 'Social Theory and Social Structure', ch. xiii.

21. J. K. Galbraith, 'The Great Crash' (Penguin, 1961) pp. 77 f.

22. See above, Ch. 6, n. 12.

23. P. Gay, 'The Dilemma of Democractic Socialism' (Collier paperbacks, New York, 1962).

24. D. E. Butler, 'The Study of Political Behaviour' (Hutchinson, 1966) pp. 61-2.

25. Popper, 'Poverty', pp. 105 ff.

26. Radzinowicz, 'Ideology and Crime', pp. 33-4.

27. 'New York Times', 21 Nov. 1967.

28. J. S. Mill 'Civilisation', in 'Essays on Politics and Culture', ed. G. Himmelfarb (Doubleday, New York, 1963) pp. 45-56.

29. H. Lefebvre, 'The Sociology of Marx' (Pantheon, New York, 1968) pp. 40-56.

10 Science, Social Science and Ideology

Over the last several chapters, we have developed what amounts to an answer to our initial question about the scientific status of the social sciences. We have seen that the logical requirements of adequate explanation can be met in the social sciences, although the differences between the subject-matters of the natural and the social sciences make important practical differences, and will, of course, make a great deal of difference to the content of the explanations. We have seen, too, that holding this view does not amount to saying in a simple-minded way that there are no important peculiarities of the social sciences — for we have seen several — or that these should aspire in the nineteenth-century manner to the status of 'celestial mechanics'. But now we must end by assessing the claim that these peculiarities so alter the status of the social sciences that they are necessarily to be evaluated as ideology not as science. There are so many and such different accounts of the ideological nature of social science that almost any one would merit a book to itself. (1) But our task here is not to review all that could be said on either side; all we need to do is outline the *kind* of claims that are being made and denied. Thus we commence by seeing, as simply as we can, what is claimed when it is said that a doctrine is part of an ideology, rather than a part of science; then we can go on to consider first the argument which is couched in 'contingent' terms, to the effect that we *can* know the truth about what goes on in social life, but that there are various circumstances which will systematically make it harder for us to do so, and secondly the 'non-contingent' argument, which seems to assert that the truth about social matters is in principle unavailable, hence that there is no possibility of escaping from the hold of ideology. And what these two, otherwise very different, accounts have in common is that both imply that when the claim to

220

'objective truth' made by social science has been rebutted, what is left is a valuation of the world in various ways.

An 'ideology' has come over the past century to mean a secular and political creed, and especially it has come to carry the implication that the truth of what is said to belong to an ideology is relatively unimportant, compared with its effects on those who hear it and believe it, or compared with the social origins of the creed. Unfortunately the term is not always used in this sense; (2) sometimes it means no more than 'pertaining to ideas', so that to talk of an ideology is only to talk of a set of ideas; usually, however, talk of ideology is meant to be talk about those ideas which are selected and held for their effects on the converted and unconverted, not for their truth. And almost invariably in everyday speech, ideology loses all connection with truth and falsity, and just means the political creed of whoever is said to possess the ideology in question. There is a simple reason behind this diversity of meanings, and it will help us make our way through the various claims we have to evaluate if we see what this is. When we ask why a person holds a belief, we may be looking for one of a variety of different answers. We may in the first place want to know what evidence there is for the belief, i.e. what reasons there are for holding the belief to be true, and derivatively which of these reasons, if any, the person who holds the belief would have appealed to. Thus, to take an example as old as Herodotus, (3) people are prone to believe that their own moral beliefs are shared by everyone else, everywhere; this belief, though false, is easily accounted for by the fact that in a given society there usually is a high degree of moral consensus, and thus the only evidence available to most people suggests that it is in fact true that everyone holds the same moral views – their reasons for believing what they do are not irrational, in that they have only evidence of agreement, and no evidence of disagreement; naturally, as Herodotus pointed out, when those who ate their deceased ancestors were introduced to those who cremated their deceased ancestors there was a good deal of mutual surprise and confusion. But there is another kind of question we can ask about beliefs, namely how a person or a group came to acquire the belief or beliefs in question, irrespective of the reasons which can or cannot

221

be given for the belief. Thus we could account for the hypochondriac's terror of damp evenings in terms of the excessive amount of cossetting and protecting that his mother gave him when he was a baby. Or we may account for a friend's distrust of all Yorkshiremen and his belief that they are all dour and mean in terms of a long-forgotten piece of unkindness from a Yorkshire relative. This second question, about the origins of a belief, is obviously a rather different question from that concerning the justification of a belief; but it is important to notice that it can either run in harness with such questions or independently of them. For when we ask about the origins of a belief, we are very often asking why it is that a person or a group of people was in such a position that he or they took some state of affairs as evidence or justification for the belief. Since we know that the evidence on which Herodotus's moralists founded their belief in the uniformity of moral judgement was not in fact adequate, we also ask why they believed it was — and we are told about their limited experience. And when the hypochondriac says that he thinks damp evenings will cause all sorts of illnesses, although we know that there is no adequate evidence for this belief we employ our insight into his upbringing to explain why he comes to accept some sorts of evidence more readily than everyone else — in terms of his emotional predisposition to see dangers everywhere. We thus ask both sorts of question together, employing our knowledge of the situation to explain why some kinds of evidence were thought to be acceptable; it is, of course, true that where a person believes what is true, for seemingly impeccable reasons, we are not likely to ask how he comes to be in a position to do this — though we can do so. It also seems to be the case that of some beliefs there is rather little question of justification or evidence, and that all we can ask concerns their origins — candidates for such beliefs vary widely from sociologist to sociologist, according to their estimate of how like and unlike beliefs about straightforward matters of fact these are; but ultimate moral principles for Weber seem to have been such, totemic beliefs for anthropologists like Frazer and Malinowski, and religious beliefs generally for Durkheim. Since what is believed cannot in the nature of the belief rest on appeals to evidence, the only kind

222

of explanation at issue is sociological or psychological. (4)

We can now see what is being said when proffered explanations in social science are characterised as ideological: they are being explained, or explained *away*, as beliefs held only because of their social origins or purpose, because some prior examination is thought to have discredited their status in terms of the reasons logically supporting them. Generally, the notion of ideology is more specific than this, and involves a third strand in the argument; this is the claim that a social class or other group will so select the evidence, or so slant the kind of language in which the belief is couched, or so order their moral preferences and their beliefs about these preferences, as to protect their own interests in what they say about the world, especially the social world. (5) That is, when we were offered an explanation of why a person or a group holds a given belief, and this explanation is couched in terms of that person's or group's social position, the assumption usually is that the holding of the belief conduces to the promotion of the person's or group's interests. And this, as we can now see, is why the connection arises between ideological and evaluative considerations; for when we say that a claim about the world is part of a given group's ideology, we are probably saying that the claim has evaluative consequences of an immediate kind favourable to the group whose ideology it is. Thus when it is said that the social sciences are, either necessarily, or only usually, ideologically charged, what is claimed is that the theories put forward by social scientists are proffered in order to defend the interests of some group or other, and that their efficacy in so doing accounts for both their production and their reception. The most famous of such accounts, and the most influential in terms of the fears it has stirred among social scientists ever since, was Marx's account of the status of classical economics in 'bourgeois society', an account which is elegantly summarised in George Lichtheim's 'Marxism'. (6) Although Marx's early attacks on 'ideology' were directed against Hegelian and Young-Hegelian theories of the state, theories whose religious and philosophical premises served as an opiate to drug the discontented, he generalised the attack to include not only religion, but moral beliefs, political science and economic theory as part of ideology. (7) They all had the

223

common feature that they served to hide the truth of exploitation and misery from the working class, by painting a picture of the world in which the existing incumbents of powerful positions were doing the best job they could, and were only taking their due reward for so doing.

In launching this attack, Marx not only struck some very shrewd blows against his German socialist contemporaries and against English liberalism, he also launched into sociological theory some terrible confusions. For what Marx never made clear was how to distinguish between ideology and the truth about social life. Marx himself plainly never doubted that there was a clear distinction to be drawn; but in trying to draw this line later writers have become entangled in some very awkward questions about the relativity of social truth and the apparent subjectivity of all social theory and observation. (8) On the face of it, the claim that a doctrine is ideological and not scientific ought to be susceptible of a simple enough test — at any rate in principle. We have already in this book analysed at some length what such a test is: where we are offered an explanation, we cast the explanation into the hypothetico-deductive mould and try to derive from its assumptions testable predictions about social life. When we have done this, we can perform the appropriate tests and see whether the generalisations on which the explanation was based can stand up to the evidence. If a proposition has *no* testable consequences, then it is not a scientific proposition at all, and it will very likely turn out to be a moral demand which we may either accept or reject; or it may be a metaphysical proposition which can be turned into the kind of methodological claim which can be indirectly tested by way of the fruitfulness of its recommendations or which can be rejected as meaningless. This in outline is the Popperian view which most contemporary social and political scientists would accept. Thus when Professor Dahl attacks the 'power-elite' analysis of contemporary American politics, he dismisses it as ideologically overcharged in that it cannot be cast into a form which is susceptible of empirical testing. (9) Equally, one of the objections to 'functionalist' accounts of contemporary American society has been that their major premiss was a covert evaluation of American society as a good thing, and thus that their explanations of how institutions and activities contrived to keep American society going always ended up as evaluations of those forms of behaviour from a conservative political stance. (10) Again, the work of Professor Goffman has shown that when we explain the operations of mental hospitals from the viewpoint of the sane who set them up, we get a very different picture from any we should obtain once we set out to explain them from the standpoint of the insane who are imprisoned in them. (11) Since the essence of science is generally supposed to be its 'objectivity', the fact that we have two such different accounts of the same situation makes us wonder uneasily whether the official account is not 'ideological' in the sense of being intended to brainwash us into acquiescence in the way we treat the insane, and not at all an objective account of what happens in asylums. (12) In raising this question, we plainly set out with the assumption that what we want from the scientific story is a coherent and objective account, which, if it does not 'look the same' from all angles, at any rate allows us to co-ordinate the views from all angles on some non-controversial and non-evaluative basis. We agree readily that a patient's experience of treatment is different from the doctor's experience of giving the treatment; but basically we assume that there should be some one account which will tell us what it is they have this diverse experience of. To the extent that Goffman's work implies that such agreement would be very hard to come by, that it would not appear spontaneously where psychiatric medicine is concerned, and that where it did appear it would be the result of successful coercion by the self-declared 'sane', he both draws attention to the usual conditions of objectivity in science, and disturbs our belief that the reports of doctors and administrators can be simply accepted as the truth. But even an argument as sceptical as Goffman's still leaves the line between truthful scientific accounts and ideologically motivated accounts as clear as before. A writer such as he who 'debunks' our ordinary views is in no doubt that such debunking gets us nearer the truth than before.

But when we confront the issue of whether it is so obvious that we can apply the tests outlined above, doubts creep in. These doubts are of two kinds — though they are very difficult to keep distinct. The first doubt is contingent, that

225

is, it is the doubt whether as a matter of fact social scientists can live up to the demands of the Popperian view. Of the various ways in which such doubts have been discussed, those of Marx, (13) Weber (14) and Mannheim (15) are justly famous stances on different sides of the issue. Their arguments begin from a common starting point, which they share indeed with many other sociologists of the present day — the observation that a person's social position determines to a large extent what kinds of moral and political creeds he espouses, what kinds of beliefs he will hold about the way in which society ought to be organised. This is not simply an allegation of bias, for it goes much deeper. It is not simply that the social position of a writer or a scientist will prejudice him in favour of some beliefs and against others. It is also the assertion that a person's whole way of life is bound up with the way he thinks, in such a way that thought and action together form an integral whole. Thus in Marx's analysis, it was not mere prejudice which made the feudal nobility see the world in terms of reciprocal obligations, sanctified by Catholicism and adorned by the morality of courtly love, chivalry and honour: such a view of the world was an essential element in the feudal world, and to sacrifice it would have been impossible, save with the sacrifice of the entire feudal world as well. To see personal allegiances, not in terms of honour, but on the basis of profit and loss would already be to be a bourgeois. And thus, so long as the feudal world remained intact, a man could only see the world in terms of its categories. Now, Marx's account of how economic circumstances determine an intellectual and moral superstructure has been the source of immense difficulty ever since he first gave it; but a number of things about it are clear enough for our purposes here. The main point is that it is part of the 'sociology of knowledge'; (16) that is, it is an account of how as a matter of fact the social, economic and eventually political circumstances in which we live make it harder or easier for us to discover the truth about social life. Because in any understanding of the world we have to select some aspects and ignore others, we are necessarily vulnerable to the preselection of significant detail which the existing social organisation of our society involves. It is thus the case both that the social world will be organised according to

226

some particular kind of principles, and that we will be predisposed to see some principles embodied in it, to the neglect of other principles, which are perhaps even more significantly at work. Now, it seems clear enough that Marx thought that sociological knowledge — and in this category we must place such things as economic theory and political science — was especially vulnerable to this kind of blinkering; it is a matter for dispute whether he believed (as many Marxists have done since) that the natural sciences also are perverted by the class-structure of a given form of society, but whether he did so or not, it is plain that he thought that the social sciences were peculiarly vulnerable. And Marx goes rather further than this, for he went on to argue that the dominant social class will hire intellectuals, artists, priests and philosophers to put about its social view as *the* social view, its account of the truth as *the* truth. (17) It is for this reason that Marx often refers to ideology as false-consciousness, for when the non-dominant class sees its own situation in the terms which the dominant class has imposed on it, then it *mis*perceives its situation, and cannot be aware of the truth about its condition.

It is worth remarking that much of Marx's account of the matter has become sociologically commonplace far beyond the ranks of Marxist sociologists. The concern of the American sociologists Cooley, Thomas and Znaniecki for what they termed 'the definition of the situation' attests to the obviousness of the phenomenon noticed by Marx. (18) What a person or a group will do in some situation largely depends on how he or it has defined that situation — this is an obvious consequence of what we earlier said about the role of reasons in human action; the reasons a person will act on must depend on the way he visualises the situation in which he acts. This means that any group will be better able to control a situation when it can make *its* definition of the situation come to be *the* definition of the situation. Of course, this does not amount to saying that a group or a person has to impose its definition by brute force — we are all familiar with cases where a well-established appearance of weakness enables a person to make the most of his opportunities. The interest of the American sociologists was in the way in which immigrants made their way in American society, but fundamentally the kind of phenomenon was much the same. The European proletariat studied by Marx was in a position where it had to be able to fight for better conditions of life, and where a common consciousness of its condition and its needs would have been a vital weapon in this fight; but it was a weapon which was hard to forge in the face of prevailing social and intellectual views. The immigrant groups had to make their way upwards in a competitive American society where a common consciousness would again be useful, but was in danger of erosion by the views of the existing inhabitants of America, and was open to moral threat by the incumbents' assumption of their own superiority. And today it is not surprising that advocates of one or other form of Black separatism in America concentrate their attention on the extent to which the existing American language and the existing network of idiom, metaphor and presupposition all hamper the self-esteem and hence the progress of the Black American. (19)

But, of course, sociologists have varied a good deal in their accounts of how we are to get at the truth about social life. Where there seems no real question of truth, as in, say, the belief of Sicilian immigrants that everyone worth making friends with comes from two or three villages in a small area of Sicily, sociologists have been content simply to chronicle the extent and efficacy of such solidary sentiments. But in the case of sociologists who have been concerned with the social bases of developed social science, the situation has been much more difficult. The Marxist problem runs as follows: in what sense, if any, is it true that bourgeois social theory is bound to be ideological, i.e. to be value-loaded in favour of the bourgeoisie's interests? A well-meaning bourgeois social theorist can surely complain that his concern for the truth is being denied before he has had a chance to reply to the charges against him. Surely, he might say, he could accept any well-attested facts which the Marxist economist or sociologist brought to his attention. Indeed he might go onto the offensive and point out that Marx himself had praised the agents of the bourgeois British government for the care with which they had amassed the statistics which he employed to such effect in 'Capital': (20) for bourgeois and proletarian alike, the facts were the same; bourgeois social science and proletarian social science alike were to be assessed not in terms of the motives and the social origins of those who produced them, but in terms of the compatibility of the theories with the facts. If he were sufficiently irritated by the charge, our bourgeois social scientist might go on to read his Marxist critic a lesson about the ill-effects of introducing ideological considerations into science; neither Lysenko's effects on Soviet genetics, nor the purges' effects on Soviet economics were very good advertisements for a concern with the ideological aspects of science and social science. Less thought about the social origins of the thinker and more thought about the empirical testing of his thoughts would be an improvement of a vitally necessary kind. It is doubtful that Marx himself would have been vulnerable to such a critique; he himself was well aware that his own position as a bourgeois critic of the bourgeois order would have been paradoxical and inexplicable on any rigid account of ideological influences in social theory. His argument was only meant to hold for the most part and in the majority of cases; it was not meant to imply a kind of bourgeois original sin whereby any member of the bourgeoisie would be inexorably tainted and quite unable to tell the truth about social life. Rather Marx meant that since the truth meant unmasking the exploitation and wholesale cheating practised by the bourgeoisie, it would be irrational to suppose that large numbers of bourgeois would commit large quantities of the resources of the bourgeoisie to such a task. It was in this sense a contingent matter that social science was in danger of being corrupted.

Marx did, however, suppose that the proletariat would see the social world more clearly than their oppressors; and this doctrine has caused a certain amount of outrage. (21) It is again plausible to think that Marx meant something fairly simple — that in a classless society ideology would disappear because the clash of interests which had given rise to it had also disappeared; ideas would cease to be judged as weapons because there would be no one to fight. Whether this was in fact what Marx meant is a difficult question to decide because it hangs on estimating the extent to which Marx remained under the influence of the philosophy of Hegel. In

229

Hegel's philosophy there are hints of the claim that at a certain point illusion had vanished, and a revelation of the truth had been given to Hegel; and Marx's youthful writings do contain statements which convey the impression that he accepted Hegel's general orientation, but that he wished to dismiss Hegel's claim to be the beneficiary of the revelation and substitute the proletariat for Hegel. This is obviously a very non-matter-of-fact account, and quite incompatible with the one I have so far given; it also rests on a philosophy of history whose empirical relevance is at best doubtful. But we do not need to delve into the depths of Marxian exegesis; the only lesson I wish to draw from this problem is that Marx's account, whether or not its *content* is anything like that of Hegel's philosophy, is often couched in such a way as to resemble it in *tone* and *manner*. (22) Though this tone and manner are not necessarily a clue to Marx's own meaning, they are a clue to the hostility with which Weber and Mannheim reacted to it. And it is their reactions which concern us now.

The position adopted by Weber and Mannheim is so splendidly sensible that there is little wonder at its great popularity. They both started from the belief that the great danger to objectivity in social science lies in politicial commitment. (23) It is not to be wondered at that they thought this, when they lived in a Europe torn internationally by rival nationalisms and in a country torn internally by class war. But neither was at all ready to believe that the proletarian view of society was the only true one, and that the truth would be freely available on the farther side of socialist revolution. Both thought, as seems plausible, that a group which used ideas as weapons now would continue to evaluate them for their effectiveness rather than their truth in the future as well. And neither of them thought that intellectuals would improve the quality of their ideas by rushing to join a cause — no matter which cause. Mannheim in particular thought that utopian politics, a politics based on messianic inspiration, looking for the millennium, and thus in his eyes replicating the essentials of other-wordliness, was quite incompatible with the search for the truth about this world. To believe that truth will be grasped only by commitment is to abandon science for the illusion of revela-
230

tion. Both Weber and Mannheim put their limited trust in the intellectual, described by Weber as 'freischwebend' — floating free of class allegiances, since in the Marxian sense intellectuals do not form a class, though they can be and usually are recruited to some class cause or other. Upon the free-floating intelligentsia the weight was to fall of establishing an objective social science. (24)

But it needs to be stressed how cautious were both Weber and Mannheim in this connection. Neither of them believed in the possibility of a complete divorce of social theory from moral evaluation. (25) For both of them social theory begins in the desire of theorists to bring about goals; for only with such goals in mind does the theorist have any reason to select some facts as significant and worthy of study. And although they both accepted that social theory could affect such value-choices — if only because we may come to see that our goals are unattainable, and thus decide to settle for something other than those goals — they considered the value-choice essentially non-rational in that it could not be logically deduced from the facts. (26) But this element of arbitrariness and subjectivity was the only one which can enter social theory. Thereafter, we must base all answers to the question of how to achieve our values on the hardest, most objective causal investigations possible. And such causal inquiries yield results which social scientists *have* to accept, whether their values agree with our own or not.

Mannheim goes farther than Weber in emphasising the influence of values on the way we organise our factual evidence, and thus suggests that we should not expect *an* objective view, but simply several objective views. Thus, to take a recent object of some curiosity which has involved a good many evaluations of one and another sort, we may be concerned to explain the cause of apathy about politics in America in recent years. Now, the first discoverer of the phenomenon, Professor Berelson, saw apathy as an essential element in preserving the stability of democratic politics: (27) visualising American democracy as a self-regulating mechanism, he saw stability as dependent on apathy, because the function of apathy was to keep conflict within tolerable limits; a large degree of unconcern gave the system its chance to adapt slowly and steadily to the demands made upon it. More critical writers, less impressed with the merits of American democracy, saw apathy as both cause and effect of the political system's inefficiency and injustice; (28) because important needs were not met, American society gave up on politics; because Americans gave up on politics their needs were less than ever met. Now, such explanations both make sense of the facts we have, one in terms of how well the system is working and one in terms of how badly it is working; but they can each be explored further, and the research and policy implications of each can be pressed. The result may never be *an* objective account, because we may indefinitely disagree about what ought to be going on, and thus about what the significance of the facts is; nonetheless, we shall achieve objectivity in the sense that we shall not hide the facts for the sake of the values we happen to hold, and we shall not confuse the goals of the theorist with the truth about the world. If the goal of *the* truth is illusory, no matter, we shall at any rate discover truths.

This has some implications for the practice of social science which ought to be explored before we turn to the more disturbing claim that the search for the truth is in principle a mistaken activity. A comparison of the different images of scientific activity held by Professor Popper (29) and Professor Kuhn (30) will effect this transition for us. On the account of the search for objectivity and value-neutrality given above by writers like Weber, the scientific community must form an 'open society' in Popper's sense. (31) Since causal inquiries require us to submit all proffered hypotheses to empirical testing, the institutional setting for science — including social science — requires us to recognise no authority save that of truth. Any hypothesis can be put forward and its truth-claims scrutinised. To lay down truth by fiat is obviously detrimental to the practice of science and indeed logically incompatible with the scientific attitude. This in turn explains why it is so wrong for the intellectual to allow himself to be captured by a movement espousing some particular creed: if the movement regards some beliefs as articles of faith — and it would not be a political movement if it did not — then these are removed from the arena of scientific scrutiny and the scientist loses out to the believer.

232

This explains why Lysenko was a disastrous influence on Soviet genetics: since he was attracted for non-scientific reasons to pre-Mendelian genetics, he would not allow anyone to perform the experiments which would prove him wrong. The social and political analogue to Popper's claim was produced a hundred years ago in Mill's essay 'On Liberty'; in that essay he called for 'experiments in living' as a way of testing our beliefs about how people could and ought to live. (32) If people wished to live differently, then we should not try to stop them, so long as their doing so would not harm us directly; what we ought to do was allow them to perform any experiments whose costs they were willing to bear, as we could thus see what new truths might emerge about social life — and even if none did, we should better understand the old truths. What all this rests on is the fundamental assumption that the business of science, social and natural science alike, is the confrontation of hypothesis with fact; and the less obstacle there is to this confrontation, the greater the chance of establishing the truth and thus distinguishing science from mere ideology.

But the whole presumption on which the past few pages have been based is called in question by Professor Kuhn's account of science. We have been assuming that if the social scientist can emulate the practice of the natural scientist sufficiently closely, he will produce social science rather than class ideology. But what Kuhn has done is to undermine this assumption by assimilating the status of the natural sciences to that of ideology. Up to this point, we have tacitly assumed that the natural sciences provide a standard of objectivity to which it is safe to appeal when asking whether the social sciences can achieve objectivity. But now we must confront the suggestion that the practice of science, both in crisis and normality, has been a paradigm not of the life of the open society but of a totalitarian community. (33) Kuhn's arguments are a somewhat perplexing mixture of factual and philosophical considerations, and he rarely makes it explicit whether he is appealing to sociological and historical considerations about the way in which scientists have actually carried out their work or to philosophical, *a priori* considerations about how we can intelligibly describe our experience of the external world. For our purposes this defect in Kuhn's presentation has a positive exegetical advantage in that we can first look at the arguments of an apparently factual kind, and then go on to consider the philosophical arguments, because these latter tie in with some important considerations which we ought to draw from our earlier discussion of the views of Professor Winch. Kuhn's factual case is simple enough, though its full effect requires it to be read in his own words: scientists have always aimed at a condition of 'normality', a condition where their universally accepted theories and experimental techniques generate a steady supply of 'puzzles', such as can be more or less decisively solved within the framework available. A theory or set of theories of sufficient scope to supply this framework of normality is termed a paradigm; its major properties are its generality and range, together with such a distance from the facts that its implications can only be brought out with the aid of numerous supplementary hypotheses about how its truth could be known in practice. A candidate for the status of paradigm in social science might be the utilitarian image of men as acting for motives of self-interest so that their social life approximates to market behaviour. Such a paradigm sets out the general shape which any explanation must follow, but does not determine what the explanation of any particular phenomenon will be. We have to develop supplementary hypotheses, such as perhaps the law of diminishing marginal utility of all goods, or develop accounts of the kinds of thing that will be perceived as costs or benefits. The paradigm cannot be directly refuted, because there are always so many supplementary hypotheses between it and the evidence; but it might be set aside as unfruitful. The life which Kuhn outlines for a paradigm is thus that it is the ideology of the scientific community. In its shadow scientists can develop explanations of a more or less satisfactory kind, but it they cannot challenge save at those times when normality has broken down and crisis occurs. At such a point, scientists behave like the citizens of a totalitarian state by shifting their allegiances *en masse* to a new paradigm, so long as that promises a new normality. And this is indeed a revolutionary movement, for just as the leaders of a revolution deny legitimacy to all the actions of the old regime and regard its servants as criminals, so here the scientific community has no

234

mercy on anyone who would choose to practise in the old way. He will have no audience, no research workers, probably no job; he will be 'read out' of the profession.

Now, what Kuhn's factual evidence does tend to establish is that scientists do not as a matter of fact behave as if they accepted Professor Popper's account of the open society. (34) It is a complicated business to assess Kuhn's evidence; but its implications are clear enough. The natural expectation of a Popperian science would be that its history would be reformist rather than revolutionary; theories would be tested and modified and even sweeping advance would be made steadily rather than suddenly. But this seems not to happen; theories put up with all kinds of 'refutation', and are unmercifully distorted until suddenly the faith of the scientists goes, and they seek a new picture of the world to guide their work. It is much more like religious conversion than Popperian pragmatism. However, such an argument is non-conclusive as an attack on Popper's account — the basis of our own account — of what the object of science is. We should expect people to work through long periods of normality, exploring all the implications of a given way of organising the phenomena before they suddenly decided that they had accumulated too many impossibly hard cases and therefore ought to start challenging the wider assumptions on which their work had rested. Equally, we should expect to see a similar state of affairs in the social sciences: we are likely to try to play around for a long time with hypotheses about the way in which consumption varies with income before we start thinking seriously of throwing out the whole of Keynesian economics. And where we do decide that Keynes is not much of a guide, it is very likely to be because we have pushed his views into a new and testing situation — perhaps the economics of an underdeveloped economy where the concept of the multiplier has no application, or there is nothing resembling a local criterion of full employment. And none of this tends to show that we cannot make the distinction between fact and ideology stick, because even if it is true that theories are refuted in larger units and more rarely than we should expect *a priori*, it still remains true that what goes on is a process of testing theories against facts, and thus true that the essential distinction is preserved between what

235

does happen and what we want to believe is happening.

It is at this point that we have to turn to the arguments of principle. These have two branches: the first concerns the subjectivity of observation, and is offered by Kuhn among others; the second concerns the subjectivity of what is observed, and naturally has no place in Kuhn's concern with the natural sciences, but is important in the context of the social sciences. The subjectivity of our observations is employed as a way of explaining why it is that theories remain unrejected for long periods of normality in science and why we reject entire world-views at those times of crisis called revolutions. For what Kuhn suggests is that the notion of appealing to the facts is vitiated by the organisation of human perception and intelligence: we cannot see such things as facts, but only facts-as-interpreted; we see, not what is *there* in any simple sense, but what is seen-as-there. And for this reason, we cannot claim that the appeal of a paradigm is that it makes the same old facts seem newly comprehensible. The facts which the new paradigm makes comprehensible are new facts, and the scientists who have made the revolution live in a new world, one which is as subjectively structured and organised as was the old. (35) The impact of an extension of these views to the social sciences is obvious. It looks as if the dividing line has been taken away between facts and theory and between social science and ideology. For if the facts appealed to have no existence save in the theory of the scientist, then the science of social life is not to be explained as a rational attempt to understand the external world. It must be understood — if it can be understood at all — either as an ideology in some class-based, Marxist sense, or else as some wider kind of ideology whose satisfactions are cultural or aesthetic. And this conclusion is plainly rather a shocking one to have to reach.

Fortunately, it is also an incoherent one. The incoherence goes deep, but hinges on one vital slip. This is the slide from saying, what is true, that all statements about the facts of the case involve some presuppositions, and saying, what is false, that the facts cannot be enough to make us decide between two theories. It is, of course, true that any description of the world, or some no matter how insignificant part of it, must *make* some assumptions about the world which it does not

236

state. It is nonetheless true that we can state these assumptions, but not in terms which take it for granted that they hold good, and ask whether they are justified. We cannot describe the world independently of *all* assumptions, and if this were required for objectivity, then we should indeed be unable to achieve it; but we can certainly describe the world independently of any particular assumptions which we wish to question. It may very well be true that both natural and social scientists have been insufficiently self-critical about the assumptions which they make; and no doubt we are all much less careful than we should be about distinguishing how we are accustomed to saying things are from how things are. Nonetheless, nothing Kuhn says shows that the distinctions we require cannot consistently be made. Indeed, his own account of the nature of anomalies is only intelligible on the assumption that the extremer conclusions drawn from it are false. (36) Only because we are able to make the distinction between the facts and our more or less accurate conceptions of the facts can there be either puzzles or anomalies, for these arise only where our theories and the world which our theories try to explain can be brought into confrontation. If Kuhn's image of the new theory bringing its own facts with it were wholly correct, there would be no possibility of either puzzles or anomalies; and the processes Kuhn so lucidly describes would be quite unintelligible.

But in the case of social theory there is a further argument, which all our arguments up to this point have failed to touch. And the existence of this problem shows that in our earlier accounts of why Marx or Goffman disturbed social theorists, we did not dig quite deeply enough. It will be recalled that when we discussed the implications of the account given by Winch of the way in which social science is concerned with the standpoint of the actor, we saw that this implies that social facts involve to a large extent the reasons and beliefs of human beings. This point was made by Winch in his analysis of economic exchange: it is not just a question of bits of metal changing hands — the processes of buying and selling have to be *meant as* such processes for them to *be* such processes. (37) And equally, when we observe such out of the way phenomena as those of the Melanesian cargo cults, we are not misled by the superficial similarities between such behaviour and our own behaviour when waiting for aircraft; we look to the religious meaning with which the actors invest their behaviour. As the name of cargo *cult* well enough indicates, we have the sense to assign such behaviour to the realm of religion and ritual, not to that of trading and transport.

It is therefore an important fact about human behaviour that what our actions are is to a large extent a function of what we believe them to be, a point brought out by Winch's insistence on rule-guidedness. It is equally the case that our actions display our values, in the sense that within the context of our rules and our beliefs that constitute a given activity, our values determine the 'thing to do' — in other words the right or correct thing. This seems to damage the objectivity of social theory in the following sense: people following rules and choosing what to do for the appropriate reasons only make their choices as they do because they hold certain beliefs already about the point or purpose of what they are doing; and this, as said earlier, means that they already hold a social theory. If they hold the same social theory as an observer of their behaviour — and it should be recalled that in our day to day dealings with each other, we are both actors and observers of each other, and do hold the same social theories at least over a very wide range of activities — then they will presumably give identical accounts of what is going on, and in this sense the observer's story can be verified with reference to the 'facts'. But if they hold different 'theories' and give different accounts, it seems implausible to hold that we can settle the dispute by some account of the facts neutral between observer and agent. If we allow primacy to the theory of the agent, we seem to swallow the unacceptable aspect of Winch's arguments, which would turn anthropology into an uncritical record of the ideological preconceptions of alien societies. If we allow the observer primacy we seem always to be negatively evaluating the rationality of the agents whom we observe; thus Durkheim's characterisation of all religion as the recognition of the sacred nature of social authority implies the falsity of the believers' own characterisations, and thus — although he denied this — presents their lives as irrational.

If, on the other hand, our account of the behaviour of the
238

people we are studying does agree with theirs, this does no more than show that they and we agree on the criteria for evaluating actions; it does nothing to show that our theories are true to the 'facts'. In the case of mental illness, for example, Goffman does not merely show that when we treat 'mental patients' we often treat them like 'criminals'; what it also shows is that the term 'mental patient' is one which we try to get the mental patients to attach to themselves, so that they will then behave *as* mental patients, and thus accept our evaluation of their activities. (38) In other words, we try to get them to think of themselves as semi-criminals, so that they will repent of the trouble they cause us. Social life is a matter of people playing roles, and what we are now saying is that there can be any number of social dramas in principle, since there can be any number of scripts; all that matters is that roles should be coherent and actors should follow their 'scripts'. And at this point, social science becomes a strange enterprise. There do not seem to be any facts to appeal to, for what 'the facts' will be depends entirely on what parts people can be persuaded to play; we can either record the parts people are currently playing, and thus record the going ideology, or else we can set up a counter-ideology by writing a different play. But truth and falsity seem far away. Of course there is truth and falsity of a sort, namely true and false statements about what people believe concerning their own social roles, and the reasons for their own behaviour. But there seems no room for that notion of truth which will lead beyond these beliefs and refer to the facts which would show that these beliefs were true or false. And this is an apparently paradoxical result of Marx's insight into the truth that what people believed to be the reasons for their behaviour could become the reasons; hence that an agreed story about a social order will wear the appearance of truth — for between the story of how it works and its workings there will be an exact correspondence. For this perception makes it very difficult for the notion of *false* consciousness to gain a foothold. If social life is so much in the minds of the actors, what is there to be falsely conscious of? If what they believe themselves to be is what they are, how can they make mistakes about themselves? A working class which believes itself to be contented *is* contented, whereas a working class which believes itself to be angry *is* angry; if consciousness and being are so closely linked, what room is there for truth? (39)

Once again, the answer must be that a good horse has been ridden to death. It is obviously of the utmost importance that the tendency of social science to become merely ideology is so hard to check for the reasons outlined above — as Weber and Marx could have agreed on, if on little else. Nonetheless, a close look at the sociologists who have been impressed by the kind of argument above presented shows how far they have been from espousing this wholly subjectivist view. For once again, we can reflect on the nature of puzzles and anomalies. People's beliefs are not only beliefs about their own states of minds, they are also beliefs about the factual consequences of each other's behaviour, and about the factual results of people playing the roles their society allots them. In other words, their beliefs go beyond the merely subjective, and can be falsified by the way the world turns out; it is, of course, true that the more general a theory a person entertains, the less likely it is that any particular circumstances will shake it, but this is no matter. All moral codes, all religions, all ideologies make some — often minimal — claim about the world beyond the intentions and evaluations of believers. All social theories are thus vulnerable to the ravages of the facts which may push them beyond the stage of merely having puzzles to solve to that of presenting anomalies; and at this point, the revolutions which occur are not scientific ones, but political and social revolutions. (40) Weber's bureaucrat who believed that the world was amenable to more and more organisation and more and more routinisation will be proved wrong when the unintended consequences of such routinisation pile up disastrously; Marx's free-trader who believed that tariffs were disastrous and free trade both moral and successful will find himself both shouted down and bankrupt in the end; in this sense, the facts retain their hard, objective status — mistaken social theories will eventually founder on these rocks. It may well be almost impossibly difficult for social scientists to remain objective and not to allow their hopes and fears to colour their beliefs; but. there is a world of difference between setting out to do something very difficult, and setting out to

240

do something which makes no sense. It is the argument of this book that social science is difficult.

NOTES

1. G. Lichtheim, 'The Concept of Ideology and Other Essays' (Random House, New York, 1967) pp. 3-46.

2. Ibid., pp. 3 ff.

3. T. A. Sinclair, 'A History of Greek Political Thought', 2nd ed. (Routledge, 1967) p. 40.

4. See A. MacIntyre, 'Secularization and Moral Change' (Oxford University Press, 1967) for such an account.

5. Marx, 'Selected Writings', p. 93.

6. Lichtheim, 'Marxism', pp. 154-62.

7. Marx, 'Selected Writings', pp. 97-8.

8. L. Goldmann, 'The Human Sciences and Philosophy' (Cape, 1969) pp. 35 ff.

9. R. A. Dahl, 'A Critique of the Ruling Elite Model', 'Am. Pol. Sci. Rev.' (1958) 463-9.

10. R. Dahrendorf, 'Out of Utopia', 'Amer. Jnl Soc.' (1958) 115 ff.

11. Goffman, 'Asylums', pt iii.

12. M. Foucault, 'Madness and Civilization' (New American Library, New York, 1967) for an equally disturbing account.

13. Marx, 'Selected Writings', chs 1, 2.

14. Weber, 'Methodology', pp. 1-112.

15. K. Mannheim, 'Ideology and Utopia' (Routledge, n.i. 1966).

16. Lichtheim, 'Concept', pp. 33-6.

17. Marx, 'Selected Writings', pp. 93-5.

18. Martindale, 'Nature and Types', pp. 349-52.

19. LeRoi Jones, 'Home' (MacGibbon & Kee, 1968).

20. K. Marx, 'Capital' (Foreign Languages Publishing House, Moscow, 1961) preface pp. 9-10.

21. Mannheim, 'Ideology and Utopia', pp. 65-6.

22. Especially K. Marx, 'Economic-Philosophical Manuscripts' (Foreign Languages Publishing House, Moscow, 1963).

23. Mannheim, 'Ideology and Utopia', pp. 33-8.

24. Ibid., pp. 136-46.

25. Ibid., pp. 165-71.

26. Weber, 'Methodology', pp. 22-5.

27. Berelson et al., 'Voting', pp. 305-23.

28. C. Bay, 'Politics and Pseudo-politics', 'Am. Pol. Sci. Rev.' (1965) 39-51.

29. Popper, 'Conjectures', intro. pp. 3-30.

30. Kuhn, 'Structure of Scientific Revolutions', pp. 23-42.

31. Popper, 'Open Society', i 172-7.

32. J. S. Mill, 'Utilitarianism', etc. (Everyman ed.) p. 115.

33. Kuhn, 'Structure of Scientific Revolutions', p. 166.

34. A. de Grazia, 'The Politics of Science and Dr Velikovsky', 'Amer. Behav. Scientist' (1963).

35. Kuhn, 'Structure of Scientific Revolutions', p. 134.

36. Ibid., chs vi and x.

37. Winch, 'Idea', pp. 117-18.

38. Goffman, 'Asylums', pp. 304 ff.

39. H. Marcuse, 'One-Dimensional Man' (Beacon Press, Boston, Mass., 1964) pp. 52-7.

40. Wolin, in 'Politics and Experience', pp. 150-2.

Bibliography

Footnotes in this book indicate textual references in the usual manner; here is a very short bibliography intended to suggest some useful background reading to the various topics discussed.

Chapter 1
A. J. Ayer, 'Language, Truth and Logic' (2nd ed., Gollancz, 1946) is short, exciting and only rivalled by B. Russell, 'The Problems of Philosophy' (2nd ed., Oxford University Press, 1967) as an introduction.

Chapter 2
P. F. Strawson, 'Introduction to Logical Theory' (2nd ed., Methuen, 1964) is a distinguished work; W. Salmon, 'Logic' (Prentice-Hall, 1968) is shorter and simpler.

Chapter 3
E. Nagel, 'The Structure of Science' (Routledge, 1961) is a masterpiece and a monument to scientific empiricism; C. G. Hempel, 'The Philosophy of Natural Science' (Prentice-Hall, 1966) and R. Harré, 'An Introduction to the Logic of the Sciences' (Macmillan, 1966) are excellent shorter works.

Chapter 4
In addition to the above, S. E. Toulmin, 'The Philosophy of Science' (rev. ed., Hutchinson, 1967) is unusually original at an introductory level.

Chapter 5
D. F. Pears (ed.), 'Freedom and the Will' (Macmillan, 1963) usefully discusses most of the philosophical issues; D. E. Broadbent, 'Behaviour' (Methuen, 1968) is a good general account of recent psychological theory, while N.

Chomsky, 'Language and Mind' (Harcourt, New York, 1968) has some excellent asides on the nature of psychological theory.

Chapter 6
P. G. Winch, 'The Idea of a Social Science' (Routledge, 1958) is a small book with large implications; it is best read in conjunction with one of his targets — E. Durkheim, 'The Rules of Sociological Method' (Free Press, Chicago, 1965) or J. S. Mill, 'A System of Logic' (Longmans) bk vi.

Chapter 7
M. Weber, 'The Methodology of the Social Sciences' (Free Press, Chicago, 1949), though old, still contrives to steer a careful course between exaggerations; S. F. Nadel, 'The Theory of Social Structure' (Cohen & West, 1957) suggests great ambitions for sociological analysis, but with due caution.

Chapter 8
R. K. Merton, 'Social Theory and Social Structure' (rev. ed., Free Press, Chicago, 1957) pt i is the contemporary 'locus classicus' for a defence of functionalism; in addition to the critics cited in the text, R. P. Dore, 'Function and Cause', in 'American Sociological Review' (1961) is clear and effective.

Chapter 9
In spite of its tone, K. R. Popper, The Poverty of Historicism' (2nd ed., Routledge, 1960) is still essential reading; but G. Lichtheim, 'Marxism' (Routledge, 1961) ought to be read to restore the balance.

Chapter 10
G. Lichtheim's essay 'The Concept of Ideology' (reprinted in a book of that name, Random House, 1967) is the best available introduction to the problems at issue; H. Marcuse, 'One-Dimensional Man' (Beacon Press, Boston, Mass., 1964) is a justly famous analysis of contemporary ideologies.

Index

actions   130 ff., 159
alienation   87
Almond, G.   64, 96, 154 f.
analytic-synthetic   distinction
      27 ff., 57 f.
   and theories   86 ff.
analytic truths   42, 62, 67
angels   62
anomie   7, 85, 128
anthropology   144, 146, 157,
      175
apathy   231 f.
arguments, how appraised   24 ff.
      and explanations   24, 48
Aristotle   65 f., 92, 97, 140, 204
arithmetic   35 f.
astronomy   14, 204, 209
Augustine, St   205
Austin, J. L.   133
authoritarianism   70
Ayer, A. J.   6, 102
Azande witchcraft   160 f.

Berelson, B.   231
'black box' theory   92 f.
bossism   189 f.
Boyle's Law   77 f.
Broadbent, D. E.   104
Burke, Edmund   10, 117, 197

Caesar   177 f.
cargo cults   237 f.
Carnegie, A.   178
causal laws, see generalisations
causal sequences   46, 48, 60 f.,
      68, 73, 79, 96 f., 110 f.,
      140, 156

mechanisms   70 f.,   113 f.,
      186 f., 190 f.
   and theories   73, 79 ff., 94,
      96 f.
causation   16,   49 ff., 67, 158,
      164 ff., 199
causes   51, 213
   and   reasons   117 ff.,   146,
      199, 210 f.
'charter'   187 f.
choice   120 f., 145, 209 f.
Chomsky, N.   91, 126 f.
Comte, Auguste   8,   149, 151,
      205 f., 215 f.
conceptual   connections   130,
      140, 156 f., 166, 211
   revision   11, 100, 122, 167
Cooley, C.   227
Copernicus   11, 95
consistency   33 ff., 146, 161
conventions   136
counterfactuals   55 f., 78, 200
crime rates   175, 213
criteria   6 f., 131
   and   identity   134 f.,   143 f.,
      151
'cultural relativism'   153 ff.
cybernetics   103, 193

Dahl, R. A.   30, 224
deduction   25, 32, 34 f., 48, 50
   and induction   36 ff., 43
definition   5, 67 f., 129
   vs.   empirical   truth   29 ff.,
      57 f.
definition of the situation'
      227 f.
democracy   29 f., 40 f., 62 f., 73
245

demography 158, 162
Deutsch, K. W. 93
Devlin, Lord 29 f.
Disraeli, Benjamin 19
Downs, A. 73, 83, 93 f.
Durkheim, E. 7 f., 83, 87 f., 128, 174 f., 193, 205 f., 215 f., 222, 238

Easton, D. 13, 64, 80
economics 8, 14, 19, 31, 50, 60, 84, 108, 146, 152, 157
 in 'bourgeois society' 19, 223
 and political science 41 ff., 93 f.
 and psychology 108 f.
Eddington, A. 89 f.
'emergence' 150
empiricism 13, 52, 56, 60, 102 ff.
entities, theoretical 83, 86 ff.
epidemiology 36
equilibrium 175
existentialism 162
experiment 14 f., 62, 64, 126, 200 f.
explanatory force 77 ff.
explanation 20 ff., 24, 46-73, 197
 causal 51 f., 58 ff.
 in context 47 ff.
 and deduction 46, 48 f., 53 f., 63, 69 ff., 78
 probabilistic 69 f.
 teleological 140, 168 f., 173, 183 ff.
 varieties of 128 f., 146 ff., 169
See also prediction

falsification 34 f., 46, 61 ff., 86, 224, 232, 235 ff.
 of social theory 141, 237 ff.
feed-back 168, 184, 193
feudalism 226
first-order questions 4 ff., 18, 24 f.
Firth, R. 39

246

formalisation 35, 41 f.
Frazer, J. 144, 161, 222
Freud, S 85
functional prerequisites 192 f.
functionalism 158, 167 ff., 172 f., 180, 182-94, 224

Galileo 65 f.
Garfinkel, H. 136
Gay, P. 212
generalisations 38, 41, 49 f., 64, 101 f., 129 f., 141, 164, 199 ff.
 dispositional 77
 enumerative 55 ff.
 nomothetic 55
 probabilistic 40, 68 f., 202 f.
geometrical theory of optics 79 f., 82
geometry 42 f., 153
Gladstone, W. E. 164
Goffman, E. 157 f., 225, 237, 239
Goldstein 179
Guerry 175, 213

Hanson, N. 202
Hart, H L. A. 140
Hegel, G. W. F. 230
Heisenberg 142
Hempel, K. 46, 52, 82, 184 ff., 198
Herodotus 3, 221 f.
Hobbes, T. 15, 102 f., 149 ff.
holism 103, 158, 172, 174 ff.
Homans, G. 21, 179, 194
Hume, David 102, 111
Hypothetico-deductive model 46 ff., 61 ff., 128, 146 f., 199 f., 224 f., 232 f.
 criticisms of 59 ff., 68 ff.

ideal types 90 ff.
ideology 125, 162, 197, 220, 225, 227 ff., 237 ff.
 definitions of 221 ff.

and natural science 227, 232 ff.
indeterminism 20, 61
   in social science 19 f., 206, 209 ff.
individuals 172, 176 f.
induction 13, 79
   See also deduction
in-filling explanations 83 f.
initial conditions 49, 200, 206 f., 215
intellectuals 231 f.
interests 154 ff.
internal understanding' 139 ff.

juries 38 f.

Kant, I 67
Keynes, J. M. 235
kinetic theory of gases 76 ff.
Kuhn, T. S. 18, 71 f., 80, 142, 232-7

Laing, R D. 159
language 131 ff., 134 ff.
   and causality 132 f.
   innovation in 135
Laplace 46
laws, covering 49, 51, 55, 111 f., 200 ff.
   as hypotheses 61 ff.
   as recipes 60 f.
   vs. trends 198, 213 ff.
Lazarsfeld, P. 33
Levy, M. 183
Levy-Bruhl, C. 153
Lichtheim, G. 19, 223
Lipset, S. M 40
logic 10, 25 ff., 32
   vs. matters of fact 26 ff.
'logic of the situation' 177 f., 210
Lombroso 213
Lysenko 229

MacIntyre, A. C. 112, 153 f., 159

Malinowski, B. 167 f., 187 f., 222
'manifest functions' 189 f.
Mannheim, K. 226, 230 f.
maps 76, 96
Martians 166 f.
Martindale, D. 125
Marx, K. 19, 87, **97**, 197, 205 f., 211 f., 215 ff., 223 f., 226 ff., 237, 239 f.
Marxism, 162 f., 210 ff.
mauvaise foi 162
meaning 16 ff., 131
   and causes 132 f., 140, 164 f.
Merton, R. 189 f., 210
metaphysics 67 f.
'methodological individualism' 172, 177 ff.
methodology 13, 67, 149, 198-203
Michelet, J. 3
Mill, J. S 13, 17, 37, 46, 102, 108, 128, 206, 215 ff., 233
mind—body problem 109 f.
models 64, 76
Molière, 77
Montesquieu 97
multiplier 152 f.

Nadel, S. 88, 139, 161, 176
Nagel, E. 46, 86, 184, 187
necessary conditions 112 f., 185
necessity 51, 57 f.
Newton 65, 82
normative theory 81
norms 131, 138, 175 ff.

objectivity 221, 225, 230 ff., 239 ff.
'observables 72 f., 88
operationalism 76, 84 ff., 90 ff.
Oppenheim, P. 52
organic analogy 191 f.

paradigms 18, 71 f., 80 f., 91, 94, 142, 233 ff.
   shifts 234 ff.

social contract and 80 ff.
Parsons, T., 21, 80, 87, 128, 191
participant understanding
151 f.
pattern variables 87
philosophy 1 ff., 24 ff.
and first-order subjects 2 ff.,
9 ff., 17 f., 21 f., 24 f.,
144 f., 155 f., 167
Plato 173 f., 204 f.
political science 62, 80, 93 f.,
154 f.
Popper, K. R. 37, 46, 49, 111,
173, 177, 198, 207, 210,
213, 232 ff.
prediction 14, 56, 141 f., 207
as aim of social science 198,
204 ff., 209
and explanation 198 ff.
long- and short-range 208,
212
and probability 202
probability 40, 68 f.
'problem of induction' 38
psycho-analysis 162 ff.
psychology 102 ff., 108 f.
mechanistic 130 f.
and physiology 103 ff.,
114 f., 119
and sociology 8, 103, 108,
110, 115 f., 174, 179 ff.
punishment 100, 120 f., 156

quantity theory of money 83
Quetelet 175, 213

Ranke, O. 3
rationality 117, 159 f.
'realism' 76, 84 ff., 87 ff., 95,
110 f., 146 f.
reasons 117 ff.
reductionism 21 f., 102, 105 ff.,
115 f., 150 f., 173, 179
regularities 13, 16, 172, 174
and causal laws 58, 60 f.
in human behaviour 101 f.,
120 f., 128, 139 ff.

248

religion 7 f., 118, 127 f., 144,
168, 188, 204 ff.
responsibility 120 ff.
revolutions 14, 41, 112, 240 f.
scientific 11, 71 f., 234 f.
Ricardo, D. 19
ritual 144, 238
Robbins, W. 108
Rockefeller, John D. 178
roles 138, 161, 175 ff., 239 f.
Rudner, W. 166
rules 131, 135 ff.
guiding action 128, 137 f.,
140, 169, 237 f.
vs. regularities 133 ff.,
138 ff.
Ryle, G. 89

Saint-Simon, C. H. 205
Sartre, J. P. 162.
Schumpeter, J. 62
science 9 f., 36, 66 f.
natural and social 6 f, 12-22,
47, 76, 81, 84, 125-38,
141 ff., 146 f., 232 ff.
self-fulfilling predictions 18 f.,
208, 210
self-regulation 168, 175, 193
Skinner, B. F. 132
Smelser, N. 181
Smith, A. 19
sociology 8, 17 ff., 20 ff., 80,
174 f.
and history 180 f.
of knowledge 18, 226 f.
S.P D. 211 ff.
'stepping back' 118
structural properties 181 f.
subjectivity 236 ff.
sufficient conditions 112 f.,
184 f.
suicide 84 f., 128
syllogism 25, 33 ff.
synthetic a priori 67
system-maintenance 168

Taylor, C 130